# Feminism for girls
## An adventure story

Edited by
Angela McRobbie and Trisha McCabe

Routledge & Kegan Paul
London, Boston and Henley

First published in 1981
by Routledge & Kegan Paul Ltd
39 Store Street, London WC1E 7DD,
9 Park Street, Boston, Mass. 02108, USA and
Broadway House, Newtown Road,
Henley-on-Thames, Oxon RG9 1EN
Set in 10 on 12pt Journal by
Columns, Reading
and printed in Great Britain by
Robert Hartnoll Ltd, Bodmin, Cornwall
Selection and editorial matter

Library of Congress Cataloging in Publication Data

Feminism for girls.

1. Adolescent girls — Great Britain —
Addresses, essays, lectures. I. McRobbie,
Angela. II. McCabe, Trisha.
HQ798.F45      305.2'3     81-11921

ISBN 0-7100-0961-5        AACR2

The manuscript was typed by Wendy Bradshaw

# Contents

# 1 Introduction

*Angela McRobbie* and *Trisha McCabe*
Illustrated by *Phil Goodall*

**Dangerous girls!**

To the world at large it might seem a bit strange, linking the Women's Liberation Movement and feminism with ideas of adventure. Hardly surprising, when most of the mass media do their best to reduce anything to do with women's liberation to the antics of a minority fringe group. As far as they are concerned, we are all dull, boring, and quite united in our lack of humour. With this kind of publicity to contend with, it does indeed take an adventurous girl to give feminism more than a second thought. But what exactly is the basis of this war waged on women who refuse to conform to society's image of how women should look and act and be? This is a question that touches on the whole way in which sex and gender are understood in our culture. It also relates to the way in which any challenge to the patriarchal *status quo* is greeted with fear and dismay if not outright terror. In this sense it is possible to interpret these stereotypical characterisations of feminism and feminists (bearing grudges, unpopular with the boys) as something which is created right across a range of institutions, precisely as a response to this threat, and as a clearcut defence of patriarchy — the power of men over women. If the women who challenge this power, who question the inevitability of their own subordination and the 'naturalness' of their inferiority, are reduced to a group of eccentrics, then half the battle is won. The threat is deflected and diluted — what woman in her right mind would want to join with this mob? Yet such unrelenting ridicule suggests something deeper. The fears, perhaps, of a patriarchy which is somehow beginning to lose its grasp, but doesn't know quite where to put the pressure on. The easiest way to deal with it is to hit back wildly, caricature it, trivialise it . . . and then hope it goes away. This anti-feminist promotional campaign depends then on transforming some of its representatives, those women who are no longer captured by suave masculinity, by machismo and charisma and charm ('your sex life complications are not my fascination' as the song

1

by Grace Jones puts it), into 'unfeminine' oddballs, women who are going against nature.

The problem for us is that these vindictive images do feed into popular (mis)conception, they do penetrate consciousness and create prejudices. Two recent examples of this will suffice. At an interview for a job, one gentleman thought he was paying me a compliment: 'You don't look like someone who bears grudges,' he said, 'do you have a happy personal life, are you a' (nervous cough) 'a, women's libber?' Even more obvious was the uproar surrounding newsreader Anna Ford's claim that 'body fascism' was virulent in television and ensured that only young and attractive women got jobs and succeeded, where such criteria simply were not relevant for men. The popular press took this comment, made at a Women In The Media conference, as an insult to men and to themselves as indeed it was intended. They responded in terms of 'how dare she bite the hand that feeds her', and then resorted to suggesting that 'she's got a nerve to speak', and then the usual, 'She's got extremely large hands and a big bottom.' So she's not really so 'feminine' after all! Later that week on television Robert Robinson mocked her, 'Whatever next?' he said, 'Plain women reading the news!'

But there is something more to this than just a childish ritual exchange of insults. For so many years any kind of media recognition, any kind of visual publicity, has been the epitome of success for a woman. 'Getting your picture in the paper'; whether as actress, model, television presenter or pop singer, the result has been the same. Made-to-measure images, glamour, smiles and 'thank you very much, I owe this all to my manager, my producer, or to the talent scout who saw me on "Opportunity Knocks" ', and so on. Women have been so flattered to succeed in these spheres that they have rarely dared to voice any complaints that they may have. Until recently they haven't ever publicly challenged the authority which has kept them in their places and which continually reminds them that there is always a large army of eager young women just dying to take their place. So when one of these figures does articulate her exasperation, not only is she risking her career, she is also directly accusing all those men who work around her. And she can be assured of having a far from easy future with them. Fortunately, she's not quite alone. The fact that Anna Ford made these statements at a Women In The Media conference, and that she has the support of this group behind her, is evidence enough of this. So perhaps patriarchy, in this case the media, really does have something to fear. For example, the tabloids may resist it wherever they can, but women's magazines *have* changed. They have been influenced by ideas from the Women's Movement and they no longer depict women as only house-wives, only dolly birds. Controversial issues, previously avoided by magazines like *Woman* and *Woman's Own*, can now be discussed with some frankness. Careers are recognised as worthwhile and important, and there *is* life beyond *House and Gardens*. Magazines like *Cosmopolitan* are clearly not feminist, but at least they have jettisoned completely the idea that happiness for a woman lies only in housework and childcare. Of course, what they offer instead, the new Superwoman, is as much a myth as any other. Some women argue that this is just another male fantasy, a view of women who are ever-available sexually and unhampered by domestic responsibility. Quite true, except that it at least provides its readers with the idea that there are alternatives and that marriage and settling down are not the only possibility for women. Recent issues have carried strongly feminist pieces written by increasingly sympathetic women journalists, so perhaps the rest of the mass media has good reason to flex its patriarchal muscles.

Our aim in putting together this collection is not so much to create new and feminist myths, but rather to demolish those which flourish so freely in everyday life. We want to unmask the fears they hide, and expose their rationale. But in carrying out this work we will not be suggesting that seeing through such representations and understanding their basis is enough to rid ourselves of them. Patriarchy is about power relations and never in history has power been redistributed without a bitter struggle. Even trying to live apart from, and in opposition to, society's myths about women is hard, to say the least. This is because these notions have, over history, become built into the very fabric, the cement, of Western society. They provide people with 'basic common sense'. When real life seems a great deal less reliable, less certain, these values are referred to for support: 'It's only natural after all isn't it?' The saying 'a woman's place is in the home', plays a similar kind of role as the Royal Family or Hollywood movies. Happy families and happy endings. Until, that is, housework becomes insufferably boring, the baby's cries intolerably endless, and the husband's absence (football, work, drinking, friends) simply unacceptable. Only then does the myth begin to crumble, the glamour fade and the resentment mount.

It is our belief that alternative myths have little to offer in terms of finding ways of struggling against women's oppression. Myths are circular, they foreclose discussion because they're complete, coherent and polished. They take the easiest route to the simplest answer. One of the most familiar and damaging to women goes something like this: women are physically weaker than men; they bear children and are responsible for feeding them; men have always been aggressive; they have provided for their families whilst the women have stayed at home and looked after the young. This pattern has been seen to serve as the very basis of society, from the earliest stages onwards. It is therefore natural and consequently right. (A crude summary of a well-worn argument.) Biology is destiny, whisper these myths, just below the surface. 'Really?' we ask. Yet if women are so weak how come they have for centuries managed to combine back-breaking hard work (tedious and repetitive — carrying water, fuel, washing, scrubbing, cleaning) with childcare, child education, with care of the family, the husband, with servicing him and his needs, with paid work in factory, office, or shop? If women really were that weak then the species would have died out centuries ago, and anybody who needs further convincing of women's strength need look no further than those first-hand accounts collected in Sheila Rowbotham's and Jean McCrindle's book, *Dutiful Daughters.*

Of course, other factors do come into play. Rich, middle-class women have not had to work and struggle just to make ends meet in this way. Biology, far from being a static quality, in fact seems to be an exceptionally elastic quantity. Or maybe it's just more accurate to recognise that biology is so tightly tied up with culture and its oppressions that it's virtually impossible to separate the two. We learn to become girls; we learn femininity just as boys learn to be men. And society invests a great deal of energy in ensuring that these processes don't go wrong.

If we're not interested in feminist mythology, where does the adventure start? We can't promise that struggling for women's rights is the stuff that glamorous movies are made of. So where does the adventure come into it? In fact we use the word loosely. Adventure is founded on initial confusion, even fear. It demands enterprise and ingenuity. It necessitates tactics and manoeuvres. Unlike myths, adventures are open-ended, there are no foregone conclusions. We won't be offering a step-by-step guide to the feminist 'Good Life'. We prefer to deal with clues, suggestions and ideas, all of which are based on a number of basic assumptions. First, that girls and young women are capable of a great deal more than they're ever allowed to imagine (this being one of the ways in which they are oppressed). Second, that they need space and autonomy from men to work out the hows, whys, and wherefores of this situation, and third, that this process of exploration and discovery can be fun. Challenging authority, questioning what seem to be God-given rights and undermining patriarchy *can* bring about change, they can also be rewarding and exciting experiences. And just like a good story, when the picture falls into place, the relief is great, it makes you smile.

There is, however, a limit to the usefulness of the analogy. Everyday life goes on where fiction ends, and the adventure is invariably partly of the girl's or woman's own making. This book, a collection of pieces written from different feminist perspectives, cannot possibly provide all the clues, never mind answer all the questions. And this is how we want it. We offer neither a manifesto nor a set of demands or statements and we would be doing an injustice to the Women's Movement in trying to summarise all its aims, all its points of tension. As a result, this introduction is itself a little unconventional. What we want to do is actively to apply one of the central tenets of feminism. The claim that the personal is political. We will try to interlace parts of our own personal histories with this particular project on adolescence, with our work outside this volume and with our commitment to the pieces inside it. We'll describe how and why the book came about and what kind of problems are inevitably experienced in such an attempt. And we'll try to deal, briefly, with some of those issues which seem to us to be of fundamental importance to women. What we'll hopefully avoid is the patronising attitude often adopted by people writing about adolescence. We don't consider ourselves grown up — wise and adult as the word is commonly meant. This is because 'growing up', as it is presented to girls, is about becoming settled in outlook, stable in disposition. 'Maybe some day you'll get those silly ideas out of your head,' my mother used to say. But growing up for girls is little more than preparation for growing old prematurely. Real life is more complicated than the stages and the phases which psychologists so willingly label us with. Getting into the Women's Movement can mean learning to reinterpret our past as well as re-assess our present. It means holding onto some images and abandoning others, even if we still remain complex and possibly muddled persons.

Amidst such speculation and hesitation, what can we hope for? First, a realisation that women and girls can work together, that they can overcome the obstacles which society puts in their way and which aim at keeping them apart. Mutual help and support have characterised women's culture for centuries, even though its official history is only beginning to be written. Second, a confidence that has to be fought for. Without seeing everything in society as a conspiracy against women, it is none the less easy to see that it hasn't been in society's and men's interests for girls to be frank and outspoken about their needs, their desires; about what they want and what they can do (particularly in times of high youth unemployment — but more on this later). Third, access to knowledge and information and to those channels which encourage such exchange in a free and democratic way. We need to know more about other women's situations, more about our rights, about contraception, about power and politics and even about nuclear power. We have to know what we need before we can hope to find ways of getting it. Maybe this is where a new kind of adventure starts.

*Angela McRobbie*

## What is feminism?

Considering that this is obviously a crucial question for a book like this, it seems a bit odd to say that we don't really know the answer. But then you've already been warned that this book is about clues and questions, not answers. Feminism is a word you may be familiar with,

though feminists are more often called, or rather put down, as 'women's libbers' — or something even less polite. The image of 'women's libbers' that we all get from the media, and from most other people, tends to be of 'bra burning', ugly (or at least unattractive), screaming women who only cause trouble and make a fuss over nothing because they can't get a man. Hopefully, it will be clear from this book that in fact feminism is about women, all women; it's about the way we live our lives, the things that happen to us and the things we make happen, being able to talk together, act together, and support each other. It's not about what you look like, how you have your hair cut, whether you wear Doc Martins or high heels, dresses or trousers. It *is* about having *choices*, about not having to wear high heels because you're small, not having to wear flat shoes because you're tall. Feminism is about being who you want to be — and finding out who you are in the first place.

Some of us find the idea of women's liberation frightening, off-putting, fascinating, exciting, intimidating. None of us felt confident about it when we first got involved. For young women it's probably more difficult. Have you ever sat in a meeting, or in a room full of older women, and not known what they were talking about? Or been bored out of your head? Or felt out of it because they didn't notice you? Or felt intimidated because it seemed as if everyone but you understands — about childbirth, marriage, sex, children, relationships? Feminism can often seem as if it's for older women, it's got nothing to do with *your* life.

There is one basic reason why, although most of us have felt like this at some time, this can't be the case. There's no single feminism. Because feminism is about all women, and for all women, it means different things to all of us. It takes different forms, it's concerned about different things. If you're having a relationship with a man, the most important thing to you could be getting hold of decent contraception. If you're pregnant, it could be getting an abortion, or good ante-natal care. If you have kids, it could be nurseries or childcare. If you go to a youth club, it could be getting a go on the pool table, or getting events or space just for girls. If you're at school, it could be learning woodwork or learning how to cook for yourself — not always for a family. If you're black, it could be stopping the school from treating you as less important than the white girls. If you're married, it could be forcing people to see you in your own right. If you're a lesbian, it could be stopping other people from always assuming you're heterosexual, being able to say you're not. If you're low paid, it could be equal pay and training that matter most to you. We're all in very different situations and at every point in our lives our priorities, the issues that affect us most, are different too. But we also care about other women, and know that every struggle by any group of women makes us all stronger. So we've got the right to demand support and to get it — something that young women need to fight for, even from other women. We do think that young women and older women can work together, but it has to be on *your* terms, since girls often have different needs and are seen as less 'grown up' than adult women, with fewer rights and never taken seriously. I remember adolescence as probably the most difficult period of my life so far, not because *I* was disturbed, but because of boys, parents, teachers!

On top of all this, if you read through the lines in this book, you'll see that the different chapters, though they're all written by feminists, have different perspectives. The fact that we're all women doesn't mean we agree with each other all the time. So different chapters will be arguing different things. Within the WLM (Women's Liberation Movement) there are lots of different politics and women put their energy and time into the areas that they see as the most important, or relevant, to them. We have big disagreements, not to mention rows. Women aren't nice to each other all the time! Our ideas can be so different that it can make it difficult, or impossible, to *always* work together. And feminists outside of the WLM may have different ideas again. But that doesn't mean we shouldn't listen to each other, or that we aren't all fighting for the same thing. The however-many thousands of women that are involved in the WLM in this country (and there are millions more, in every country of the world) obviously don't agree on how to end women's oppression, or exactly what kind of society we want to build. The WLM is a movement, not a political party or a social set, precisely because it can encompass so many different political positions. The movement has broad aims — not a political programme — and what we have in common is that we all want women's liberation, we all want changes, and we all want choices.

For all of us, our ideas come from who we know, what we read, what we see and listen to. We aren't born with ready-made ideas; we learn them, develop them, adapt them. But some ideas are around a lot more than others; we hear them more often, we look at images of them more often — and ideas are catching. Not many of us 'catch' the ideas of feminism, because they're just not around as much. We're trying to spread the germs and hoping you catch them! Or at least know they're there. How many other books, magazines and films are spreading the feminist germs? How many magazines have you read recently that discuss feminism seriously or sympathetically? How many people do you know who think women's liberation is important, or a good idea? How many television programmes and advertisements show women as strong, positive, independent, making decisions for *themselves*? Then again, how many magazines only talk about how to get boyfriends, which clothes and make-up styles are 'in', what you should look like? How many people have you heard say women's libbers are making a fuss over nothing, going too far? How many times have you seen

Page 3 staring at you on the bus?

One reason, we all wrote this book is because we think that the ideas of feminism — the differences as well as the similarities — should be around and available — in schools, colleges, techs, because if you're going to say that feminists are talking rubbish, at least you should know what we actually *do say*. But we also wanted to show that you don't have to believe any one thing to be a feminist, there's no signing on the dotted line, that if the issue is choice then we also have to be free to choose our own ideas. And if it's about all women, then it's also about listening to each other and learning. Not learning the right answers, but learning that there aren't any — not until we make them.

Most of us don't really get the chance to make up our own minds because we don't get all the sides of the story, especially not the sides that threaten the people who want to make up our minds for us. The mass media, the books you read, the films and television programmes you watch are usually written, produced and controlled by men. Feminists are women and we have the other side of the story. Not only that, but feminism's story has different sides — and you might not have heard all, or even any, of them before. Being a feminist is a bit like washing out your ears, opening your eyes, and telling everyone else to shut up for a bit. Above all, it's about taking risks, being open to new ideas, being prepared to explore new possibilities, discovering what women's lives are like, what your life is like, and what you haven't recognised in yourself. Women's oppression is normal, it's 'common sense' that women can't walk down the road at night alone, need a man for protection, automatically want marriage, children and a 'home of their own'. It's only if we start to make it *not* normal, *not* make sense, ask questions, that we start to find out what women *are* and can be. So it's time to decide what kind of women you want to be, what options are open, it's time to give yourself *space* — forget the washing up and the babysitting and think what *you* want to do. Taking risks and asking questions is dangerous, but it can also be exciting and fun. Young women spend most of their lives having decisions made for them. Maybe it's time for you to make a change for yourselves.

*Trisha McCabe*

## Politics, personal life and publishing

How is a book like this produced? We think it's worth trying to answer this question in some detail. Why? Because conventionally the whole process of writing books, researching and publishing is presented as something which is above most people's heads, a mystified activity requiring mysterious skills. Typically, you have to be exceptionally clever, talented, or at least highly educated before you can put pen to

paper with any hope of seeing what you write appear in print. Likewise, writing is seen as an intensely personal and isolated activity, carried out in solitude and demanding gifts like inspiration, insight, style, even genius.

Of course, writing and publishing do demand skills and abilities which have to be learnt and can take several years to master. And writing does tend to be something done alone, although, (as two of our chapters here show), this need not necessarily be the case. Our aim in this short section is to normalise the whole procedure and hopefully to make it more accessible to other women and girls. We'll describe the background to this particular collection, the way it was conceptualised, the problems we encountered and the kinds of people who have contributed to it. We will not be saying that any of these processes was straightforward or easy; nor will we be suggesting that everyone can or should want, automatically, to do this kind of work. The point is that discussing, collaborating and working collectively are especially important for women. It certainly doesn't save time; frequently it would be quicker to work alone — its advantages are possibly less immediately visible and more long-term in effect. Ideally, it would mean that *more* women and girls have *more* self-confidence about writing and that, in a sphere very much dominated by men, they too would have the pleasure of seeing their texts available and on the counters.

It is certainly the case that men have dominated the literary world, but historically, writing (everything from novels to love-letters) has played a vital role in women's culture — as has reading. We want to suggest that the value that women have, through the ages, placed on these forms is very much worth holding on to and actively encouraging. As Gill Frith suggests in her article, becoming aware of women's oppression demands that we learn anew 'how to read'. Learning also anew 'how to write' and how to make women's writing as widely available as possible is a necessary part of this 'consciousness raising'. But still there are limits to the kinds of consciousness raising that we as *white* women have been involved in, be it talking, reading or writing.

One of the most difficult areas in writing a book like this for girls is that in our society we tend to immediately think of white girls. To try to counteract this racism we have to be careful not to fall into adding a token chapter about black girls. In some ways, this is what we've done, and we are aware of the problems this raises. The chapter by Pratibha and Val in fact challenges lots of the assumptions that we, and all white people in a racist society, make about black women. I found that chapter challenging and threatening to read; it was hard work. It seems likely that most white readers will feel the same, because the article shows how, as white people, we benefit from racism, however much we may try to be anti-racist. In many ways this is the only type of chapter that could have been written in a book that is predominantly about white girls. Black girls can't just be added on as a footnote or an appendix, as a special case. It's more important to have a chapter like this because it makes clear an unwritten assumption, which is that the other chapters are, in fact, about white girls. I think that Pratibha's and Val's chapter shows us how the rest of the book should be read; it indicates that we, as white women, have to be aware that girls or women 'in general' in fact means white girls and women. It makes us aware of the insidious ways in which racism operates, by almost making black girls invisible — or at least masking the fact that the other chapters are about whites. As I said before, reading that chapter is hard work for white women — though for black girls reading this book it's probably a breath of fresh air — and it's difficult not to take it as a personal criticism of us as white women. But then again, maybe it's about time that we *did* take it personally. Racism is our problem and we have to start making changes.

Originally, the idea was that this book would comprise of a set of readings. These would be chosen from already existing feminist work, particularly that which dealt with adolescence. But after a few informal conversations we began to realise that there was a great deal of new work on girls in the pipeline, work which we could publish for the first time and which would bring completely fresh perspectives to the subject. We immediately set about commissioning pieces. This we did in an admittedly haphazard way, not advisable in retrospect, but fortunately not too disastrous. The women we discovered were willing to contribute were mostly researchers, but they did include an ex-secretary, a number of teachers, youth workers, and a German social worker. Altogether, this now seemed a more exciting project than scanning years of women's literature for relevant passages.

After we worked out exactly who would be contributing, two all-day sessions were organised and were attended by most of the writers. In the first session basic guidelines for writing were discussed — like clarity and accessibility, and several women summarised the main points they would be raising in their papers. Some months later the group met again, this time to listen to draft versions of completed contributions and to iron out problems that had arisen on the way. Next came the slow process of waiting for chapters to come in — discussing them, editing them, sending them back for comment, suggesting rewrites and so on. At the same time we had to collaborate with the women who had undertaken to be responsible for the illustration, an important dimension in a hopefully 'popular' book like this. Each chapter, when completed, had to be sent out to an artist, and if the writing was delayed then so, in turn, was the artist and if when it did arrive the artist was already busy then it had to wait. Only three chapters, all of which were possibly the most difficult to write, demanded a lot of discussion and rewriting and this went on, quite literally, for weeks. It meant contributors coming from London and Sheffield to Birmingham on at least five different occasions. On top of this two chapters got lost in the post, one on the way from Jamaica, the other, less exotically, somewhere between Sheffield and Birmingham! Eventually we got them all to the typist and to the illustrators. It has taken almost eighteen months, exactly a year longer than we had anticipated. At the risk of sounding melodramatic, organising this book has given us sleepless nights, vast telephone bills, and countless migraines (more of an ordeal than a gripping adventure). At the risk of sounding clichéd, we still think it was worth it.

Most books include, either in the foreword or else in the introduction, some kind of personal dedication to the people who have helped on the sidelines, who have given advice, emotional support, and friendship. They are usually mentioned fleetingly and, when the books in question are written by men, these shadowy figures are most often wives or girlfriends. Instead of simply reproducing this pattern, we want to show just how doing this work has invaded our personal lives. The people we have depended on know this and it would be little more than tokenism to 'name' them. As editors, our role has obviously been more demanding, more involved, but as a product, the book has been the result of a whole set of working relations, some harmonious, some stormy. Inevitably, friends have been involved in all the debates, they have read the chapters, discussed them and helped to solve some seemingly intractable political problems.

One such weighty problem related to the whole question of editorship, and what it demonstrated conclusively to us was the extent to which any purely neutral 'professional' definitions of this role are blown apart when the personal politics of the Women's Movement are involved. Traditionally, the task of the editor is quite clear — to commission articles and maintain a balance between taking risks and guaranteeing 'good copy' on time. Certainly, the job doesn't end there, but when there is an issue at stake, the focus is generally on the text or the script itself. But while clarity, good writing, the flow of the argument and the overall coherence of the piece are vital, regardless of politics, external issues do intervene when the book comes out of the Women's Movement.

One of us commissioned a chapter, yet it does not appear in this volume. There is no point in rehearsing all the ins and outs of the arguments which resulted in this decision. This simply isn't the place to dwell on the various positions represented within feminism; it's sufficient to say that one of us wanted to publish it, the other didn't. A battle raged for at least six weeks until it was clear that one of us had to concede.

It would be easy to say, 'Well, we learn by our mistakes.' Or that we should have been more systematic or rigorous about how we commissioned, or that *if* we had discussed our differences in relation to this chapter earlier . . . and so on.

Yet even the most watertight set of editorial principles couldn't legislate against issues like this emerging. Nor could they guarantee that they would be any less stubborn. Whatever the decision, one of us was bound to feel a little jaded. Perhaps all that can be said is that feminism can't and doesn't (nor should it) protect us from conflicts and disagreements between women. It would be both unrealistic and absurdly romantic to expect anything else. The adventure of feminism may be embarked upon with wildly optimistic expectations, but the exhilaration shouldn't blind us to the way in which it can at times tear us apart. Sisterliness and solidarity would be meaningless if they implied that we had to stop disagreeing with each other.

What we *have* clearly agreed about is who the book is aimed at and the importance of keeping this readership firmly in view throughout our quarrels. Once again, we started out with fairly inflated notions of our readership. In fact, girls aren't often encouraged to read 'seriously' unless it's for 'O' or 'A' levels, so it was probably a little unrealistic of us to imagine hordes of girls fighting to get their hands on a copy of *Adventure Story*. It is rare to come across books quite unprompted; usually it's a matter of someone telling you about *Wuthering Heights* or *The Joys of Sex*. Girls do tell each other about books, but they, in turn, are 'turned on to them' by groups as divergent as elder sisters, grandmothers, youth workers, teachers, even boyfriends, though we hope in this case to bypass this particular tradition. The point is that all sorts of influences act to push girls in one direction or the other and books don't just magically appear in front of them from nowhere. Realising this, we tried to stretch out our 'catchment area' to include women working with girls. Teachers, mothers, social workers and youth workers. We also hope that it will have some relevance to women returning to education after years of housework and childcare. As Dorothy Hobson's chapter shows, adolescence is an important turning point in most women's lives and is very definitely remembered as such. For the housewives in her sample, it represented their last taste of freedom, adventure and warm friendship. If our book and its various contents can also speak to women like these, perhaps attending evening classes in sociology or modern studies, then we will be more than thrilled.

What all this indicates is that, like it or not, we are in the business of education. But this doesn't just mean studying in the narrow sense to pass exams, it means learning in a much broader way to understand how society works and what it does to women. To have the confidence to challenge we must possess knowledge as well as conviction.

*Angela McRobbie*

### Are women really oppressed?

We talk about women's oppression a lot in this book, but what do we mean, exactly? It's actually a lot more difficult to recognise oppression than it is to assume that it doesn't really exist. One of the reasons for this is that women's oppression is 'normal', 'natural'. But is it? Is it normal for men to rape women? To batter women? To kill women? Violence is one issue that clears up the question of whether women are really oppressed or not. For me, personally, starting to see my own fears of the dark, my fears about walking down the street at night, of spending the night alone in the house, as something that isn't just personal has been both scary *and* confidence-building. Scary because it's 'common sense' that women generally shouldn't be out alone at night, wear hemlines that are too high or necklines that are too low, lead men on, or accept lifts from strangers; otherwise we ask for it — don't we? Scary because questioning common sense always is. Scary because it means that men can go where they want, when they want, wear what they want to and not worry about how to get home. They can do what they want, too, and we all know that men are aggressive, easily aroused and potentially violent. That is how they are taught to be. Confidence-building because I know now that it doesn't have to be like that, women don't just have to put up with it and 'be careful'. Is it natural for one half of the population to have to always 'be careful' because of the other half?

Of course, not all men rape women, so is it really a question of women being oppressed by men? Most men are nice men, especially the ones you know, they wouldn't do anything like that. So it's not men — just some men. But what do *you* do if you're on your way home at night and a man, or a group of lads, are walking towards you? Cross the road? Walk faster? Grit your teeth and feel terrified? Just ignore them — but feel a bit scared none the less? It doesn't really matter whether he's a 'nice man' or not, because in that situation *you* can't tell. Every man you meet is someone to be scared of *just because he's a man*. As long as some men do attack women, then every woman has to be frightened of, or at least wary of, every man. Is that natural? But not every man — it's OK if you know him, the boyfriend you rely on to walk you home, your friend's dad who picks you both up from a party. Unfortunately, though we all tell ourselves that, most rapes are actually committed by someone you know. Your boyfriend, husband, next-door neighbour, workmates or classmates — they are all more likely to attack you than a stranger who leaps out in the dark. Is that natural?

So what do we do? The short answer is usually not so much as we'd like to. We don't tend to question the fact that parents, boyfriends, husbands put limits on our freedom, stop us doing things that we might otherwise like to do because of their fear that we'll be attacked, assaulted or abused by *other* men! It sounds odd putting it like that, but it's not because of other women is it? So one half of the population, men, keeps the other half, women, scared, dependent on other people, and without the freedom to even walk down the street and feel safe. Is that natural?

But then isn't it all biological after all? Men are stronger than women and more into sex — they get frustrated easily (or at least some of them do) and women are easy prey. Well, for a start I don't think rape is about sex, as such. If sex is about caring about another person, and wanting to give them pleasure, getting pleasure from that person — in other words, mutual — then violently attacking someone, enjoying terrifying and humiliating them, often beating them up, seems the opposite of sex to me. Rape is about power and violence, not biological differences. Just because someone has a penis, and someone else a vagina, does that mean that it's 'natural' for the man to want to stick it into a woman, any woman, against her will? And physically and psychologically destroy her as a person? Is it natural for men to see women as a hole rather than a human being? Is it natural that, with a whole body, women are actually treated as a walking vagina, one part of our body defining our whole being?

All this may seem a bit extreme, but it doesn't seem like that to me any more. One reason for this is that I've been learning self-defence for the last eighteen months, and it's made a big difference to my life. It's forced me, and the other women in the class, to recognise that we *are* scared, that women from six months old to ninety years old get raped, that most women are attacked or raped at least once in our lives, that it can and does happen to any of us (and the age range in the class I go to is from twelve to sixty) and that *we have to do something about it for ourselves*. I can't afford a car (though that doesn't necessarily make you safe), I do have to be out after dark, I don't want to have to rely on a man to walk me home — and that's not safe either — and I don't live with a man. So I'm scared; at night, outside, and at home. Even during the day sometimes! Because I've also learnt that rapes don't just happen after dark, or outside your own home.

You could say that doing self-defence has made me paranoid. I sometimes think that myself, because what's actually happened is that I've been made more aware of things that I'd really rather not have known about. But I've also learnt that I have the right to say no, that it's not OK for men to hassle me, that my body belongs to me and no one else. I've also taught self-defence to girls and seen similar things happen. Girls who have been raped, whose friends got attacked on the way home from school, who've been frightened by flashers or who are 'just' scared. Learning to fight back means developing a sense of your own personal space that belongs to you; it makes it possible to see that men in the street, fathers and brothers and boyfriends don't automatically have the right to boss you, grab you, hassle you. Men haven't got the right to persuade you to go further than you want to. They don't have the right to touch you unless you want to touch them. And other people don't have the right to say 'What did you expect?' because you should expect everyone to respect your body. And that means you must be able to respect it yourself.

I'm still scared — and I feel angry because I no longer accept it as 'just natural'. I don't want to spend the rest of my life being scared if I meet a man after dark. If I live alone, I don't want to wait around at parties for someone to walk home with when really I just want to go. I don't want to go on being careful about where I live, whether it's secure, can I afford a telephone just in case? I don't believe that any woman has never experienced this kind of fear. I don't believe any man knows what it's like to live with that fear. None of us can stop being scared until men stop being aggressive and seeing women as available any time for whatever they — the men — want.

### Action

Do we have to put up with these limits on our freedom? With not being able to enjoy leisure in the same way as boys — not being able to explore new places, new parts of the city, stay out late, afford a night out if you need a taxi at the end of it? If your answer to that is no, then it's important to recognise that the action we can take is limited. It would be totally irresponsible to say that if you do self-defence you can wander the streets at will in safety. After all, being frightened is probably the biggest block to being *able* to fight back, not physical strength or lack of techniques. And it's not much fun being scared and maybe having to fight just so that you can say you're independent. Self-defence is *something* of a solution for individual women; maybe you should ask for classes at school, instead of PE (after all jumping over horses or whatever isn't something you'll need to know how to do in everyday life — though being fit is). Or why not advertise for a woman to teach a class in your area? We have to rely on each other — check out your local women's centre or ask at a martial arts club if anyone (preferably a woman, they understand what you need to know better) could teach a class. Demonstrating or marching against rape can also help, it makes us feel stronger and brings violence against women to the attention of other people. Women throughout the country have organised 'Reclaim the Night' marches to protest against rape and assault, and the feeling of walking down the street at night, with lots of other women carrying torches, shouting, being angry *and* having a good time, is hard to describe. Where I live, we marched one night and all the kerb crawlers (men who follow you around in their cars — even during the day!) had to turn around and get away fast, they were scared by the sight of so many women. It makes a change; *you don't feel scared.* It also makes you realise how frightened you are the rest of the time, but in a way that shows you that we don't have to go on accepting our fear, we can protest and show that we're angry. Women who are raped, whose husbands or boyfriends beat them up, even women who are frightened of rape or are threatened with violence *aren't allowed* to do what they want to. They aren't equal to men because their freedom is limited by men. I think this applies to all of us, if we're all threatened with violence at some point, and scared at others. None of us are as free as men, nor are we ever completely safe. So what is oppression? One group of people denying another group freedom — the same freedom as themselves. It seems to me that not having the freedom to control your own body and therefore your own life is a pretty fundamental and everyday form of oppression. Why should we put up with it? I can't think of one good reason. I can think of every reason not to.

## Practical hints

There's not a lot I can say on paper, as the main advantage women who fight back have is that men don't expect us to. Nevertheless, all the things our mothers told us to carry at night are useful. Anything you can use as a weapon is important and worth having handy. *Attract attention* if you are attacked. Shouting rape won't, in our experience, help — shouting fire or throwing something at a window might. Practise screaming — yes, really, because women tend to freeze when they're attacked and can't get any sound out at all. If you're walking alone and see another woman, or other women, ask to walk with them — it doesn't matter if you don't know them, they'll understand. Wearing shoes you can run in, or taking off high heels to run, throwing anything you're carrying at him, and keeping fairly fit are all important. If you do get raped and want to report it, take a friend to the police station, do it straight away. Police aren't always sympathetic and women are more often 'put on trial' for rape than rapists are. You can also ring a Rape Crisis Centre for advice, someone to talk to or someone to go with you to the police. Even in this case you may still have to fight for your rights; being confident about having the right to say no in the first place makes this a lot easier.

'However we dress, wherever we go, yes means yes and no means no.'

This may be just a slogan — but if we believe it ourselves we've made a start in making it a reality.

*Trisha McCabe*

## Sixth-form semi-feminism: poetry, punk and promiscuity

Quite a large amount of space in this book is devoted to the setting up of two kinds of arguments. One of these is about the extent to which girls and young women are hard done by, in the school, in the family, by the mass media, in job opportunities and in love and romance. The concern of the writers is to demonstrate vividly the kind of discrimination and oppression which is experienced every day in a multiplicity of ways. And the objective? To make this kind of account available, to promote discussion, and to help bring about change. A shared recognition that this is something worth taking issue about, challenging and actively struggling against. The second kind of argument is less concrete. It's concerned with this process of active change. It's suggesting that what happens to girls needn't, and that, contrary to popular belief, women's subordination is not just based on 'human nature'. Reading between the lines, these articles are making suggestions. Like, for example, start a girls' magazine! Put as much emphasis on friendships with girls as those with boys! Encourage mothers to question *their* roles in the home! Think about the positive aspects of breaking with convention. 'YBA Wife?' as one feminist campaign puts it! Importantly, neither of these sets of arguments want to rob girls of their femininity. Rather, they want girls to redefine it and claim it as their own, independent of boys. So, really, it's got nothing to do with washing off the make-up and throwing away the mascara. More a matter of choice, doing it for yourself and not doing it if you don't want to.

In this section I want to shift the focus a little. I want to suggest that despite all our arguments about what society does to girls, anyone who works with them knows that they are not the docile, passive creatures we might well expect them to be. Social attempts at subduing a considerable proportion of the population, in this instance girls, are invariably frustrated. Girls (and boys) are not just human putty, to be moulded into shape at will. Rather, they are parts of human and social groups; sexes, classes, ethnic groups, cultures and subcultures, with all the values, attitudes and resistances which these entail.

They *do* challenge that which is perceived to be unacceptable, even if the way in which they challenge is not, perhaps in our view, the most immediately damaging, the most 'political'. But every day girls 'talk back' to teachers, to authoritative figures. They don't always let themselves be pushed around by employers, by families and by boys. For girls, both the most symbolic and the most concrete escape from authority is one which the authorities are very well aware of, so much so that it's officially recognised as a social problem in its own right, 'running away from home'. Girls do demand the right to leisure even if the only place they can find it is in the school and during school time! When they get married they don't all become good, loving, wives and conscientious mothers. If they did, the divorce rate wouldn't be as high as it is. More and more women are unwilling to put up with the mental and physical bullying which their husbands often see as part of normal married life. More and more women are demanding, and perhaps even getting, better, warmer, and more equal relationships within marriage. Men are being forced to take notice.

So here I want to single out, for a moment, the girls who *do*. Not the girls who have already become 'young feminists', but rather those who experience their gender and its implications in complex and confusing ways, but who individually and often quite alone are unwilling to capitulate, who resist the seemingly natural outcome of their sex in small but obstinate gestures, who are stubbornly opposed to the assumption that there are a great number of things girls can't do.

Some years ago I began some research on white working-class girls — their family lives, their leisure, their sexuality and their career opportunities. I argued that they didn't just go along with their prescribed careers as wives and mothers, as underpaid part-time workers and full-time domestic labourers; rather, that the way they worked out the often contradictory demands put on them was extraordinarily complex and complexly subtle. It was full of delaying mechanisms, so that even if in the end oppression did get the better of them — and in many ways it did (at a time of increasing youth unemployment where young unqualified girls are among the most vulnerable groups), they none the less manipulated the structures where they could. They didn't expect much of boys and men and if their romances or marriages 'didn't work out' they weren't going to hang on to him. Nor were they willing to put up with the thought of a lifetime of drudgery. Of course, even this account drastically simplifies. What I'm trying to suggest is that the girls were caught in both a class and a gender trap — so much of what happened to them was beyond their control — yet they did act upon aspects of this oppression, they were neither inadequate nor under-socialised as the text-books would have it. They certainly didn't conform to middle-class norms; they didn't perform well at school, nor did they behave 'like ladies' in and out of school. But they did use all the resources they could to voice their disaffiliation. School uniforms, magazines, pop culture, language, gesture and culture, these were all part of their armoury of resistance.

What I didn't manage to encompass in my research and what, as far as I know, has not as yet really been commented on by feminist writers, is a kind of gender disaffiliation which is nearer both to my own personal experience and, I suspect, to that of many active feminists today, and much more difficult to locate and describe precisely. So I'll start off with some loose comments.

One of the ways in which class domination (at its most crude the power of those who 'own' over those who don't) operates, is to make escape from one's class destiny difficult if not impossible. The working-class girl is destined for a working-class career and often even the greatest amount of resistance to this merely has the effect of securing it. The more she rebels against the boredom of school subjects and the authority of the teachers, the more likely is she to find herself eventually in the most boring kind of job, and dependent on her husband's wage as hers isn't enough to cover the cost of her own keep. The result is that girls who do avoid their own particular class and gender destiny are both unusual and invariably isolated in their 'deviance'. Even those who escape by what sociologists call 'upward mobility' experience intense feelings of alienation. It's been shown time and time again that when, under the old grammar school system, working-class girls made it into the predominantly middle-class atmosphere of the grammar school, they were most likely to drop out early and fail academically. Feelings of social inadequacy overcame and stifled whatever academic interests they had originally harboured. (One of Dorothy Hobson's interviewees describes this quite poignantly.)

For middle-class girls, however, the leap into unconventionality, though often frowned upon, is both financially and ideologically less traumatic. What I want to suggest is that in the post-war years the main recruiting grounds for our contemporary 'bohemias' — artistic fringes where unconventional values are celebrated, 'radical' alternatives actively pursued, experimental sexuality endorsed — are the 'delinquent' lower-middle-class ends of the old grammar and new comprehensive schools. And this goes for boys as well as girls. I'm not suggesting a direct escape route into feminism, more a meandering path through things like poetry, social issues, even school drama, which often ends up in a kind of semi-feminism. The interesting thing is that these are all spheres that traditionally girls can do well in. And since the early 1960s, state funding of 'the arts' has made it possible for some girls to find careers here, in a way that wouldn't have been possible thirty years ago when post-war bohemia first raised its head as an ambiguously male adventure. One which found explicitly masculine expression in writers like Jack Kerouac and William Burroughs in the United States and, less exotically, John Osborne in England.

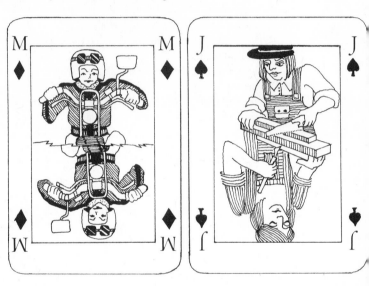

It's difficult to say how many feminists today embraced this path through 'culture' and 'bohemia'. Maybe now it seems like an unnecessary detour, but when I first read Sheila Rowbotham's *Woman's Consciousness, Man's World* and her account of finding a relatively unknown paperback called *Protest*, an anthology of the new angry (male) writers, I felt quite thrilled because, some years later, I too found it remaindered in Woolworth's on my way home from school. And the 'Howls' of protest which it included within its covers, from Allen Ginsberg's long poem 'Howl' to Norman Mailer's 'The White Negro' had a similar effect on me. I too was overwhelmed by the force of the disaffiliation that these essays announced — even though not one of them was written by a woman. It also made me question why my school English literature course never got past D.H. Lawrence. Perhaps importantly, many of my girlfriends at school were also, in the late 1960s, beginning to question the value of the 'straight life'. One wrote a school play about Vietnam, others started surreptitiously to smoke marijuana, some even talked about living with people rather than getting married! By the early 1970s, in Glasgow (things always arrived in Glasgow at least five years late), hippiness had become a full-blown ideology. At that point I don't think anybody noticed that it was still men who were doing things: organising events, playing in bands or setting up business as hippy entrepreneurs. A few women (those considered to be very cool) dropped out altogether and had babies, but somehow, either remnants of Catholicism or remnants of our parents' insistence that we finish what we started and get some kind of qualification, or simply a sense of the need to survive economically, kept all my women friends enrolled in higher education.

My point in documenting this is not to evoke feelings of nostalgia. I do think that this kind of route was and is both quite typical and important for the women involved. I can't imagine feeling closer to anybody than I do to two of these women. Ten years later we are all feminists, one a playwright, the other studying to be a women's rights lawyer. Of the rest of this group, all are financially independent — some have rejected marriage and stable relationships altogether, they have boyfriends and lovers, own their own flats and are, well, common-sense feminists. Of course, we have all had the privilege of (lower) middle-class backgrounds where a career was seen as a good investment, should your husband run off and leave you, or even die and leave you a widow. We have all angered our parents, even grieved them. We have threatened their respectability and rejected their religious beliefs. They still try to, and do, exert an influence on our lives. Recently my mother, upset that I didn't want to send my little girl to a Catholic school, adopted a new tactic in her repertoire of well-intended emotional blackmail. 'Even Communists in France send their children to Catholic schools,' she said.

Nor do I think all this represents a historical accident — the side-effects of hippy-trippyness. For a start, it refers to a social phenomenon which is continually being reproduced. As all teachers will testify, being 'into' poetry and punk, David Bowie and anti-fashion, being a bit different, not fancying the local heart-throbs, but definitely fancying the idea of adventure, escape, living in a flat, drinking coffee and finding people who 'understand' — all of these continue to be rallying points for generations of girls. And some examples? Well it's always easiest to look at the most immediately visible figures, those who have 'made it' in (and through) precisely these terms. Kate Bush's lyrics and songs, their yearning, but explicitly sexual, romanticism; their celebration of the exotic; their overwhelming literariness ('Wuthering Heights' of course); Toyah Willcox's choice of acting roles, from tarty girl in 'Quadrophenia' to Miranda, sensual child, in *The Tempest*; her school-girl shock tactics; her punk persona. Julie Burchill's vitriolic punk journalism, and her giveaway autobiographical fragments (an adolescence apparently of séances and superior self-imposed isolation). Most of all,

Patti Smith's arty poems and rock lyrics; her schoolgirl crushes on archetypal bohemians; her escape from gender into androgyny, and her consequent wariness of established feminism. None of these women are feminists, they frequently even define themselves against it, yet in many ways they betray all the features of this kind of semi-feminism I'm trying to describe. They're undoubtedly individualists, but in a society where, for women to succeed, they have to struggle against the odds, it's hardly surprising that these women should resist being categorised, labelled and compartmentalised and then possibly dismissed. My point in considering these pop/punk figures is to show how in society at large and outside official feminism things are and have been changing for quite some time. Women in the public eye need no longer subscribe to a wholly traditional and glamorous stereotype. And all of these women have constructed a style, be it literary or visual, poetic or musical, which exists quite apart from, and in contradiction to, what 'nice girls' are taught to do. One way or another they *threaten*, and I can't help but think this is an extremely useful tactic in the long-term struggle to redefine what it means to be a woman.

*Angela McRobbie*

### Women's space

One of the things we've learnt in the Women's Liberation Movement is that it's crucial to have space for women only, and that we have the right to meet and talk without men being there. This has always aroused some hostility, especially from men, who can't understand why we might not want them there. But we have found it impossible to talk about us as women, and about how men oppress us and put us down if they're there. In our society the only women-only spaces are toilets and bathrooms — if you go to any school or youth club you'll find girls in there: talking, smoking, putting on make-up, doing the things they can't do anywhere else. There are no female equivalents to the men's clubs, pubs, football matches or even the streets to hang around. When you have a problem at school and want to talk quietly to your friend about it, where do you go? In a club, whether it's a youth club or a night club, the toilets are usually full of women, talking. Women need space to ourselves — men already have that space. Feminists often have discos for women, women's bars to go to for a quiet drink with no hassles, meetings and conferences where men aren't allowed. Why? Because it's important to know that we don't need men to enjoy ourselves, that women are interesting people we can get to know much better if their men aren't around, that if we enjoy dancing, whether it's working out a disco dance or just moving around, we can do without the lads laughing at us. And we can talk without having to adapt our

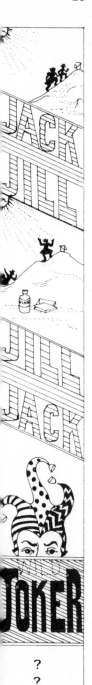

conversation, without having to listen to men going on and ON. Have you ever noticed how in a mixed group of people the men talk much, much longer than the women. The other week I was going to work — it's a half-hour train journey — and this man I didn't know wanted someone to talk to. I decided to wait and see how long it would take him to notice that I was just nodding and not saying anything. Half an hour later, he said, 'Thanks for the chat, it was nice talking to you!'

What's started to happen relatively recently is that on the one hand, young women have demanded that space for them too, in schools, youth clubs and within the WLM, and, on the other hand, women who work with girls have questioned their own practice, their attitudes to boys and girls. Women teachers, youth workers, social workers — and mothers — have found themselves putting more energy into boys, because they cause more trouble; giving them more attention because they demand it, offering them more facilities to keep them occupied. In short, reproducing the same old attitudes to boys and girls and assuming that the girls are quite happy because they keep quiet (or quieter). In trying to change that, feminist teachers, mothers, and youth workers have found that if girls get space and attention then they'll make demands too, have ideas, organise and experiment. If you make an effort then girls are just as interested, and just as interesting as boys.

But young women don't need telling this. Girls in schools have started girls' groups, meetings just for girls. They have organised to get the right to wear trousers to school, just like boys, have questioned sexism in their lessons, fought for the right to do woodwork or metalwork and found women teachers who'll help them to put on plays, write articles and read things about what it's like being a girl. In youth clubs, young women have demanded space for themselves, access to pool tables, darts, table tennis, organised and enjoyed events and activities that are relevant to them. They've found they can enjoy being just with girls, at girls' nights, days, weekends, or in girls' groups — even girls' clubs! They've felt able to try out things they would never have done if the boys were there: self-defence, riding motor bikes, using video and film — the list is endless. Instead of saying 'I can't', girls have found out that they *can*, have explored new ideas and opened up new possibilities for themselves.

In some ways we hope this book will help to do the same thing; open up ideas and ways of exploring what women are and can be. It hopefully shows that there *is* support from other women when young women want to make changes, and that we can work together. We're saying that young women have rights too, to their own space and their own ideas. Our ideas certainly aren't a blueprint, but we hope they will be a springboard to start from, to jump from. What you do with the ideas is up to you, whether or how they affect your life is obviously

your decision. However you decide, if you do want to make changes it
also clear that it's not simple, that sometimes you don't just have to as
— you have to fight. We think that control over your own life and spac
to yourself is something worth fighting for.

*Trisha McCab*

# Part I

# Experience

# 2 Little women, good wives:

## is English good for girls?

*Gill Frith*

Illustrated by *Suzy Varty*

I have been teaching English in comprehensive schools (mixed and single sex) since 1970. I started teaching in what you might call a spirit of naive optimism — believing that comprehensives were in themselves the answer to society's ills. I came to realise that the inequalities (of sex, race and class) which exist *outside* the school system also have their effect *within* the school system; classrooms are not 'neutral' and nor are the subjects that we learn in them.

**What has feminism to do with school?**

Since the Sex Discrimination Act in 1975, it has been against the law for schools to discriminate against either sex. The school must offer equal opportunities for boys and girls. For example, girls must be allowed to do metalwork and technical drawing; boys must be allowed to take domestic science and needlework. Is everything all right now, then?

It isn't quite that simple. In 1979, a Department of Education and Science survey commented gloomily that:[1]

> equality of opportunity for the sexes had not in practice been easy
> to achieve. The choice of subjects still tended to reflect traditional
> sex roles, with fewer girls on science courses, more girls on child
> development courses. In college 'linked' courses, in the 4th and 5th
> years, the boys largely selected technically based studies, while girls
> were mostly found taking commercial subjects and courses such as
> hairdressing.

Why is this still happening? The DES survey concludes that the reasons are 'above all, the attitudes and aspirations of parents and the pupils themselves'. In other words, nothing to do with the school?

Schools are all different, and some schools are much more sensitive than others to the need for equal opportunities. You'll have to consider the next points in the light of your own school experience. Were both sexes given equal treatment? Did differences in uniform, play areas, punishment, sports activities, make girls and boys more conscious of the *differences* between them? Were certain subjects more likely to be taught by men, and others by women? Did textbooks or teaching materials give the impression that some subjects were more appropriate for one particular sex? Were most of the senior posts in the school held by men? The important point here is that if the organisation of the school shows differences between the sexes, students are likely to respond accordingly.

It's not surprising that this should be so. Schools are a product of their society, and they reflect the values and assumptions of that society. Teachers, too, are not immune. They are people: they have themselves, both men and women, been influenced by their upbringing, and may, consciously or unconsciously, have different expectations for girls and for boys. Of course, not all teachers are the same. You may have come across teachers who said quite openly that they thought women were inferior to men, or who called girls by their first names and boys by their surnames, or 'flirted' with their students. The effects of this are obvious, but there can be more subtle distinctions. Teachers may, even without realising it, take it for granted that girls will do their homework, listen quietly, present their work neatly; that boys will call out, move from their seats, push each other, take less trouble in presenting their work. As a teacher, I often used to gear lessons to the interests of the boys without even thinking about it; the girls wouldn't make a fuss. When I later tried consciously to treat all my students equally, I still found it hard. Teachers, like other people, find it difficult *not* to be affected by the assumptions of the world in which we live.

You may feel that there's an argument missing here. Isn't it *natural* for girls to be quiet, docile, enjoy dress-making and looking pretty; *natural* for boys to like football and fighting and messing about? The problem is that it's impossible for us to know what is natural and what isn't. By the time boys and girls reach the secondary school they have absorbed a barrage of influences from television, magazines, books, advertisements, friends and relations, all telling them in hidden and not so hidden ways what is 'proper' behaviour for boys and what is 'proper' behaviour for girls. None of us likes to think that we are not an individual, that we are the product of social conditioning, and indeed if social conditioning were really that effective, the differences between girls and boys would be far greater than they are. But unless we understand how much of our behaviour is 'learnt', we will never really be free to choose for ourselves.

In school, the problem is that in implicitly accepting that there are different codes of masculine and feminine behaviour, the school helps to *perpetuate* those values; it may even assume that the differences between boys and girls are greater than they really are. One young teacher on a school trip was extremely surprised to see girls joining in fights and football games with the boys. He said:[2]

> The amazing thing was that most of the girls were involved, and
> girls that I didn't think would be involved in that sort of thing, and
> in fact in school would definitely not be involved. . . . They were
> mixing with the rest and they didn't want to be left out of it,
> which I don't think we find in school so much. The girls don't mind

being left out. They would rather be left to their quiet life, because
I think we have put it across that that is the accepted role of girls in
the school, and it is the boys that have all the fun, and the girls
don't object to it because it is a socially accepted role.

What message, then, do girls receive in school about their sociall
accepted role? Do girls learn that it is 'feminine' to be quiet, obedien
hardworking and domesticated? Do boys learn that it is 'masculine' t
be strong, adventurous, wild and dominating? I am not suggesting tha
this is all a villainous plot on the part of schools to make girls fee
inferior. You might think that girls in fact *benefit* from some of these
assumptions: they are less likely to get into trouble. Nor do boys alway
have an easy time of it. As I write, there's a song on the radio whic
leads up to the conclusion: 'Sometimes you have to fight to be a man
What if you don't want to? Boys may not be happy with their 'sociall
accepted role' either. But there is a difference: behind the differen
expectations for boys and girls lies the assumption that girls will be
economically dependent, boys will be economically independent, tha
girls will be future wives and mothers and boys will be workers. It's no
surprising, then, that the subjects they choose reflect this — eve
though most boys will be husbands and fathers as well as workers; mos
girls will be workers as well as wives and mothers.

### English: a subject for girls?

Why worry about English? Surely English is the exception to what
have been saying: it's a subject which girls are successful at, and usuall
enjoy; it's an academic subject which isn't directly connected with
being a wife and mother, a haven, a refuge, where girls can work with
boys on equal terms. At fifth-year level, where English and maths are
compulsory, boys do better at maths, and girls do better at English; a
'A' level, when the subject is optional, the number of girls taking and
passing English 'A' level is twice the number of boys.[3]
What is it about English, though, that appeals to girls — that has ever
led to English being seen as a 'girls" subject? After all, English is essen
tial for almost any career; it is as important for boys as for girls. Th
reasons may go back a long way: to early childhood, when girls are
encouraged to read and draw, rather than run and shout; to the nine
teenth century, when girls were expected to rest, to preserve thei
energies, not to 'overstrain' themselves. You can see this in the com
ments that some people make about English: 'Every teacher is a teache
of English.' 'You don't *do* anything in English.' 'English is *easy*.'
English, then, is seen as an 'amateur' subject, connected with intui
tion and the emotions; a subject which doesn't involve learning a 'block

of knowledge', like history, or working things out, as in maths or science, or making things, as in woodwork. In English, you can keep your hands clean and your clothes tidy. You don't have to compete as directly as in other subjects where there are clearly 'right' and 'wrong' answers.

Also, it's generally accepted that girls find it easier to write essays than boys do. When a number of examining boards began to move more and more towards 'multiple-choice' questions, (the student is given several possible 'answers' to a question, and asked to tick the correct one) they found that the boys' performance suddenly improved. In subjects where they had been equal, the boys shot ahead of the girls; in subjects like English language, where girls have always done much better than boys, multiple-choice questions closed the gap. When a paper involves written essays, on the other hand, girls do better.

It is possible that the reasons for this again go back to early child-hood: that, by playing with 'boys'' toys, and helping their fathers with 'man's' jobs, the boys are developing abilities which will be useful later for science and maths as well as technical subjects. By playing with dolls, sitting quietly reading or drawing, helping their mothers, girls are not only paving the way for domestic subjects; they may also be developing the verbal abilities they will later need for writing essays. When girls enjoy English, then, are they simply fitting in with their traditional role, preferring an essentially passive activity? I shall return to this question later.

Let's get back to the idea of English as a 'refuge', where girls can get on with a subject they enjoy, on equal terms with the boys. How far is this really true?

What happens in the English classroom does not happen in isolation. The English classroom is part of the school, and if boys and girls learn elsewhere that there are different standards for 'masculine' and 'feminine' behaviour, this will affect the way in which they behave in the class room, and the way in which their teachers respond to them. In English teachers may, often without being aware of it, have different expecta tions of the ways in which boys and girls will approach their subject: that girls will like poetry and boys won't, that girls will write thorough careful essays and boys will be more slap-dash, that girls will listen and boys will answer questions, that girls will be interested and boys will have to be persuaded to take an interest.

Let's have a look at how these assumptions may affect what goes on in the English classroom.

## Reading: between the lines

Here are some comments from teachers:[4]

1    'The girls will read anything so I always choose a book that will interest the boys.'

2    'Nearly all the books have male characters because the girls don't mind reading about males, but the boys won't read about females.'

3    'Boys are very particular. They won't have anything to do with things they consider "sissy" you know. So we read lots of stories about adventures and spies, that sort of thing.'

4    'Well the boys have so much trouble with reading. They find it so difficult. They don't want to do it. You have to help them and encourage them all the time.'

You can compare this with your own experience. Did teachers choose books more likely to appeal to the boys? If so, how did the girls feel about it? Does it matter?

This girl thinks it does:[5]

When we were given our class reading book, the class went in uproar — the girls did anyway. The book was called *The Goalkeeper's Revenge* and, when sifting through it, I saw a paragraph saying,

'This book is for boys, about boys. Rugby, fighting, trolley driving and football.' That is typical of my school's attitude on girls — we are classed second, while the boys must have what suits them.

I think it matters, too: not only because the girls may be bored, and because it reinforces the idea that certain subjects are more suitable for boys, but because reading is one of the ways in which we learn about the outside world, and what sort of behaviour is expected of us. What do girls learn from their reading?

Once again, it begins in the primary school. Changes are, slowly, being made here, but many of you will have learnt to read from books which not only had a strong middle-class bias, but also presented children and adults in stereotyped sex roles. Peter does things; Jane watches. Mummy stays in the kitchen and wears an apron. Daddy goes to work and reads a newspaper.

In the secondary school, if books are chosen to appeal to boys (and even if they aren't), most of the books that girls read are written by men. So girls learn about what girls are like, about their appearance and personality and behaviour and sexuality, through men's eyes. Let's look at some examples.

In the late 1960s, a small revolution took place in English textbooks. Suddenly, glossy paperbacks with stories by writers like Stan Barstow, Alan Sillitoe, Bill Naughton were available, and you could hear the gusty sighs of relief echoing round staffrooms all across England. Here at last were stories that were real, were *relevant*, stories about working-class life 'in the raw', stories to bring new life into English teaching. New? There was nothing new about the ideas of male and female behaviour in these stories, however, unless it was the frankness with which they were expressed.

Stan Barstow's 'The Desperadoes',[6] for example, tells the story of a gang of boys, led by Vince. At the beginning of the story the gang see a girl, Iris, with her boyfriend.

She wore very brief, scarlet shorts which displayed her long, handsome thighs, and a white high-necked sweater stretched tight over her large shapely breasts.

Finch was hopping about as though taken bad for a leak and making little growling noises in his throat.

'. . . We'll take her pants off an' make her ride home bareback', Finch giggled.

'Aye', Vince said, 'an' if laughing boy has any objections we'll carve his initials round his belly button.'

As the story goes on the flavour of sexual violence develops. The boys go to a strip show, explicitly described, and release their frustrations by beating up an old man. Vince falls for the girl, who belongs to a particular male fantasy/stereotype: beautiful, cool, remote, clever, middle-class, with secret and unpredictable passions.

> As they walked along between the parked cars and the wall of the building Vince stopped and turned her round with his hands on her shoulders, feeling their smooth warmth through the blouse.
> 'Don't get panicky', he said. 'I'm just gonna kiss you.'
> 'Who's panicky?' she said as his mouth came down on hers.
> She was quiet at first, acquiescent but passive, her mouth cool and unresponsive under his. Then she parted her lips and put her arms about him.

The idyll is interrupted by Jackson, the dance-hall bouncer, who shines his torch on them, calling Vince a 'mucky little bugger', just as Vince is thinking about 'things like steady courtship, marriage, a little home with someone to share it and be waiting for him at the end of the day'.

The girl, humiliated, disappears; Vince and his mates wait for Jackson on the hillside to beat him up. Things go wrong; Jackson seems able to take on the entire gang, and Vince 'in a kind of daze' knifes him. The story ends with Vince, standing alone on the hillside above the dead body of Jackson.

I read this story to a number of groups and thought it was a big success. Everyone listened intently: if the bell went in the middle, there was a loud groan. Then one day, when I was reading it, I realised that beneath the encouraging murmurs of the boys, there was a deep silence: the embarrassed silence of the girls. At first I thought they were embarrassed by the explicit 'sexy bits', but gradually I realised that the embarrassment was created by the whole *atmosphere* of the story: the linking of sex and violence, the portrayal of women as sex objects, the contrast between the girl in the strip-show who is just for sex, and the girl Iris who is for marriage. In every way, the story created an impenetrable barrier between boys and girls. The boys may well have been just as embarrassed and disturbed by this as the girls, but it would have been more than their lives were worth to admit it. They were *expected* to enjoy it.

While this story may be an extreme example, the attitudes it conveys are present in many other stories frequently used in the classroom. In Bill Naughton's collection of stories, *Late Night on Watling Street*,[1] the disrupting influence of women in men's lives is a theme which runs right through the book. The men are shown as extremely sexist in their attitudes, exploiting or ignoring their women; the women are 'strong' in the sense that they trick, outwit and make fools of the men, but because this is seen only through the eyes of the men they have little individuality and the reader cannot identify with them. We are invited to laugh at the sexist attitudes of the men, and to smile ruefully when they get their come-uppance.

> I mean I never had to ask for a dance. I used to stroll up to the corner where all the girls stood in a circle, the cream of the town's dancers, and I'd run my eye over them, and the one my eye rested on would come running into the arm of my tight-sleeved, pinstripe, barrelled jacket. Sometimes in their eagerness two would run out to me. If there happened to be a stranger, or one a bit posh, I might say, 'Lend us your body, baby', but no more than that. (*Seeing a Beauty Queen Home*)

> She was a bit of a drip was old Myra, but absolutely gone on me. If she hadn't have been I don't suppose I'd have looked on the same side of the street she was on, let alone take her out. But I'm like that I am. I can't turn my back on a woman who looks up to me and thinks I am somebody, even if, what you might say, I can't bear the sight of her otherwise. I must admit a bit of the old flannel goes a long way with me, especially if a woman tells me I dress well. I do like anything like that. (*Spiv in Love*)

Perhaps the most extraordinary story in this collection is *The Little Welsh Girl*. The narrator and his mate, Jimmy, meet Jenny, the little Welsh girl, in an all-night cafe. She is broke and has nowhere to live; they feel sorry for her and take her home with them. She stays on, but there is no sexual relationship. The two men don't 'fancy' her; she dresses badly, and 'She wasn't a bit like a London girl. She had this nice rosy sort of skin, all freshified and smooth, but I like women with pale skin and lots of powder on and plenty of lipstick: it looks more natural somehow to see a woman done up.'

They buy her clothes and make-up. Gradually, however, Jenny takes over. She cleans and tidies the flat, until the men feel that the place is not their own. They decide to get rid of her, and trick her into leaving. Two years later they meet Jenny again, with an old 'Toff'.

> She looked real smashing. She was wearing a lovely little fur coat, what Jimmy, who's working amongst hides, said was the real thing. She had on a blouse trimmed with white frilly stuff. And she'd a nice warm smell of scent and drink and that.

It is clear that Jenny has become a prostitute.
This is how the story ends:

As we was supping our light ales, Jimmy says: 'We was a couple of goms, you know. If I'd have known she was going to turn to brass —'

'Just what I was thinking', I says. 'We could have sent her out on the bash ourselves.'

I'm not saying that stories like this shouldn't be used in the classroom. In fact, they can be very useful if we can manage to confront and talk about the issues they raise. We can learn a lot from seeing how books provide a particular image of 'the perfect girlfriend', the 'perfect wife', the behaviour of men and women towards each other. We can see how the same images appear outside the classroom, in magazines, films, television programmes, and about the way this influences our lives. We can think about whether there are other possibilities: whether people should try to live up to these images. But how far do the books we read in the classroom provide an alternative view of women?

There is one other kind of woman in Bill Naughton's stories: the long-suffering mother, who provides a stable background for her children. The mother figure appears in plenty of other books to be found in the classroom. Apparently, there are two kinds of mothers: the 'bad' mother who goes out, drinks, has boyfriends and neglects her children (to be found in *Kes*, *Zigger-Zagger*, *A Taste of Honey* and other popular examination texts) and the 'good' mother who stays at home, cooks and cleans. She may be bitter, especially if she has a husband who drinks, but she is there when she's needed. It is very rare to find a 'good' mother who is seen to have any life of her own.

Do you think I'm being unfair? In *Lord of the Flies*, another popular examination book, there are no girls at all: they are simply invisible, and this 'invisibility' can be seen in subtler forms in other books. Look back over the books you read at school: in children's adventure or family stories, how often were the girls the leaders, taking decisions, being practical, rather than getting emotional or in the way? In books for older readers, how often did girls appear, not as girlfriends or wives or mothers, but as *people*? How often were female characters shown having conversations which were not about relationships or babies or appearances?

Perhaps one reason why 'boarding-school', 'ballet' and 'pony' books, so often popular with girls and frowned on by teachers, *are* so popular is that, albeit often in very clichéd ways, they do show girls using their initiative and having varied personalities. In an all-female society, girls are not seen as sisters or girlfriends: they take decisions, argue, play tricks on their teachers, succeed in competitions, get into trouble, have future careers. Maybe Enid Blyton's books are popular because they do at least show girls getting involved in adventures, even if she does carefully balance the 'tomboy' with the 'soft' feminine girl. The tomboy is itself an interesting conception. It provides identification for girls who want to run, shout, climb trees, get their hands dirty, but the very name suggests that the girl is an oddity, like a boy, not a real girl — it is a temporary aberration, which the girl will 'grow out of' as she gets older. But at least it provides an acknowledgment that girls are *different*: they don't all like the same things, behave in the same ways.

Does this mean that girls should only read novels written by women? It isn't as easy as that. A few years ago I started teaching in an all-girls school, in the halcyon days before the cuts, when we had money to buy new books, and one day we gleefully realised that the girls didn't *have* to plough their way through ancient copies of *Shane*. We bought new books, written *by* women, *about* girls and women: books like *The Country Girls*, *The L-Shaped Room*, *Fifteen*, *Sam and Me*, *Rebecca*, *London Morning*. There were some real advantages. The girls loved the books: we had considerable trouble getting them back as they were passed from group to group. The leading characters in the books were female: some showed strong, determined girls dealing with interesting problems. But slowly doubts began to creep in. It wasn't so much a question of what the books were about, as what they were *not* about. Was it right that we should be reading so many books with 'girly' subjects like romance and pregnancy? Weren't we just contributing to the idea that girls' lives occupy a special enclosed area in which war, aggression, adventure, sport, play no part? Did the books *really* give an alternative viewpoint?

One of the books, *Fifteen*,[8] begins like this:

Today I'm going to meet a boy, Jane Purdy told herself, as she walked up Blossom Street toward her babysitting job. *Today I'm going to meet a boy*. If she thought it often enough as if she really believed it, maybe she actually would meet a boy, even though she was headed for Sandra Norton's house and the worst babysitting job in Woodmont.

The entire book revolves around getting a boyfriend, clothes, making-up, baby-sitting, being one of the crowd, and it was one of the most popular of the books we bought. It's not surprising that this should be so: if girls are encouraged by the world around them to think of themselves in terms of marriage and romance, then that's what they'll want to read about. The problem is that so few of the books question the traditional picture, and that doesn't apply only to the books you read in school: elsewhere in this book you will find discussion of the images of women to be found in girls' magazines and romantic fiction.

There *are* alternatives. More and more writers like Louise Fitzhugh, Betsy Byars, M.E. Kerr and Rosa Guy are writing really good books in

which the characters do not have clearly defined sex roles.[9] The problem
is that the further you go up the age range, the more difficult it is to
find books which break away from traditional sex roles, and from the
fourth year onwards, most teachers have to choose from a limited list
of books prescribed by the examination boards. Some, as I have said,
have very stereotyped views of women: others are more stimulating.
The nineteenth century, when women really began to write, produced
great writers like Jane Austen, George Eliot, the Brontës: we don't
need to agree with everything they have to say about womanhood to
find these books interesting today. Some male writers, like Thomas
Hardy, have written powerfully about the problems encountered by
women. Whatever you are reading, the important thing is this. Writers
do not present 'real life': they present a particular *interpretation* of
real life. Reading is *not* just a passive activity. We have to learn to 'read'
with a questioning eye: to ask ourselves: 'What image of men and
women, their behaviour and relationships, does this writer give us? Is
this the way it is? Is this the way we want it to be? Is this the way it
*has* to be?'

**Writing: doing what comes naturally?**

As with reading, so with writing: along with the idea that boys have to
be 'coaxed' into reading, whereas girls take to it like ducks to water,
goes the idea that girls enjoy writing, boys find it difficult. One
researcher conducted an experiment in which she asked a group of
teachers to mark a selection of children's writing. She found that work
which was thought to be by a boy got a higher grade, and more compli-
mentary comments, than the *same* piece of work when it was thought
to have been written by a girl.[10] I don't think this necessarily shows
that teachers are prejudiced in favour of boys; rather it shows that they
have lower *expectations* of boys, and therefore they reward their
achievements more highly.

It may be that girls enjoy writing more than boys, and that the
*content* of their writing tends to be different. If boys often choose to
write about cops and robbers or war, to write funny stories, science
fiction stories; if girls often write about romance and emotions, personal
stories — after all, these are the interests they have been encouraged, by
their reading and their upbringing, to develop. You can judge for
yourself whether this is true. Is there a difference, though, in the way in
which girls and boys *approach* their writing, and the way they express
their ideas?

The following extracts are taken from reports on the year's English
work, written by 3rd year students. In this section, they were asked to
choose pieces they had written during the year, to describe the piece

and the way they went about writing it, and to say why this particular piece was significant. They were asked to take particular care because this report would be kept as a record of their work. Can you tell which were written by boys, and which by girls?

1  The Elephant.
This was a descriptive poem, which took half-a-piece of A4 paper, but there was an illustration at the end that increased the length to three-quarters of a page of A4 paper. This piece of work is

significant, because I felt as if it was my most successful poem, and that I had described the elephant, and its environment, exactly how I wanted to.

First of all I noted any words that described the elephant, or connected it to the environment. Then I numbered each section so as to put it in a specific order. Next I wrote my notes out into sentences, so as to check all my spellings. All this was done in rough, so my last task was to write it up onto A4 paper. Although this poem was planned very thoroughly, it did not take me long. Altogether with both the planning and the writing it took me approximately two hours.

2   Title: From one to the other. Length 22 pages.
Type: Imaginative long story.
It was significant because from the beginning of writing the story I knew exactly what I wanted to write and how to write what I wanted to say. I had never written a very long story before and I enjoyed writing it. The characters I wrote about almost became real live people. They were stuck in my mind as I wrote the story. I wrote the whole story out in rough and then I went through to check as many spelling mistakes as I could. The idea came to me after I had read a book called 'Into Exile'. Altogether it took me six weeks to write.

3   Title: Haiku.
Type of writing: Haiku.
Length: 3 lines.
Why it was significant: It was significant because it was a new type of writing.
How I went about writing it: I thought about it and then wrote it in rough.
How long it took: It took 1 lesson to write.

4   I wrote a book called 'Fools Chase'. It was only fifteen pages long with six chapters, each chapter being two to three pages long. It is a book to be read by children. It took a bit of thinking about it to keep it going because I could of ended it a couple of times. If I had an Idea I jotted it down and tryed to add it to the story. The trouble was I couldn't sit down and write. I couldn't write very much before I had to have a rest from it. At times I felt like completely changing the story, or starting again. I wrote it in rough before putting it into best. It took me about 6 weeks to write that with doing other things inbetween.

5 Increasing your vocabulary. Factual. 1 hour. Its significant because
it learn't me something. I look the words up in a dictionary and
wrote it down. 1 piece of paper.

If you found this difficult, it isn't surprising, because I cheated. All
the writers were, in fact, girls, and all were from the same group. The
important point is this: the ways in which these girls approached and
thought about their writing, the language they used, even the form in
which they chose to organise and express their thoughts, show immense
variety. There may be differences *between* the sexes, but the differences
*within* the sexes are just as great.

All the same, when I chose these pieces, I based my choice on
certain ideas about 'masculine' and 'feminine' writing. They go something like this:

Boys are more casual and detached, prefer short, practical writing,
express themselves more concisely and factually.
Girls are more involved in their work, fluent, thorough, prefer longer,
imaginative pieces, express themselves more tentatively and emotionally.

As you can see, the above pieces cross all of these categories, yet all of
them were written by girls.

The group was in an all-girls school. If there had been any boys in
the group, would they have responded differently? You might find it
interesting to gather some examples of writing, read them out to a
group, and see whether you can tell which are written by boys and
which by girls. Or you could read extracts from novels, without giving
the name of the author. Could you tell which was written by a man,
and which by a woman? What criteria were you using to help you
decide?

What exactly do we mean if we talk about 'masculine' or 'feminine'
writing? Is it a question of subject matter and point of view, or is it
something about the words themselves, and the way they are put
together? There are all sorts of problems here, which women writers
have tried to deal with. When we talk about a 'feminine' style, do we
mean that it expresses the feelings, the way of seeing the world, which
comes 'naturally' to a woman, or is it the language which women have
learnt, from the society in which they live, to be the language of
femininity? If a woman wants to avoid the traps of writing in a
'romantic', 'passive' style, should she then 'write like a man'? But how
then can she really express what it's like to be a woman? There are
plenty of women novelists and poets writing today, and it's worth
looking to see how they have dealt with these problems. It's difficult,
because the woman who can write about a woman's experience, free
from conditioning and learnt assumptions, has not yet been born. It's
not just a question of describing the world as we see it and experience

it — our language has been formed by a society which has particular ideas about the roles of men and women, and the language itself reflects it. Look at these sentences:

'God created the world in six days; on the seventh day; she rested.'
'If a child shows promise, the teacher should encourage her or his potential.'
'When Primitive Man discovered fire, she took the first step towards civilization.'

What are the assumptions which make these sentences sound awkward or odd?

The novelist Virginia Woolf said, about the problems which face a woman writer: 'To begin with, there is the technical difficulty — so simple, apparently; in reality, so baffling — that the very form of the sentence does not fit her. It is a sentence made by men; it is too loose, too heavy, too pompous for a woman's use.'[11]

Styles may have changed since 1929, when this was written: but is the problem still there? When you feel that 'you know what you want to write, but you don't know how to say it', is it because the *language* for what you want to write is not available to you? Try, for example, to write a story in which it is not clear whether the narrator is a man or a woman. Is it possible to write in a 'neutral' style?

Writing is anything but a passive activity. It is hard work. It is a challenge, but it is a challenge worth meeting. Once we understand that language is not a simple tool, that there are different *ways* of using language, we can start to *use* language, instead of letting language use us. We can play with language, fight with it, experiment with it. Mandy McLoughlin's piece, 'The Golden Pathway' which follows this chapter is just one example. She wrote it at school, for her fifth-year examination folder. It is an angry piece, but it is also an exciting one, because it reminds us that through our writing, in and out of the English classroom, we can explore and challenge our experiences as girls and women, can try out new ways of looking at the things we take for granted.

### A quiet life

Her voice was ever soft,
Gentle and low, an excellent thing in woman.
(William Shakespeare, *King Lear*)

Sir, a woman's preaching is like a dog's walking on his hinder legs. It is not done well; but you are surprised to find it done at all.
(Dr Johnson)

*Talk* is a crucial part of the English lesson. Through talking we explore and test our ideas, try out ways of using language and communicating. This is not only valuable as part of the learning process, but also vital because in our lives we *talk* more than we *write*. It's not surprising that teachers are concerned when they feel that girls are less willing than boys to talk in the classroom. Look at these statements:

1    Boys dominate discussion; the girls won't talk.
2    Women are chatterboxes; they talk too much.

If women love to talk, why don't girls talk more in the classroom?

Let's look at some of the reasons why this should be so. From an early age, we learn not only the vocabulary and grammar of our language, but also the appropriate ways of using it: what is 'polite', what is 'acceptable'. What boys learn about spoken language, however, is rather different from what girls learn. If a little girl plays quietly, doesn't talk a lot, that's 'natural'; if a little boy behaves in the same way, he needs to be stimulated. Fathers often talk more boisterously to their sons than to their daughters.

From listening to adults, reading, watching films and television, we learn the 'rules' of conversation. Have you learnt to accept that:

Men: talk loudly, boast, swear, show their anger, go straight to the point, state their point of view forcefully, tell jokes, interrupt, use slang.
Women: talk quietly, listen, are polite, considerate to the listener, use good grammar, express themselves cautiously and emotionally.

I'm not saying that people necessarily *follow* these rules. But do they feel they *ought* to follow them? Compare 'What a load of bloody rubbish' to 'Oh dear, that isn't very nice'. Either of these statements could be made by either a man *or* a woman, but I don't think you'll have much difficulty guessing which is supposed to be masculine, which is 'feminine'. This applies to *what* we talk about as well as *how* we say it. For example, if boys avoid emotional subjects or make jokes about them, isn't this because from the first 'Now be a big boy, boys don't cry' society has taught them to repress these feelings? If girls don't tell jokes in public (even if they laugh and joke in private), is this because most humour depends on laughing at those very subjects which society has taught them to hold sacred?

As they reach adolescence, girls also learn how to be popular with boys. Here's Val in *London Morning*,[12] trying to conceal her working-class background and to behave in the ladylike, feminine manner which she believes her boyfriend expects:

I kept taking a furtive glance at my reflection in shop windows as
I walked down the Old Kent Road and approved of the smart
young lady under the big, black umbrella. I was thinking about the

article I had read last night in a woman's magazine. 'You should walk as though you had an imaginary pile of books on your head. . . . Men like women to speak in soft, deep tones.' I was quietly saying to myself: 'How do you do, Clive? I'm sorry to have kept you waiting,' when I was suddenly interrupted by 'Ah, there you are.' And he was there.

The rules for a girl who wants to be popular are clear enough. She should listen, talk softly, talk about what the boy wants to talk about, ask questions, look interested, flatter him. She should not use rough language, interrupt, disagree, talk too much. Thus girls learn to conceal their interests and personalities.

Women have the reputation of being great talkers, but try listening to conversations in the pub, on television chat shows and interviews, in lessons, at meetings. Who does the most talking? What sex are most politicians, trade union leaders, television announcers? Women may talk a lot in private, but most *public* speaking is done by men. This has two important effects. One is that women who speak up in public have to take over a language generally thought to be more appropriate to men. They run the risk of being called bossy, nagging, illogical, hysterical. It may be partly suspicion of women who take over a 'masculine' role, but it may also be that it is actually *difficult* for women to adapt the 'rules' they have learnt to the 'rules' of public speaking; they have to learn a different 'language'. They have to overcome embarrassment, fear of ridicule, of making a mistake.

The other point is that 'men's' subjects come to be seen as more *serious* than 'women's' subjects. Politics and football are 'public' subjects; home, family, relationships are 'private', 'personal' subjects.

Given all this, it's not surprising if boys find it easier to talk freely and spontaneously in the classroom. It may be that girls, having learnt to be more tentative, show more consideration for the listener; but these are not 'public' virtues. In public discussion, you have to dominate if you are to be heard.

**Seen and not heard: some students' views**

Before I began to write this piece, I thought that I should ask the students what *they* thought about English. With the help of two teachers (one in an all-girls' school, one in a mixed school),[13] I asked two fourth year groups what they liked, disliked and 'didn't mind' about their English lessons. The results made me question some of my preconceptions. If I had written down before I started what I *expected* the survey to show, it would have looked something like this:

Girls enjoy creative writing, reading stories and poems more than boys do. Boys prefer factual reading and writing, and structured activities such as grammar work.

Girls prefer 'passive' activities such as reading and writing. Boys generally prefer 'active' ones such as drama and making tapes.

Girls are more inhibited and prefer discussion in small groups; boys are more outgoing and enjoy whole class discussion.

Here, then, is a summary of the results:

1    The fourth year girls showed more enthusiasm for creative writing than the boys. The boys showed rather more enthusiasm for making tapes.

2    No one (including the boys) said that they *did not* enjoy creative writing.

Neither boys *nor* girls showed much enthusiasm for reading poetry.

The boys were no more enthusiastic about grammar work than the girls.

The boys did not show much interest in factual writing.

The boys showed no less interest in reading stories than the girls.

3    There was an interesting difference between the girls in the single-sex group and the girls in the mixed group. The 'single-sex' girls showed more enthusiasm for practically everything, though this could be because they were an enthusiastic group, or had a particularly good relationship with their teacher. The most striking difference, though,

was in their attitudes to whole-class discussion and drama: the 'single-sex' girls were much more enthusiastic. In the mixed group, neither boys nor girls showed much enthusiasm for these activities, but the girls disliked them more than the boys.

I have talked about the dangers of classifying people as 'boys' or 'girls'. Each answer was different, but the picture as a whole made me think about two things. First, could it be that girls feel less vulnerable, more willing to take part in 'out-going' activities, when they are on their own? That, away from boys, they feel less obliged to act 'as girls', more able to act as individuals? Have you found, yourself, that girls and boys, men and women, talk and behave differently according to whether they are in mixed groups or in groups of their own sex?

Second, we have to be very wary of *assuming* that boys and girls 'prefer' particular activities. If boys are bored or dislike a topic, they can express their disapproval by making a noise. If boys shout, jeer, make jokes, well, that's how boys behave. What do girls do if they're bored? Writing letters, reading magazines, talking quietly in little groups, painting fingernails, may be just as much a *rejection* of the lesson as shouting, fighting, playing up. The fact that girls are 'quiet' does not mean that they are *acquiescing* in the lesson any more than the boys are. The difference is that the girls' behaviour does not disrupt the lesson, so it may simply not be noticed; also, it is a rejection which reinforces, rather than challenges, expectations of feminine behaviour. Girls are quiet anyway, so who notices if they don't take part? This is particularly important in discussion. If girls don't talk, they may be making the only protest available to them; but silence is 'invisible'.

It is not easy for teachers to overcome the problems of discussion. After all, people should have the right *not* to speak, not to be forced into taking part. If teachers try *too* hard to 'get the girls to talk', they may emphasise, or even create, barriers between boys and girls; those girls who do talk freely may become self-conscious. One answer may be small-group, rather than whole-class, discussion. This doesn't tackle the real problem, though. Somehow we have to overcome the idea that certain subjects, certain ways of speaking, are 'taboo' for women; to have confidence in the way we talk, to make ourselves *heard* as well as *seen*. How can we do this?

### English: work or play?

In the fourth year, students do not *choose* to do English: they just *do* it. So I also asked two groups of sixth formers to write about why they had *chosen* to do English 'A' level, and what they enjoyed about it.

Once more, I was surprised. Although these students had *chosen* to do English, the difference between boys and girls was much more marked. The girls showed much more enthusiasm for reading novels, and, to a lesser extent, poetry, than the boys did. The boys showed a definite preference for creative writing. Is this to do with the idea that writing is *doing*, is active; reading is *receiving*, is passive? Again, the girls in the single-sex school showed much more enthusiasm for discussion than the 'mixed' girls, three of whom specifically mentioned that discussion was a problem.

When asked to give reasons for their choice, many of the boys emphasised that English was a useful subject, that it went with their other options, that they had been encouraged by their exam results. Very few girls mentioned these reasons, but almost *all* the girls mentioned enjoyment of English as an important factor, and half of the 'single-sex' girls also said that they wanted to increase their enjoyment of literature.

These comments illustrate the differences:

> I feel that English is a useful subject to learn at 'A' level as it is not only accepted as a good 'A' level to obtain, but it improves one's abilities in English, which are helpful and satisfying in later life. (Boy)

> I had no choice. It was the only subject open to me with the other two 'A' level subjects that I wanted to do. (Boy)

> I have always enjoyed reading and towards the end of the fifth year I had begun to realise that there was a great deal to learn from novels apart from the basic story. However, I didn't feel I could find a way into novels without the help of a structured course like 'A' level and I think it has succeeded in making me appreciate literature more fully, which was what I wanted originally. (Girl)

Since most 'A' level courses are primarily, even exclusively, literature courses, it seems at first as though the girls, with their romantic emphasis on the pleasure of literature, are an English teacher's dream. Many of the boys, on the other hand, with their concise, down-to-earth comments, seem to have chosen English for all the 'wrong' reasons. And yet — don't they have a much better understanding of the education system, a more realistic appraisal of long-term career prospects?

This impression is confirmed when you look at what happens to students who go on to University to study English. More girls pass 'A' level, more girls do English at university; but more boys get top degrees, and go on to further study.[14] When you look at English teachers in university departments, there are far more men than women. Of course, there are lots of things you can do with English 'A' level, apart from going on to university; but does this suggest that when English is *pleasure*, the girls do well; when it becomes connected with *work*, the boys shoot ahead?

There's another point, too. Two-thirds of those who do English at 'A' level are girls — but how far does the 'A' level course take account of this? Would you expect to find these comments in a book or examination paper:

'The poet should use language appropriate to her meaning.'

'What is the responsibility of the writer towards her society?'

'The dramatist expresses her point of view through her characters.'

Unless you are writing about a particular woman writer, you are expected to refer to 'the writer' as 'he'. Also, at 'A' level you are almost always limited to the 'set books' prescribed by the examining board (unlike CEE, for example, where the choice is much more flexible and can be adapted to the students' interests). In 1977, the popular JMB board set *one* work by a woman (Jane Austen) among their twenty-five texts. This is fairly standard. From the 'A' level lists, you could be forgiven for getting the impression that there were *no* women poets, and only one twentieth-century woman writer (Virginia Woolf). Writers like Elizabeth Barrett Browning, Katharine Mansfield, Olive Schreiner, Sylvia Plath, Doris Lessing, are 'invisible'. Thus girls at 'A' level are even more likely to learn about what it means to be a woman through the eyes of men; they are certain to acquire the idea that 'serious' writing is done by men. Is it surprising that the boys showed more interest in creative writing than the girls?

**Why choose English?**

What am I saying, then? Does this mean that girls should all give up English and do science instead? I hope you will have realised that that isn't what I'm saying at all. It *is* important that in the future more girls should take scientific and technical subjects. There are changes to be made; we all need to remind ourselves that girls are *not* all the same, and neither are boys. Having said that, there are good reasons for choosing English.

Whatever the reasons why girls do well at English, we can make *use* of that fact. English gives us a unique chance to look at the *images* of men and women in our society, and to question those images. It gives us the opportunity to look at *language*, at the way we learn to express ourselves, and to test the limits of that language, in speaking and writing. English gives us a chance to see how men and women have shown the problems of girls and women at particular stages of our society, or have had particular assumptions about the way men and women should behave. Once you are *aware* of the problems, you can read with a discerning eye, measuring the writer's viewpoint against your own. We can compare this with the way in which, in our present-day world, women learn what a 'woman' is. Feminism, like English, is about learning to 'read'; to read the hidden messages, all around us, every day, telling us what women 'are', what women 'ought to be'. It is a good partnership.

## Notes

1 *RSLA — Four Years On*, Department of Education and Science Report on Education No. 95, October 1979.
2 Ann-Marie Wolpe, *Some Processes in Sexist Education*, Women's Research and Resources Centre Publication, 1977, p. 40.
3 See *Statistics of Education*, vol. 2, HMSO, 1977.
4 Dale Spender, 'The Facts of Life: sex differentiated knowledge in the English classroom and the school', in *English in Education*, vol. 12, no. 3, Autumn 1978, pp. 3-4.
5 Debra Peart, 'Schoolgirls Up Against Sexism', *Spare Rib*, Issue 75, October 1978, p. 6.
6 Stan Barstow, 'The Desperadoes', *The Human Element and other stories*, Longman Imprint, 1969.
7 Bill Naughton, *Late Night on Watling Street*, Longman Imprint, 1969.
8 Beverley Cleary, *Fifteen*, Penguin/Peacock, 1962.
9 Interested students and teachers will find the following publications very helpful:
   *Spare Rib List of Non-Sexist Children's Books* (available from Spare Rib, 27 Clerkenwell Close, London EC1R 0AT).
   *Children's Book Bulletin* (4 Aldebert Terrace, London SW8 1BH, three issues a year).
10 Dale Spender, *op. cit.*, pp. 4-5.
11 Virginia Woolf, 'Women and Fiction', in *Virginia Woolf: Women and Writing*, ed. Michele Barrett, The Women's Press, 1979, p. 48.
12 Valerie Avery, *London Morning*, Pergamon Press, 1969, p. 127.
13 Thank you to Leonie Barua, Donald Fry, Julia Sokota, and their students.
14 See *Statistics of Education*, vols 2 and 6, HMSO, 1977.

# 3 The golden pathway

*Amanda McLoughlin*

This is a shortened version of a story written in 1979 by sixteen-year-old Amanda McLoughlin for her English language examination folder. At present, she is unemployed, but is hoping to train as a nurse. It *is* an angry and bitter piece, angry not just with the men she 'meets' but with everyone — other girls, parents, people in authority.

We think that this comes in part from her feeling of being forced into a mould, being expected to fit everyone's expectations. Because she feels powerless to change those expectations *and* is made to feel inadequate because she doesn't fit, her whole experience seems distorted — becomes a nightmare where she feels totally wrong, peculiar, out of place.

*Trisha McCabe* and *Angela McRobbie*

Everyone has their own individual golden pathway, one which leads to eternal life, eternal wealth, or some fantastic dream-world that everyday life cannot offer. Some people are aware of the futility of their ambitions but continue to drift nonchalantly through life, waiting for small events to brighten up their lives. Ambitions can be individual, each one unique, no one can steal them or intrude upon them. They are capable of instigating you and giving you something to live for even when the present hangs about you like a stagnant trap.

I felt there was some great element missing from my life, the ebb and flow had grown tired. I felt I needed some original spice to liven up my dull but satisfactory routine. I wanted to make new contacts, to launch away from both my school and home life. However, there was someone blocking my way, stopping me from escaping along this valuable outlet; this someone was my father. He quenched my dreams like a bucket of water would a recently lighted match.

'You wouldn't like it if you went to this place you say all girls of your age go to, if I allowed you to go every week you'd still complain of boredom. You seem to want complete contrasts and excitement all the time. Why do you always have to search for entertainment?'

You see, I longed to go to Tiffany's, it was a place I associated with laughter, dancing and meeting independent people with vibrant lives who could make me a part of their life. I wanted to desert my own world in disgust. Now I look back I had always acted on the spur of the moment, like a spoilt child really. I wildly thrived on any form of action or rebellion, despite the fact that I hadn't the willpower or mental strength to fight over a long period for what I wanted.

Julie, my new associate, encouraged my state of mind. 'It's only natural for you to get out sometimes, otherwise you'll finish up insane with emotion or too disillusioned to put up a fight,' she said. When I look back both my father and Julie were right in their own way, yet Julie's point of view seemed more inviting at the time.

One night Julie had it all worked out. She persuaded me to tell my mother that we were going to a school meeting, a deliberate lie, but

Julie had animal cunning; when she lied what she said never seemed to
be doubted, perhaps this was because she was a Catholic. Julie had
threatened her brother. She said that unless he gave us the money we
needed for our night out she'd tell her ill mother about the things he
stole. In Julie's house survival depended upon corrupt, underhand
means. The head of the house was unmistakably the mother, her stern
voice had an edge to it like a laser beam. You could do nothing to
please her, no wonder her children were so dishonest.

Walking down the road, my state of carefree excitement had passed
over. I felt guilty, almost frightened. On the bus, Julie and all the other
teenage girls going to Tiffany's looked older and more menacing, they

seemed to portray a false impression, not like their true selves, the ones I knew at school. In the house I was convinced that I'd literally thrown make-up on to my face, but comparing myself with Julie and the others I had only applied a child's portion. Julie seemed quite shocked although she tried not to show it. She said hesitantly, 'I hope you'll be able to get in. There's a new manager at the door, if he thinks you don't look eighteen you won't get in.' I was ashamed to look at Julie's low-cut dress, I'd never seen her in anything like it before. She assimilated easily with girls three or four years older than herself. Men shouted to her 'Come on Julie get ya knickers off.' I couldn't quite make out whether they meant it or were joking. Julie seemed quite used to this behaviour, but I was wondering meanwhile whether I'd put my hair-spray into my handbag. I was told it could blind an attacker and I wouldn't hesitate about using it in emergencies.

In my opinion Julie was asking for trouble but I knew or I thought I knew that Julie wasn't as sexually experienced as she acted. Anyway, the two of us arrived at the door, a large door where I knew I would be judged. I was conscious of my entire body. Stiffly I practised false reactions. I pulled my mouth this way and that, I fixed my eyes on the floor, a lampshade. I wanted to keep myself occupied. I thought if I looked absorbed in myself no one would notice me, I would be one of the crowd, confident enough of my actions but not so that I would draw attention to myself.

There was a hold-up due to one of the girls in the front. I wondered if the bouncer with that adult eye of authority in his blood-coloured uniform would stop me. Once more Julie and I shuffled down the queue, Julie attempting to match her personality with the boyish looking girl in front of me, giving sidelong opposing glances as she hauled her chewing gum to either side of her mouth.

At last it was my turn to pass through the door. Would I pass the test? The question throbbed violently in my head. 'Hey you, when's your date of birth?' a scowling door bouncer shouted. I'd half expected it but when I heard his voice I felt such a misfit. Why I replied 'The tenth of October, nineteen sixty' which was of course a lie, I don't know. 'No, sorry duck, I can't let you in,' patronised the bouncer. He pushed me out of the door like a stray dog. The more he apologised the more inadequate and rejected I felt. I was overcome by an unpleasant mixture of hatred and humiliation. The overgrown bouncer revelling in his authority nauseated me. He seemed like a bullying dinosaur harbouring a small brain. He made me want to shock him, make him notice me, then run out leaving the impression behind me that he couldn't pay me to come inside. Yet it was too late. I had lowered myself and I didn't want to be laughed at more than I could help.

I pretended not to hear Julie pleading with the stubborn bouncer to let me enter the building. I wanted to detach myself, become a martyr. I walked down the steps towards the exit door. Julie pounced on me from behind, shouting enthusiastically, 'Don't go, he said if we waited for ten minutes he'd probably be able to squeeze you in past the manager.' Julie had won the battle, but not for my benefit. She wanted someone with her for a stooge. I knew that when I left the house but I didn't care then.

After we'd spent ten minutes half-frozen, perched on a stair, we descended the rest of the flight. All was easy after that, in practice anyhow, as I still detested the thought of having to lurk in the shadows, ashamed of my very existence. Half of me still wished I'd never come. The smoky atmosphere hit me. The disco was like an enclosing cave with dazzling lights. My senses were disturbed but I was taken over by the glow of excitement.

In the toilets girls corrected minute faults in their make-up. They looked at themselves from an uncomfortable angle, their faces about an inch away from the mirror. They didn't notice, however, how overdone self-conscious and basically unnatural they looked from a distance. I looked considerably toned down and rather insignificant at the side of most of the girls, but I knew I wouldn't feel in place with the clothing they wore.

The group snatched away my last second of silence. Any ability I had once acquired to think straight had gone; the music from the top thirty lost its magic and bouncy tune when you heard it being played again and again. The disco music became meaningless, one tune merged into another. When I first saw the spacious inviting dance floor I simply was taken over by an instinctive urge to dance, but soon I'd worn out every step physically possible. Other girls seemed mesmerised and content, just swaying senselessly from side to side with vacant, empty expressions on their faces, but I knew energy was precious and I looked and felt stupid forcing myself to waste it in this way.

Sinister predators lurked in dark corners discussing quietly which girl who'd conveniently displayed herself on the dance floor would be prepared to give up the most and expect the least in return. Men were getting drunk building up courage to ask someone to dance, which was pointless because they only hovered about anyway while you did all the dancing; you couldn't talk to them, it wasn't your place to talk, you were supposed to humbly respond to their cowardly sign language. You were either willing to have sexual intercourse with them or not, that's all they wanted to know.

Meanwhile Julie had found a youth to dance with. He thought he was some smart dancer straight out of 'Saturday Night Fever'. He kept bending his tall slim figure at the knees and falling into a crouching position again and again. His dance routine was very effective and acrobatic, but surely he couldn't enjoy repeating the same steps over again, especially when the disco songs dragged on and on, repeating the same melody and then finally coming to a fading close.

During the night the oppressive, hot atmosphere mauled me more and more. A horrible sensation of helplessness gripped me. I wanted to run out into the cold, clear night and catch a bus. I knew I couldn't. Julie had the money and the buses had stopped running an hour ago. People poured on to the dance floor, smooching and feeling each other's flesh. I was confused — Julie was out of sight, everywhere I wandered men sneered at me from every direction. People appeared massive in proportion to myself. Yet I could rely on no one, not even the police, as I knew I was under-age. My head throbbed. I was as agitated as a bull in a bull-fight, though my fear forced me to humour micking, intoxicated men who remarked rudely about my figure. These people were like Dobermann Pinschers, anything could trigger them off.

A girl grabbed my arm violently. She had a thickset stature and exerted her face into masculine expressions. 'Where do you live?' she pried in an angry, unfeeling tone. My privacy was painfully being uprooted. People beyond a certain age were forbidden to enter their community, you had no status until you looked eighteen. There were social rules which I was unaware of.

I found myself studying faces. The more I thought about them the uglier they looked. I saw twisted noses, immense hooked noses which drained away strength from the rest of the face, eyes unable to focus, doped and expressionless, lacking the gleam of life. I was beginning to feel glad that I was an alien, that I didn't belong. These people weren't at harmony with the universe and I knew I should express sympathy for them. They came to Tiffany's every week, the very sameness of their routine never provided them with a breathing space to decide why they went.

I tried to talk with a man about which pop groups he preferred. I asked him what Zodiac sign he was and attempted to explain how Leos have different characteristics to Pisces. The man looked at me with disbelief and labelled me as an eccentric. I was unable to instigate any sort of conversation. He looked averagely intelligent, but he only said everyday things like 'Do you come here often? What do you think of the group?' The number one question as far as he was concerned was: How old are you?

Most men I've talked to have certain things they ask, like a tape-recorder with only one tape. After they've asked these questions they try to assess how they could use you for their own advantage.

There are two types of men who roam in and out of discos in their leisure time. One type is aged about twenty-five and shows a reactionary concern with the fashion world, as he has a dread of looking physically out of place. Consequently, he dresses moderately up-to-date and shows a rather pathetic femininity. He usually has permed hair which con veniently hides his face, which he has a noticeable complex about. He wears a casual jacket with a hood which makes him look hunchbacked and weak.

The second type has a definitely foreign and flashy, self-confident air about him. He is considerably better looking than the first type and stands out in a crowd unlike the first type, who assimilates and blends in like a part of the scenery. He usually has straight, well combed black hair. He is slim and faultless in appearance and believes truly that he is the stereotype disco-dancing star. The second type stares a great deal. He is persistent if he takes a fancy to you and he's hard to offend. Behind his flashing dark eyes, however, there lies a malign, baneful instinct, evil and seducing.

Julie had only been gone for five minutes but it seemed like five nightmarish hours. When she tapped me on the shoulder the sigh of relief came to me like water comes to a man in the desert, like a delightful shock. We walked out of the door towards Boots' chemist the place where the taxi would wait, and all my tired body wanted to do was to be cut loose of daily strain and movement and retire into my own cocoon. As I did this I knew that Tiffany's was not part of my golden pathway, and I was privileged to realise this, I thought, as glided into unconsciousness.

# 4 Schools and careers:
## for girls who *do* want to wear the trousers

*Trisha McCabe*

Illustrated by *Monica Ross*

I have been working with girls in one way or another for the last five years, in schools, colleges, work-places and youth clubs. This chapter is based on my research into girls and the transition from school to work — or more accurately now, unemployment. Girls and young women I've worked with feel it's an accurate account and I'd like to thank them for their help. Strictly speaking, the girls in this chapter should be writing it themselves. I'd like to see girls given the facilities and encouragement to make that happen.

> Question: If you could be anything in the world, what would you choose to be?
> Answer: Secretary to a famous person.

This article is about why the girl who answered this question didn't want to be the famous person. It's also about why she wouldn't have stood a chance anyway. And about why wanting to be 'His' secretary *makes sense* for girls.

The *question and answer* above is from a questionnaire carried out in a junior school, with seven- and eight-year-old girls and boys. The boys' answer to this question included professional footballer, astronaut, famous explorer. Other answers from the girls were matron, private secretary and the queen! I also asked these kids what they expected to be doing in ten years' time. The boys answered mechanic, joiner, electrician. The girls answered housewife, nurse, secretary. Both the girls *and* boys were (pretty) realistic about the second question. And both the boys *and* girls were (pretty) ridiculous about the first — which was fair enough. It was a pretty ridiculous question. Whether you want to be on 'Match of the Day' or fly round the world as a private secretary to the jet-setting and famous, obviously neither of these things are likely to really happen. The boys had about as much chance of being an astronaut as the girls had of being the queen. But what struck me then, and still does, is just how *different* — whether in fantasy or real life — the boys' and girls' expectations were. Realistically, the boys *could* make it to be a mechanic, and the girls *might* be a secretary (though they could both more easily end up as a technician or a typist), but even these are very different types of work — in terms of pay, status and opportunities. Yet even when all the restrictions were removed, and they could imagine anything in the whole world as a possibility, *why* did the boys who thought they'd be mechanics think of footballers or astronauts as their ideal jobs, when the girls who might be typists or nurses only thought as far as secretaries or matrons? And *why* did the question 'What do you think you'll be doing in ten years' time?' make *all* the boys think in terms of *jobs* (they didn't say 'I expect to be a husband or father by then') while lots of girls answered the same question in terms of marriage and the family? Housewife or mother were the most common answers from the girls. What I'd expected to find out from these two questions was how ideal, imaginary jobs compared to the work that the kids expected to be doing, that is how far 'real' expectations limited the ways in which they thought about other possibilities. The answers I actually got made it quite clear that you can't just compare boys' and girls' expectations about jobs 'career aspirations' they call it in the books, without recognising that the *way* in which boys and girls see their futures is fundamentally different. It's not just a question of *which* job, but of what *kind* of job or rather work, and in what circumstances. It's not just a question of what advice the schools give, or what jobs are available, but of what kind of messages girls receive from everywhere, and everyone, in our society. It seems to me now that being a housewife *is* work — and hard work at that (which I haven't heard careers' teachers mention) — but it's not the same *kind* of work as, say, being a mechanic. A mechanic is a description of someone's job, a housewife is a description of a *person*. The work a housewife does isn't paid, it's not nine to five, but twenty-four hours a day, and especially if caring for children is involved it's more demanding, with more responsibility — and yet *less* recognition — than any other job I can think of. So why do women do it? Why do we expect to do it? And why do schools, careers' officers, employers, shop stewards and parents assume that all women will 'naturally' be just dying to spend their days (and nights) changing nappies, washing dishes, floors and windows, cooking, shopping and cleaning for *free* rather than doing a boring well-paid job, for a full eight hours a day with nothing else to do after that but relax, go out, and enjoy yourself?

Well, maybe work, maybe life, just isn't like that for women. It can't be that we're all stupid (can it?), though obviously some people think so. A well-known 'expert' on education, John Newsom, said in 1948 in his book, *The Education of Girls*:[1]

> No woman in this age of equality of opportunity, of careers open
> to all, of equal education and political rights . . . is compelled to
> get married and accept the degradation involved. Yet she chooses
> it deliberately as her main occupation.

The conclusion is, we go into the worst job around *deliberately*, with
our eyes wide open, for some peculiar reason which intelligent men like
Newsom can't figure out.

So what's the answer? I tried reading books about schools, about
starting work, about 'careers'. But the 'schoolkids' were all boys, the
'workers' were all men (or at least that's all the writers of the books
talk about). I couldn't find much about girls — the odd paragraph or
footnote at best. So I started to ask girls about *their* ideas about school,
work and the future. (Mr Newsom hadn't thought of this one — the
'experts' on schooling rarely bother to ask the people who actually
experience it — the kids — what *they* think.) What I've found out so far
is what the rest of his article will discuss. How true it is for most girls
is your end of the argument. Most of the girls I've talked to are white
and working-class. I think the experience of school (and of being a
woman) is different for middle-class and working-class girls; it's different
for white girls and black girls; it's different for Afro-Caribbean girls and
Asian girls. One way of using this article is to discuss how — I haven't
got those answers, you have.

Last February I was talking, at a conference for fifth and sixth
formers, about girls and school, work and leisure. I'd been saying what
I thought were fairly 'extreme' things about what hard work is involved
in getting a boyfriend — buying clothes and make-up, testing them out,
earning the money to go out to discos, etc. — about the way in which
boys treat girls, about ways of getting out of having to do anything at
school — 'Sir, it's the wrong time of the month . . .'. After I'd finished
I asked if what I'd said had any relationship to the girls' own experience
of school and leisure. (It was a women-only group.) I'd expected some
criticism, but was pretty shocked by what it was. The first woman to
speak, a sixth former, insisted that I'd understated the 'problem': 'It's
much worse than that, being a girl.' It took off from there, really, and
perhaps the most significant thing about it was that everyone in the
group was able to use her own experience to judge what I'd been
saying. There was a lot of criticism of education — your personal
experience isn't usually seen as a valid way of learning or criticising;
certainly not as important as what you read in books (this book?). It
made it clear to me that my own experience is one thing that determines what, and how, I write. Your own experience determines, in
some ways, how you read and what you think about it.

So in thinking about careers I thought back on my own 'aspirations'.
When I was about six or seven I wanted to be a ballet dancer!

Unfortunately, as I got older I also got taller — too tall to be a ballerin (they're always so petite!). My ambitions had changed by then t journalism, which, amazingly, was regarded as an unsuitable job for woman at my (convent) school. The careers teacher, a nun, would onl encourage girls to go into nursing, teaching or to college or universit (or, of course, to be a nun). Actually, at one time I did want to be nun — that was in between the ballet dancer and the journalist. An now I'm doing research and writing articles like this one. This seems motley collection of 'career aspirations', so what made me pick on th lot? I can't remember anything in particular that made ballet dancin suggest itself — most likely it was stories in comics like *Bunty*, whe all the girls seem to be ballerinas, show jumpers or orphans. The nu thing is clearer. My two best friends at junior school wanted to b priests — something wildly encouraged by the school, the church an by parents. I, too, wanted to be a priest (this was after I wanted to b an altar boy) but was told, gently but firmly, that women couldn't b priests. How about a nun? (You can bake the bread the priests eat.)

The journalism idea came from a careers horoscope in *Jacki* Geminis, apparently, are pretty good at journalism — because we nev shut up and are basically two-faced I think was the general idea. So the I was, chatting at a 'careers convention' to the man from the *Hartlepo Mail*, about my chances with D.C. Thompson and glamour. It didn take long to realise that what the future in journalism held for me, as woman, was more likely to be reporting flower shows, fashion trend weddings, food prices and shortages in the shops — 'human intere stories' they call it — rather than earth-shattering world events. Ho many times have you seen women war correspondents, women reportin on major strikes, parliament, the balance of payments, the oil crisis?

So on to university — something that would open up new horizons And English literature. Of course, English is a women's subject, an there must have been eight or ten men and fifty women on my cours (Students, that is — all but three or four of the lecturers were men 'With an English degree you can always go into teaching, or top secr tarial work' — so what's new? And if I'd done sciences at school (whic hardly any girls did) the picture would have been even worse; *n* women lecturers, one or two women students, perhaps, and the re either 'helping you out' (well it's very kind of you but actually I *d* know how to do this (very simple) experiment), or blaming everythin you don't know (because you haven't learnt it yet) on your sex (blood stupid women). How does it feel to be the odd one out/a freak? 'With science degree you can always go into teaching . . . .'

The new horizons seem to stretch as far as finding a better class c husband — engagement rings are as common as degrees. Rosemar Deem quotes two fairly typical examples in her book *Women an Schooling*:[2]

61    Schools and careers

My degree doesn't really matter very much; I'll probably get married after graduation.

I would like to get an upper second, but it would upset my boyfriend if I got a better degree than he has.

Lecturers' general attitude to women students comes through too:[3] 'We expect women who come here [to university] to be competent, good students, but we don't expect them to be brilliant or original.'

Nevertheless, here I am writing this article, talking about girls, something I know about mainly because I was one, and doing something I actually *like*. But the reasons for doing it, the things that happened to me, the influences that led me to this, the luck, the chances, (the weather?) seem pretty haphazard to say the least. I don't think people make up their minds early on and, through hard work, grit and determination, miraculously 'make it'. At university being working-class (like me) was unusual. Being white (like me) was normal. So what *happens* to working-class kids, to black kids? I don't think being asked in careers questionnaires whether you'd rather mend a wooden stool or feed chickens (you must tick one or the other — aha! you want to work with your hands/work outdoors) makes much difference. But the one factor that's been there in every choice I've made, or that's been made for me, is being *female*. Well? Am I just a biased 'women's libber' or is there some truth in all this? And isn't it all different now — after all, this was between five and fifteen years ago?

### 'Well, you're interested in people's rights, and you've studied some law. I definitely think you should marry a solicitor.' Girls, careers and careers teachers

This gem from a careers officer is what I want to talk about in this part of the article. I'll argue that girls are still seen primarily as future wives and mothers, and that this often means that careers and careers education for girls are not taken seriously — by teachers, parents, careers officers, and to some extent girls themselves. Basically it seems to me that there is a *distance* preserved between girls and work which is quite unlike the way in which boys and work are thought about — i.e. *together*. One of the first questions anyone asks a man is what he does for a living. Recently I was doing a press interview about our local women's paper and the *very first* question I was asked was 'are you married?'. (The interview wasn't printed!) Work (earning money) is not on the whole seen as the main priority for girls; 'getting on' isn't as important as getting a man; the family in the future is still assumed to be girls', all girls', main concern. It's common sense, after all, you just can't get girls interested in careers!

One careers film I watched with a large mixed class was about heavy goods vehicle driving, distribution and delivery, and the only women in it were serving in the motorway cafe. The goodies on offer were: the chance to do further education and learn about 'air pressure brakes'; the fact that these jobs (drivers, mechanics, warehousemen) 'obviously require physical strength but not A levels'; that they were relevant 'since I was a little boy I've been interested in lorries, engines and that'; and that 'drivers have to spend a lot of time away from home'. All bonuses — but for whom? The girls, not surprisingly, spent the film talking, giggling, shifting around, going to the loo, looking out of the window, waving at each other and pulling faces at the teacher. Bored. Passing the time. The teacher's response was shouting at them to shut up, pay attention: 'some people want to see this film', be serious, 'You'll all be unemployed in six months'. Girls, he explained to me, just aren't interested, you can't get them to take careers seriously.

One of the problems with 'common sense' is precisely that it isn't questioned; schools can breathe a sigh of relief. Girls aren't interested so teachers don't have to make a big effort to interest them, to cover issues relevant to them. In one school I visited boys and girls were seen by the careers service separately. Girls weren't seen till *after* the closing date for apprenticeship applications. Girls aren't interested in apprenticeships, as we all know, so girls aren't told about them. It's a vicious circle with girls in the middle. Careers is often seen as a 'spare' space on the timetable when researchers like me can take girls out for a chat. And careers lessons are pretty boring and irrelevant on the whole so why bother to disillusion the teachers? If you can have a laugh without them paying much attention (girls just aren't interested . . .) so much the better. Real work is men's work — 'you can't expect boys to sit through a lesson on secretarial work, they just wouldn't have it' — and real women are quiet, gentle, caring wives and mothers, don't get their hands dirty. 'Girls don't mind hearing about mechanics — their boyfriends probably have a motorbike or something.' No one has ever said to me 'Boys don't mind hearing about secretaries — their girlfriend probably has a typewriter or something.' So why is it just girls who are assumed to be interested in their boyfriend's work/hobbies/exam results, and not the other way round? Girls' and women's lives are structured around marriage and the family — and their waged work (as well as the housework they're expected to do) is no exception:

The Perfect Secretary should be like the perfect wife — always on hand to ensure the comfort of her boss . . . employment bureau chief Margery Hurst . . . thinks 'a boss and his secretary should work at the relationship as you would a marriage'. (*Daily Mail*, 22/4/80)

Careers teacher: And how will this fit in with your family?
Julie: But I haven't got a family! I haven't thought about it yet,
I'm only fifteen.
Careers teacher: You'd better think about it, for when you *do* have
a family.
Me: Do you ask boys that question?

It's questions like these which help to construct girls' career choice
in terms of their role within the family. A career is chosen (though not
necessarily achieved) not only for interest but also from within the
scope of 'suitable' jobs for women, jobs that won't interfere with, or
take priority over, our relationships with men. As one girl put it, 'I
want to be a teacher because if you're teaching and you want to stop
you can get an allowance and go back to work later when the children
grow up.' I don't think boys choose jobs because they'll fit in with their
family, or they can take time off to look after children. Of course, it's
not just schools that define for us what we can and can't do with our
lives. Parents, employers, boys, other girls even, all have certain assumptions about men and women, about what's appropriate for each, what's
'a nice job' for a girl. Of course, we don't just accept, or interpret in
the same way, the messages that come through television, advertisements, school books, magazines, and we don't just accept what other
people tell us, but we *do* all receive them in some way, we're all
surrounded by do's and don'ts and maybe's, and the choices we make
are affected by them.

**'You, your Hotpoint liberator, and Persil automatic: together they
make a winning team.'**

I want to look in detail at one example of the messages we receive
about women and work — careers books — but obviously these aren't
isolated examples; they're part of education generally (see Anne Strong's
and Gill Frith's articles) and they're written by people who, of course,
share and interpret general attitudes in our society. Also, as I've said
before, the way in which I read these books is affected by my own
experiences — there are different ways of reading — and you'll have to
assess whether my reading fits what you think, the choices you've made.

Margaret: I think it used to be like that, women could only do some
things, were supposed to just get married and that, but these days
I think *you* decide.
Me: What do you want to be?
Margaret: I want to be a nurse, I've always wanted to be a nurse.
I think it was 'Emergency Ward Ten' that did it, and playing with

teddies, bandaging them and that. A couple of my aunties are nurses so I know what the job's like — they say it's a good job.

This girl obviously knew exactly what she wanted to do, but did she *really* decide for herself? I'm not suggesting that she chose nursing because she was brainwashed or anything — it really was what she wanted to do. But I think this is a good example of the way everything that surrounds us — television, the toys we play with as kids, the jobs our friends and family do — influences our decisions. This girl could possibly have gone into any number of medical jobs, but the first thing, and the only thing, she thought of was nursing. Doctors and nurses is a common game children play. It's exciting, satisfies some of their curiosity about each other's bodies, creates in play the responsibility for other people (albeit only teddies or dolls) that children don't often get the chance to feel. But its reference point, the thing that makes it make sense, is adult reality. Margaret bandaged the teddies while her brother probably played doctor, just as the 'Emergency Ward Ten' nurses were all women, the doctors were all men. And Margaret probably also played 'mummies and daddies' which, along with making tea and doing housework with those 'child' sized ironing boards, cookers, vacuum cleaners, etc. often also involves dealing with the cuts and bruises of her 'children'. The jobs that women do involve similar responsibilities to her job in the home — caring, cleaning, cooking and serving meals — and they're often also done for a man, whether he's your boss or your husband. When did you last see an advertisement on television that was aimed at women without reference, whether spoken or unspoken, to a man? The shampoo or make-up adverts may or may not have the woman running into his arms at the end, but either way the man who's going to appreciate the new you is just around the corner. As a disc jockey put it in one of his phone-ins 'Tell me about yourself, Mrs . . ., what does your husband do?'

I hope I've made it clear that we can't just look at careers books, or careers themselves, in isolation from other things we read and see. Looking back to how you learnt to read: when Janet was watching John sailing his toy boat, what was Janet's mother doing? Glenys Lobban, a teacher, points out:[4]

The message from most current text books is clear — female adults always wear an apron and are permanently domiciled in the kitchen while little girls do maths puzzles about scones . . . *Ladybird* is supremely sexist and supremely suitable for Educational Priority Area kids with an all white family who live in a detached house in the country from whence dad sets off in his suit and bowler hat and be-aproned mum waves from the patio. The *Pirates* initial series is

best with one minor pitfall — there is not a single female character
in the twelve books (and the evil characters are the Black Pirates).

Careers books, the way they're written and the way we read them, ar
part of everything we read at school, part of the way we learn. Not tha
I think many kids actually bother to read them, though teachers migh
But they're useful to look at because you can get at the assumption
behind what's written down, the assumptions that come through in th
way they're written as well as the things they say, about girls and work

'Singers, skaters or secretaries — whatever the job, the stories make
marvellous reading!' Careers today — new images of women?

Careers books absolutely reinforce the traditional, out of date ideas
about women's capabilities. Bodley Head concede that women can
be air hostesses, beauticians, fashion buyers, journalists, farmers,
library assistants, police women, teachers, almoners, booksellers,
dental assistants and therapists. They may also play a part in the

process of publishing, television advertising and broadcasting. Other publishers have similar lists.[5]

The Sex Discrimination Act has done very little to alter this picture of careers for girls, and it's not just from careers books that we get ideas about women's work. I remember an issue of the *Bunty Annual* with an A-Z of careers for girls. You know the sort of thing — A is for air hostess, H is for Hairdresser, S is for Shop assistant, P is for Pharmacist's assistant, V is for Vet's assistant — lots of assistants and no vets or pharmacists! It never actually got to Z because the final picture, bigger than any of the others, was W is for Wife — complete with wedding dress and proud bridegroom. The ultimate career for seven- to ten-year-olds. Other careers stuff for kids — like the rhyming ones quite common in schoolbooks: 'Glenda is a grocer's girl who sells you tins of beans; Hattie is a housewife who whistles while she cleans', or the teen magazines' 'fun' guides for adolescents: the career that's right for you, according to your favourite colour, horoscope, or the colour of your eyes — are no different. Girls' fiction, with its dream jobs, is limited to glamour and romance; the quote at the beginning of this section is from *The Girls' Treasury of Careers Stories*: 'a girl's film career from editing in the cutting room to acting on the screen'; 'a news reporter makes a difficult choice between romance and professional integrity'.

The 'official' literature used for careers teaching in schools, though more realistic, shares similar assumptions about girls' interests and attitudes; they're only interested in boys and romance, don't see work as a 'career' but only as a time-filler before marriage, are frivolous and difficult to get interested — choosing a career according to your favourite colour, or where your friends are working — which is actually a sensible consideration, but they don't see it that way. The following quote, from Tony Crowley's *Choosing A Career*, is a good example of the way a discussion of *work*, through taking a girl as an example, is changed into a rather derogatory chat about leisure:[6]

> Take a girl whose list of interests showed she spent most of her time out with boyfriends and going to dances. Suppose she chose to go to work in the local factory operating a machine. She had shown no interest in working with her hands — our 'practical' heading. But if her job was easy to learn and could be done after only a short spell of training, there is no reason why she shouldn't do it well. And if all she asks is to work with her friends and not have a job with a lot of responsibility then she could be quite happy, couldn't she? Of course, if it were a job which did take some time to learn and needed a lot of skill with your hands then it might be different. For instance, you would expect a boy who wanted an apprenticeship in joinery not only to have been quite good at

woodwork at school, but to have listed some things under the practical heading wouldn't you?

The message of this is quite clear. Girls aren't 'practical', aren't looking for 'a career', but will be 'quite happy' with a routine factory job, are more interested in their love life than their working life and don't want responsibility. Note how the tone becomes more serious once the boys and 'skill' are mentioned. There's no recognition of the fact that a factory job might be all that's going, it's better paid than office or shop work, it's boring so working with friends makes it more bearable, and who wants to spend their life doing a boring job anyway? Most girls and most boys for that matter, aren't going to have a 'career' at all they're probably going into a job where clocking off is the highlight of the day, so it makes sense to put your energy into what you do with your own time. At the moment getting any job is an achievement, and a lot to do with luck. Unemployment, particularly for school leavers is a common problem. But for girls, it's not seen as *much* of a problem. Michael Carter suggests that parents think in terms of a ' "good" job for the boys and a "nice" job for the girls.... Work, for her, is but a prelude to marriage',[7] and one careers officer explained to me that girls show little interest in training and none at all in 'the chances of promotion because they don't see it as a long term thing.' The 'normal' working life is generally seen as continuous, from sixteen to sixty-five, and the interrupted working life that most women experience, and most girls expect, is consequently seen as the exception, a variation on the norm, even though 40 per cent of the labour force is women. Have you noticed the number of letters to papers, or conversations between men, and sometimes women, suggesting that married women should stop working to give school leavers a chance? The school leavers they mean are boys — boys and men are seen as having the right to work, while for women this is assumed to be a choice, secondary to the husband's work, for 'pin money' and luxuries. Expendable.

> On 24 April 1976 the Press Association reported 1½ million unemployed and continued, without comment, that the government felt 'an encouraging factor is that in the last three months most of the increase in unemployment was among women.'

Work, as something men do, that women might do for a limited period of time, is an idea reinforced, often unintentionally, in careers books. The distance between girls and the world of work is not total; it's not that girls don't and aren't expected to work, it's the way *that* they do it — 'It's different for girls' — that is different from boys and men. (No one says 'Boys have a different attitude to work, they're a

special case.') Girls are limited in the choices open to them, but they are also expected to inhabit the role 'worker' in certain ways. If you look at the illustrations in careers books, girls are usually nurses, typists, secretaries, models. But they're also white, blonde, blue-eyed, scatty, sitting around, looking like the girls in a *Jackie* story — the drawings, not the photostory heroines, who at least look a bit normal. The token black face is sometimes included, but there's no attempt to challenge what are ridiculously stereotyped images of girls. Girls are passive (being photographed or listening to records), adorable (surrounded by men in the office), caring (playing with children in the ward — nurses have so much time!), attentive (listening to the boss). Girls aren't unconventional, noisy, witty, aggressive, active, interesting. Illustrations are as important as the written text, they present us with clear, easily identifiable images of what we are. Interestingly, in some of these booklets, e.g. *Starting Work*,[8] the post-1975 (post-Sex Discrimination Act) editions have simply had the illustrations removed. This is almost as bad as the sticky labels some careers offices have to put inside their publications saying 'Please note that throughout this book "he" also refers to "she".' Hardly a radical and determined effort to promote equality of opportunity!

So what do the texts say? One of the most subtle ways of excluding girls from many jobs is through apparently open, non-discriminatory questions. 'An electrician needs good colour vision. Do you know why?' The answer is apparently so obvious that it isn't given. Asking questions that kids have to answer for themselves is a useful way of teaching — but not if half the class doesn't have the answers. Girls often don't know why — when was the last time you fitted a plug? Who changes fuses in your family? It's likely that the boys in the class can all give the answers, making the girls feel, at worst stupid, and at best that the job of an electrician is not for them. It's not difficult to learn that the wires are two or three different colours, and have to go into the right places inside the plug. It's just not likely that girls will have learnt this at school *or* at home. Have you ever done any carpentry? I've noticed how often simple things like which way to turn a screw is something women have to *learn*, whereas men pick it up as boys. Playing with dolls doesn't give you the same skills as playing with Meccano. (How many men or boys do you know who haven't a clue how to hold a baby?)

Most of the examples used to illustrate a point are 'men's' jobs: for example, in *Choosing a Career*, the example of a job you can enter at a higher level after further education is engineering. But girls do get a look-in in careers books. *Job-Hunting with Josephine*[9] is a good example — of how *not* to get a job. Josephine provides a cautionary tale to us all — she does everything wrong. Just a coincidence that for a change we have a girl in the leading role?

"Get this: N.B. 'applicant must be 6' tall, weigh 13 stone + be prepared to strip to the waist .........."

### Now that we've got equality: the Sex Discrimination Act and careers for girls

This job is open to men and women; applicant must be over six feet tall, twelve stone, very strong and prepared to strip to the waist . . .

Most of us are aware that the equal opportunities legislation we now have is worth very little to women. There's the case of the woman lavatory attendant who claimed equal pay with the male one, and was told that 'a male attendant has to approach the job from the labouring point of view and a female attendant approaches it from a housekeeping point of view', or the woman office cleaner who was refused equal pay with the male warehouse cleaner because 'The office cleaners work in the comfortable surroundings of carpeted offices, very similar to the environment of one's own home.'[10] Then there was the case of the woman who was refused a job as a coach driver for an 'adventure travel' firm on the grounds that 'a woman at the wheel did not fit the image of

adventure travel' and that the women passengers would respond better to a male driver's leadership. In schools, the situation is worse. You can't appeal to a tribunal against sex discrimination, but have to go to a county court, and the Equal Opportunities Commission can only refer cases to the Secretary of State. Moreover, discrimination is only illegal if other schools in the area provide the opportunities being complained about. In Tameside twice as many boys as girls get grammar school places, but this was ruled lawful because of the single-sex school system, under which there are more boys' schools than girls' schools. Discrimination is often indirect, and the letter of the law rarely covers this, because ultimately it's ideas about women, and conditions under which women live, throughout our society that are responsible. If promotion, say in the civil service, depends on age, and you have to be under twenty-eight to apply for a certain job, then this does discriminate against women, because many will have taken time off work to have children, and will therefore be older than men with the same experience of the job. But it's not just the civil service being anti-women. It's also the fact that women are still the people who take time to look after children, they're still basically responsible for kids, even if the husband 'helps'.

Textbooks are not specifically mentioned in the Act, and an obvious point is that pre-1975 books are still used in most schools, while the money to replace them is disappearing fast. Sticky labels don't solve the problem — the news that he also refers to she is hardly new; how many times have we been told that 'he', 'man', huMAN, huMANity all include women? But some apparent steps forward have been made. One is the CRAC Lifestyle series booklet 'Male and Female: choosing your role in modern society.'[11] This is an obvious response to the SDA and usefully counters some stereotypes, including the 'puzzle' about the man who's driving his son to school and has an accident. When the boy is rushed to hospital for surgery the surgeon shouts 'Oh God, it's my son'. The surgeon is, of course, the child's mother, though unfortunately, as there are so few women surgeons, it's pretty far-fetched. When I say useful, I mean it's better than nothing, but that's as far as it goes. We have an ideal challenge to sex roles — a boy who is a nurse — saying 'soon I hope to be promoted to matron, or Nursing Superintendent', which is, of course, precisely what happens to men in traditionally female occupations — they get promoted over the women. Some challenge! We're told that top jobs are now open to women but warned 'Many top jobs demand a great deal from the ambitious man or woman. Family life often has to take second place to the job. It means staying later, working in your spare time, taking a lot of responsibility, and often not having much time to enjoy yourself.' What isn't recognised is that these drawbacks affect boys and girls differently, that they are precisely the things that affect women. Women and girls are expected to put the

family first, can't stay late if they've got kids, don't have any spare time — they've got two jobs already, aren't supposed to be capable of taking responsibility, and if you don't enjoy yourself, how do you ever meet boys in the first place (what's it like, being the only one without a boyfriend? The pressure is on). The authors also comment 'When we choose jobs we don't often think about how they will affect our families later on — or even whether we get married at all.' The 'we' here is absolutely male — careers for girls are clearly determined by exactly these questions: 'How will this fit in with your family?' Doing an 'unfeminine' job is risky, because it can make you less attractive to boys, and ultimately endanger your chances of marriage — or so the story goes. John Wellens, talking about engineering, points out that 'a very popular view is that engineering for girls is rather "butch" or at least distinctly unladylike.'[12] One woman careers officer I talked to, who was keen to encourage girls to do 'untraditional' jobs, commented on one girl who was doing bricklaying: 'But to be honest she looks a bit like a bloke. . . .'

Unfortunately, the answer to this problem isn't usually to challenge what we mean by femininity; why should being a woman mean being passive, not taking decisions; not doing anything strenuous — women can't carry heavy weights? What about babies and young children?; not doing anything potentially dangerous — what about chip pans (most accidents happen in the home yet we don't think of it as a dangerous place); always taking, never giving, orders? No, the answer seems to be to prove that women in these jobs are just as feminine as any others, and the Engineering Industry Training Board's pamphlet on scholarships for girls goes as far as giving us photographs just to show how attractive and 'normal' their girls are. The same careers officer pointed out that one girl doing a craft apprenticeship was 'very, very capable and she could hold her own and without not being a woman if you see what I mean, she was a feminine girl.' I'm not suggesting there's anything wrong with being attractive; just that everyone rushes to point out that women in 'men's' jobs are, as if it is necessary to justify their position in those jobs in terms of their femininity. 'Being feminine' is almost a requirement of the job. Do men who work in offices have to prove that they're just as masculine as any other man? If a booklet was produced about male nurses, with photos of them flexing their muscles to prove how masculine they were, would it be seen in the same way?

But to go back briefly to the booklet. In its discussion of family life there is some attempt to deal with sharing housework, but this isn't really considering work within the home as work. 'Men are finding that being a father is fun' is nothing new, and certainly doesn't sound like a description of full-time childcare. More like 'that nice half hour when they come home from work and play with the kids while mum gets the

tea ready'. The earth-shattering conclusion of the booklet isn't new either. Things have really changed — the old formula 'Women=Home, Men=Work' is simply out of date. 'Today, Women=Home *and* Work; Men=Work *and* Home.' So what's changed? Women are wives and mothers who also have paid jobs, men are breadwinners who also 'help out' at home. And what really annoys me about this booklet is their announcement that 'The important thing is that YOU CAN CHOOSE.'

If there's one thing I've tried to argue in this article, it's that the jobs girls do aren't simply a matter of choice. The EITB can offer girls apprenticeships, but they can't make teachers and parents encourage girls to take them. 'One headmaster actually got up and said that he would not encourage any of his girls to enter engineering. . . . He saw engineering as no environment for a girl, especially in her formative years.'[13] One girl I saw had qualified for bricklaying, but her father refused to allow her to apply for jobs because he said his mates would laugh at him if his daughter was a bricklayer. Schools can encourage girls to get qualifications, but:

> it's very difficult to persuade them to stay on at school because there's the attitude that it's only for a couple of years anyway. . . . A number of parents I've met and I've said you know your daughter is going to get 6 or 7 O levels and she's got a good chance of going on say 'well it's not important for a girl, is it?' (careers officer)

I think there's a lot of lip service paid to the Sex Discrimination Act, but nine times out of ten you know it's a boy's job or a girl's job and though we don't agree with the system, that's what the employers are taking. You can send him all the girls in the world and you know he'll wait for a boy . . . male careers advisors in this area see boys and women see the girls because the Careers Service feel boys would probably go for an apprenticeship anyway and girls were thinking of nursing probably or office work and it's easier to learn and keep up with just half the amount of jobs, instead of all of them. (careers officer, Teesside)

Employers have to advertise jobs as open to men and women, but you can't force them to take women if they are determined not to. Women with children can work full-time, but who's going to provide the creche or nursery? And then there's boys:

> I've never met a boy yet whose personal life affected him to the same extent as a girl. Even girls going to college will choose one near home so that they can see their boyfriends. The boys just say

you can come and visit; I've never known a boy choose say a
university near home for that reason.

**Equal opportunities: do we really want them? Or, women who want
to be equal to men lack ambition.[14]**

The conclusion is probably the most difficult part of this chapter to
write, because it raises so many questions, introduces problems, but
gives very few answers. Everyone's heard of the Sex Discrimination Act,
the Equal Pay Act, the Equal Opportunities Commission. And not
everyone's very happy with it. On the one hand there's the *Daily
Telegraph* wanting the laws abolished: 'Let them Bake Cake' — girls
should do 'girls' subjects', it claims; or the *Sunday Telegraph*:

> No society has ever been dominated . . . by women, and it now
> seems possible — even likely — that this male dominance is
> engineered by biological forces that are not easily tampered
> with. . . The sight of the (EO) Commission waving the SDA at
> nature's inevitabilities is at once touching and hilarious. The real
> thing being touched however is the taxpayer's pocket, and the joke
> is hardly worth one and a half million pounds. (Peter Taylor on the
> lunacy of the Equality Laws, 18 June 1978)

On the other hand, there's the Women's Liberation Movement. I've
already suggested that this legislation is worth very little more than
the paper it's written on. The Equal Pay Act allowed employers five
years before it became law to shuffle around with grades and jobs so
that women couldn't claim they were doing the same job as a man. The
Sex Discrimination Act recognises that girls in schools are vulnerable to
'discrimination', but has no teeth to do anything about it, and the
Equal Opportunities Commission has proved itself ready to back down
on anything controversial:

> Helen Whitfield wanted to take the boys' craftwork classes. . . . She
> was offered a place in the classes but turned it down saying that
> she did not want to be made an exception; the classes should be
> available to all girls. . . . Judge Perks ruled the treatment for girls
> and boys was different but equal because boys were not allowed to
> do needlework any more than the girls could take woodwork. The
> case, which was the first of its kind brought under the education
> section of the SDA, was originally backed by the EOC. However it
> withdrew its support and this is now the subject of legal action too.
> (*The Times Educational Supplement*, 22/2/80)

Equality is oh so respectable as long as you don't cause trouble.

But I'm not so sure I want to be 'equal', or that girls want to be either. At the beginning of the article I suggested that our 'failure' in the world of work isn't just because girls and women are stupid. I've suggested lots of reasons why. But one of the most important reasons seems to be that, although women are oppressed and restricted through our roles as wives and mothers, our caring and servicing, we might not want to swap that for 'getting on'. The business executive who eats, sleeps and lives work (in between games of golf?), who walks over other people to get a better deal for himself, or the car assembler who works overtime for the money, in bad conditions, without much time for anything else — maybe we don't want to be like that.[15]

Audrey Wise has suggested that one reason for female apathy about equal pay is that women workers have seen how men in exchange for high wages accept gruelling conditions of work, productivity deals, and increased exploitation in all its forms, and do not themselves wish to pay this price. Women tend to raise issues related to the social conditions of work, adequate canteen and toilet facilities, rest periods and child care provision. Equally women employed in the professions tend to seek work they enjoy and are not necessarily so anxious to reach the heights of the profession as are men.

Marie: I don't mind so much about the money, but I want to work somewhere warm and comfortable.

Women are oppressed by the conditions we live with, by being limited, stopped from doing what we want, by having to live up to the image of femininity that men (whether employers, fathers, boyfriends or the men who own the magazines we read) have created for us. But we've also learnt a few things. Girls don't behave as they're supposed to. Is it any more likely that we want what we're supposed to want? Men seem to think we want what they've already got. But do you? Do you just want to be in there with them?

Union official: We've been trying to encourage girls to go in for building apprenticeships, but they're just not interested. Once they realise it's not all glamour they drop out. You're your own worst enemies — jobs like ours aren't glamorous, but women seem to think they are.
Me: Do you take girls in groups?
Union official: No just one or two, that's all we get, and they soon drop out.

I wonder why? The general impression I get from girls who have tried these kinds of jobs is that they're lonely and oppressive. Do you want to spend your working day surrounded by men cracking jokes about women, page 3 or porno magazines, talking about getting their leg over the night before, assuming you can't do the job, helping you out maybe — with perfectly simple things any fool could do (except women). Or being one of the lads — you don't mind if they swear about other women, you're different, you've made it?

The alternative, which most girls 'choose', is to work with other women, your mates, have a laugh, joke about the boss. After all, what makes school bearable? Most girls I've talked to say it's their mates, having a laugh, the things that make it more enjoyable to go to school than stay home on your own — upsetting teachers, hiding in the bogs, nipping off for a smoke. . . . Secretarial jobs are often seen as providing the chance to meet men, being able to flirt with the men who visit or work in the office; boys at school make life more interesting, who fancies who, who's courting and who isn't. But where would you be without your mates to talk to? Would it be the same without the other girls?

Again, I'm being a bit unfair. There are people in the EOC trying to make changes. But the basic problem is that legislation doesn't actually change fundamentally the conditions we live in. Women still have the kids, and the responsibility to look after them, we still do worse at school than boys, do different subjects (metalwork for girls — jewellery making!), we're still expected to get married, have kids, and put our families first. Women still have to make a choice between a career and children, while men take for granted their right to have both. Legislation doesn't alter people's responses to a woman who does a man's job, and it doesn't change the power that husbands and fathers have to stop us doing what we want to. I know several girls and women who have dropped out of courses where they were training to be things like mechanics, gardeners, HGV drivers, engineers, because although we can, legally, enter those courses, the law doesn't change the atmosphere. It doesn't alter the fact that one or possibly two girls among twenty boys are going to have a hard time. And it doesn't recognise that girls may not want to compete on men's terms. Women do put families first, but one of the reasons for this is that we know that people we care about, children we have, are more important than the way we earn a living. That enjoying your work is more important than earning a packet. That there are more things to life than a nine to five day. That if 'getting on' means getting on on the backs of other women, then maybe it's just not worth it. We're all supposed to encourage girls and women wanting to do traditional men's work. What about the position most women are in, the work most women do, which is valuable and important, but not recognised as such? Lots of women work in 'service industries' which are very badly paid because in many ways they're an extension of what women already do, in the home: cooking, serving meals, nursing, looking after children. But why shouldn't we do jobs that involve other people and their needs and why shouldn't we be well paid for them? Men have defined these jobs as unimportant, basically because they don't do them. Why should we accept that? The only way to have a real choice about work is if all the jobs that women do, in the workplace or at home, are seen as equally valuable and important, if we don't have to either go out to work or stay at home, but can do both, if we no longer have 'women's work' and 'men's work'. But it doesn't seem to me that the way to achieve this is for the individual, ambitious, woman to make it in a man's world. OK — she's a woman, but she must be an exception. We need to make changes, though what kind of work, what kind of future, what changes you want are questions I can't answer. I can say that I don't want to make it as a woman in a man's world, I want to be a woman in a woman's world. Maybe we ought to change the world?

**Suggestions**

Changing the world takes time! So what do we do now! What kind of careers advice should girls be getting? What kind of a job do you want? I can't answer these questions, you can. My ideas go like this:
1    Most girls don't know about what jobs are available, and it's important they all get the chance to meet people doing different jobs, especially women. There's nothing more off-putting than a six-foot

bloke saying 'girls can do my job' — it doesn't make you feel confident.

2    Particularly with unemployment, it's important to recognise that it's really difficult to get any job at all and being unemployed isn't your fault — it's the fault of the people who created the unemployment in the first place.

3    It's also important for girls to have the chance to hear about and talk about *why* getting 'male' jobs is difficult. It's no good just throwing a girl in at the deep end and saying learn to swim — fast. 'You want to be a mechanic? Great, just go along to this course' just isn't good enough. Girls can do these jobs, but girls don't, on the whole. The important question is why.

4    It's difficult to answer this question with boys around. Girls and women need our own space to work out our own ideas. We're surrounded by men's ideas all the time, we don't need them there in person as well. Boys giggling at the girls' daft ideas just doesn't help. Girls being able to come out with the 'daft ideas' and talk about them together is what counts. Inside the girl who watches her boyfriend on the pool table every night there could be a brilliant player just waiting to get out, but she's not likely to find out if the 'expert' is watching. Ideas aren't any different.

5    If you do want to do something like a craft apprenticeship, it's a good idea to try and go with other girls. Groups of girls learning together, with a woman teaching — like on the EITB girl apprenticeship schemes — are more likely to be successful, enjoy their work, and stick it out. You need someone to talk to, you can discuss the problems (including the boys) with the other girls. 'Girls Rule OK' is difficult to believe when there's only one of you; girls together are together.

6    Skills — whether it's being able to repair your motorbike or wire a plug — aren't something you have to learn only if you want to be a mechanic or an electrician. They're things we need to know about to do things for ourselves. We don't have to learn them in skill centres — if you have a skill share it. If you want to learn find women who can share their skills. Advertise. And being able to knit your own jumpers is as important as being able to make your own shelves. Men haven't got a monopoly on skill.

The point is, we can do things for ourselves, we can learn and share, we can even make a living out of it — if we can do it together.

## Notes

1 John Newsom, *The Education of Girls*, Faber, 1948.
2 Rosemary Deem, *Women and Schooling*, Routledge & Kegan Paul, 1978.
3 *Ibid*.
4 Glenys Lobban in *Radical Education*, 1978, no. 9.
5 Camilla Nightingale, 'Sex Roles in Children's Literature' in *Conditions o*

*Illusion*, Papers from the Women's Movement, 1972.
6 Tony Crowley, *Choosing a Career*, Careers Research & Advisory Centre (CRAC), 1972.
7 Michael Carter, *Into Work*, Penguin, Harmondsworth, 1962.
8 Hilary Adamson, *Starting Work*, Industrial Society, 1972.
9 In Crowley, *op. cit.*
10 Jean Coussins, *The Equality Report*, National Council for Civil Liberties Rights for Women Unit, 1976.
11 Anne Jones, Jan Marsh and A.G. Watts, *Choosing your Role in Modern Society*, CRAC, 1974.
12 John Wellens, 'Girl technicians for engineering', *Industrial and Commercial Training*, vol. 9, no. 3, March 1977.
13 *Ibid.*
14 From *Spare Rib Diary*, 1980.
15 Elizabeth Wilson, *Women and The Welfare State*, Tavistock, 1977.

# 5 'They call me a life-size Meccano set':
## super-secretary or super-slave?

*Hazel Downing*

Illustrated by *Angela Amesbury*

I worked as a secretary for three years and then went to university to do a degree. I'm now writing a thesis on secretarial work. I'd like to thank Glenys Pudney for suggesting this title.

JOB WITH A DIFFEREN

ECRETARY/PA M/F for young, ambitious
any director. Interesting and varied responsi
Some travel involved. Initiative and experi
essential. Good salary. Tel: 032 855

Someone once suggested to me that if all the secretaries and typists in the country went on strike for a week, the economy would collapse. This power has remained unrecognised. Why? Well, you might wonder, why on earth should they go on strike? The working conditions are OK, the pay's not bad — well not that bad! — the hours are fairly

flexible and there are office parties; it's clean and there's no one standing over you checking and timing your work all the time. In any case,
why rock the boat, especially if you're going to leave work after a few
years to have children, and after all, it is better than working in a shop,
or even a factory. Is it? I wonder.

A lot of girls, especially working-class girls, go into office work.
They choose this area to work in for various reasons. Possibly, indeed
quite probably, they've learnt shorthand and typing at school and
decided to use these skills to earn money. Maybe for women like Janet,
it wasn't really planned:

> I couldn't decide what I wanted to do until I left school. I hadn't
> got any real plans you know. I always fancied the idea of learning
> to type, so I thought I'd go to college for a year and learn there.
> So that's what I did. It's sort of like a last minute decision.
> (interview)

Maybe the advice came from the careers officer:

> The careers officer came round and he said, 'Well, you're quite
> good at English and I think the best bet is if you do something
> like audio-typing or something like that.' Well I always did like
> typewriters and things like that as a child. (interview with Josie)

Or maybe they were encouraged by parents who didn't want their
daughters to end up night cleaning, or working in a factory. 'Do a
typing course love, you'll never be out of a job.' Sensible advice.
Certainly, the sorts of arguments women have heard in the past, but
unfortunately, with the arrival of the silicon chip, no longer the type
of advice which is very realistic.

Over the last two years there has been a lot of publicity in the
newspapers and on television, devoted to the silicon chip, or, as it is
sometimes known, the 'new technology'. Attitudes to this new technology vary and depend to a great extent on one's interest in the economy,
in other words, whether one is an employer or an employee.

Since 1978, the government has poured vast amounts of money into
research and development to encourage new applications of this technology (microprocessors) on the grounds that failure to jump on the band-
wagon will mean that Britain Will Go To The Wall. When the question
of displacement of jobs through automation has been raised, the
government has shown its concern by vague, non-committal responses,
or by not responding at all. Then there is the blind progress camp
which welcomes this latest in a string of technological advances over the
past 200 years as the saviour of Western civilisation — the silicon chip
will, they argue, free us from work and give us more leisure time. There

is, however, a vast economic and social difference between being freed from work and being made unemployed, and it is precisely the problem of unemployment and all that goes with it — poverty, deprivation, powerlessness — that is of concern to the other end of the spectrum, the trade union movement. As more jobs become automated, they argue, and as the world economy sinks ever deeper into a recession, then more and more people will be put out of work. Since microprocessing technology is being applied to areas previously free from automation, such as the service sector, areas which employ large numbers of female workers, the majority of those affected will be women.

Since 1951, the labour force in Britain has increased from 22.6 millions to 26.2 millions, an increase which is accounted for by an expansion in the numbers of women, especially married women, in paid employment. Women now make up 40 per cent of the total working population and, all things being equal, the trend is likely to continue. However, all things are not equal, especially women's status and position in the economy. Too many people still consider that women are more usefully occupied in the home, caring for children and husbands, and that those women who go out to work do so only for luxuries. But most women who work outside the home do so because they have to. They may be single parents, either through divorce, widowhood, desertion, or simply because they choose not to marry, in which case they have no male breadwinner to rely on; or it may be that they and their families simply cannot survive on one wage. This does not mean that given the choice all working women would rather stay at home. In contrast with the isolation of childcare and housework, going out to work and at least enjoying the company of other women is often a welcome escape.

Three million women, nearly a third of the total female labour force, work in clerical and secretarial work. But the office, for so long a nest of security — no lay-offs or redundancies, good pension schemes — is the main target of automation through microprocessing technology in the form of the word processor. The word processor, a sophisticated typewriter with a memory; can do the work of 2½-5 typists and at the same time replace and render unnecessary skills which have traditionally been the typist's stock in trade. Once she has learnt to read off instructions from the display screen and which buttons she has to press, the typist becomes little more than a machine minder and her work output is monitored by the machine itself. Evidence so far suggests that where word processors have been installed in Britain roughly half the original number of jobs have been lost.

Traditionally, workers in this country have not given up their jobs, their rights to a livelihood and a living wage, without a fight, and that fight has only been possible through collective struggle with other workers in trade unions. In 1951, 45 per cent of all workers were in

trade unions; that figure has now reached 52 per cent, the increase being primarily the result of a growth in trade union membership among women; from 1,790,000 in 1951 to nearly 4 millions in 1976. Despite this staggering growth, with the exception of the public sector (local government and university clerical workers for instance), women office workers still remain weak and largely non-unionised. What then can we say about the future prospects of large numbers of women in office work already, and those still at school who expect to become office workers?

This chapter will look at secretarial work in the light of the threats to jobs and skills posed by microprocessing technology and will address itself to the important question of why women office workers remain so weak and badly organised. What is it about their work or their position in society which stops them from recognising themselves as workers? And what is it about this new technology business which means they should?

### Secretary wanted: must be slim, attractive, able to make coffee and prepared to work for peanuts: a few myths

When I first started life behind a typewriter, fingers neatly poised above ASDF (left hand) and: LKJ (right hand), I had already formed an impression of secretarial work as clean, comfortable, in pleasant surroundings, with no dirt, no health hazards and no hard slog. That's not to say I thought it would be an easy ride. I was scared stiff. How could I, muddle-headed as I was, ever become a super-efficient, super-cool, super-competent secretary — for this was the image I had created. My first ever experience of office work as a temp in London didn't help either — I made so many mistakes, I had to retype things four or five times so I took all my bad copies home with me, wrapped up in a newspaper, because I thought someone went round checking the bins every night.

My picture of secretarial life was formed as a result of a whole mixture of influences: films, television serials, books, romantic girls' magazines, and above all, advertising. The image goes something like this: the brightly lit office is clean, full of potted plants, pleasantly decorated with fitted carpets. There are no trailing wires, no toxic fumes from stencil correcting or whitening fluids, no old-fashioned wooden furniture to snag tights and clothes on. The secretaries, who are all young and extremely attractive, inhabit individual offices with neat desks, filing trays which say 'in' and 'out' and neatly sharpened pencils. It is an image which is strongly encouraged by secretarial colleges, as one secretary described:

This is another thing that upheld this belief that a secretarial job was such a brilliant job to have. At the college, they were such enthusiastic people — the typewriting teacher and the tutor: 'Oh, it's lovely to work in an office' — type thing. And I got this huge impression that everyone ran around at top speed and were just so totally efficient and there was no room for blunders, and you just had to be spot-on all the time. So you came out of college thinking, I can't really do this, because they really made you feel you had to be really super-duper, an absolute brain, like a machine, running around and being totally efficient and correct all the time. . . . It really had this strange aura about it, because really I still hadn't been into an office. When I got there, of course, there's people who doddle along, there's lazy people, people who can't do their jobs — you know, just ordinary people. (interview)

The secretaries in our fantasy office are all happy in their work, ecstatic almost. They never rebel, never answer back (like at school), and fall over backwards to please the boss, to fetch and carry, developing an almost intuitive sense of when he wants another cup of coffee and thus setting it neatly on his desk without spilling any in the saucer just two seconds before he looks up from his important business to ask for another cup. These secretaries always know exactly what their bosses are doing at all times throughout the day. They keep his diary up to date and are able to answer promptly any enquiry regarding his whereabouts. They always remember to give him messages, remind him of his family's birthdays, buy the cards and order the flowers, so that, with these trivial, time-consuming details dealt with, he can turn his mind to more important matters. They are also extremely well groomed, never bite their nails, never have chipped nail polish, never have holes in their tights, or worn down heels, their hair is always clean and immaculately groomed, their make up perfect with no left overs from the night before. This is emphasised in all secretarial manuals:

As the secretary represents her employer and is in contact with many of the firm's top-level executives she must wear clothes which create a good impression. Her dress should be smart and simple in design. Careful grooming is also very important and the secretary should ensure that her shoes are highly polished, her suit or dress meticulously pressed, and on arrival at the office first thing in the morning she uses a brush so that no hairs remain on the shoulders. She should also adopt a neat hair-style, carefully manicure her nails (avoiding vivid nail varnishes) and use her make up discreetly and correctly. (J. Harrison, *Secretarial Duties*, Pitman, 1962, p. 214)

And, of course, our secretaries are always polite and never swear — ever. They never make typing errors, write shorthand at 120 wpm, read it back perfectly and are capable of designing the perfect filing system. Their lives are cushioned with flattery and praise from their supermen bosses.

I suppose it is possible that this model bears some resemblance to the reality of office life, but then it really depends on whose reality we are talking about. The image of women as servants to men, taking the blame for their mistakes, and protecting them as fervently and lovingly as they would a sick child, is a picture created largely in the minds of men. Nevertheless, it is a picture which reflects the position of subordination which women occupy in our society.

My experience, and that of most secretarial workers I've spoken to, creates a quite different picture. It is a picture which reflects low pay; appalling promotion prospects (especially for working-class women, black and white); noisy, dirty, badly heated and poorly lit offices, even hazardous health conditions; sexual harassment; humiliation, powerlessness and boredom. Once in a job, many women recognise that, in practice, it has little in common with what they anticipated. I'll now investigate why.

**The reality: hierarchical control**

Traditionally, organisations are pyramid-shaped. A carefully constructed theory dating to the beginning of this century supplies a model which goes something like this: there are a certain number of tasks to be done in an organisation, whether in the production of goods or services. These tasks are divided broadly into 'thinking' tasks and 'doing' ones and within these divisions there is a scale — some thinking tasks are more difficult than others, some doing tasks require more skills. Since, in any organisation there are usually more doing tasks than thinking ones, there are inevitably more people employed at the lower levels. In addition, since skills have to be purchased at a high price, there is a tendency to decrease the price (wages) by reducing the need for the skills either through machinery (automation) or the further subdivision or fragmentation of particular tasks into smaller components. As the old saying goes, 'knowledge equals power' — a skilled worker with extensive knowledge of the work has more power and is less easily replaceable than an unskilled worker whose services can be readily dispensed with and replaced by those of another unskilled worker. 'De-skilling' involves stripping the worker of his/her skills and knowledge and, hence, control and passing this knowledge into the hands of management. So that, for instance, in manufacturing, instead of one highly skilled person making a whole machine, the job is subjected to a

time and motion study by management and then divided up so that one (unskilled) person will put a bolt in, the next will tighten it, and so on. The same techniques have been applied to the office, with the departmentalisation of office work. Productivity increases as individual worker's skills and wages decrease.

This is no myth. It is not based on some 'natural' state of affairs because some people are stupid while others are clever, nor is it something that just happened out of the blue. It was meticulously worked out at the beginning of this century by a man called Frederick Taylor in the USA as the most efficient way for a company to increase its productive output, cheapen wage costs and increase profits, and has strongly influenced managements in this country for the last sixty years.

The office and secretarial hierarchies are no different. From the bottom the hierarchy consists of:

1    Clerk typist — a mixture of clerical and typing duties, usually invoice typing.
2    Copy-typist. Depending on the size of the organisation, she would either be in a large pool or sharing a smaller office with three or four other typists.
3    Audio-typist, considered higher than a copy typist, presumably because she needs to be able to spell, and because she uses machinery other than the typewriter. Highly productive from management's point of view and more efficient than the next category.
4    Shorthand-typist, usually working for several (usually) men, and sharing an office with other typists. The work involves no administrative duties and little contact with the boss, other than taking dictation.
5    Secretary. Some people call themselves secretaries when their work actually only fits the description of shorthand typist, or audio typist, and many employers permit this status-enhancing self-definition because they feel it 'keeps them happy' without giving them a rise. In this category, status is dependent on whether the woman shares an office with two or more, or with one secretary. Those with their own offices occupy a higher position.
6    Personal/private/executive secretary or personal assistant (or, in the days before the Sex Discrimination Act, 'girl Friday').

In addition, and not to be overlooked, is the fact that one's position in the hierarchy is dependent on the status and position of the boss. Even though they may be doing the same work, within any particular organisation the Managing Director's secretary is accorded more respect and status than the secretary to a mere manager, and is likely to be expected to supervise her lower-level colleagues.

Many women with experience of different offices recognise that the divisions are meaningless, that a typist is a typist, whether she's called copy typist or secretary. In fact, shorthand, which traditionally served as a mark of distinction between the ordinary typist and the secretary, is now being eliminated and replaced by audio typing, which any typist can do. But despite the fact that every girl who enters the office at the lowest rungs does not automatically proceed up the ladder, the myth remains to buttress the illusion of secretarial work offering an inbuilt career structure, a myth which is sustained quite clearly in secretarial manuals, to quote from just two:

> A top secretarial position is an excellent stepping-stone to many
> interesting and remunerative careers in various fields. (Mary
> Bosticco, *How to be a Top Secretary*, New English Library, 1975,
> p. 9)

> (It is) a magic carpet, an open sesame to a life full of interest — a
> life with a complete fulfilment. (S. Hardwick-Smith and B. Rowe,
> *The Private Secretary*, Museum Press, 1958, p. 6)

There's even a book by Bernard Marks of the Alfred Marks Bureau called *Once Upon a Typewriter* which details the success stories of twelve women who started life behind a typewriter:

> The twelve whose stories are told here demonstrate the
> opportunities that lead to careers in politics, publishing,
> broadcasting, banking, journalism and many other areas often still
> regarded as being a male province — such as industrial management.
> (Bernard Marks, *Once Upon a Typewriter*, Arrow, 1974, p. 1)

Certainly some women do make the top, but as Polly Toynbee commented in *Cosmopolitan* (December 1974):

> You might just as well do some research into the number of black,
> hunchbacked, left-handed orphans of the Jewish persuasion who
> had made a success in the world, and because you found a handful,
> conclude that they, too, were not at a disadvantage after all.

Whatever position one holds in the hierarchy, the work remains fundamentally the same — shorthand or audio and typing. However, the higher one gets, the proportion of time actually spent on these technical skills (for which one is ostensibly being paid) decreases. Job descriptions very rarely accompany secretarial jobs. If they do, then they demand shorthand/audio typing, general office duties, such as filing and then, tucked away at the bottom, a tiny undefined etcetera. Ms Bosticco describes it slightly differently:

> It is simply that technical skills are not enough . . . Impeccable
> shorthand and typewriting are simply one indispensable weapon
> to enable you to enter the fray. In order to stay in the battle and
> reap a victory in the form of a top job, other, far more intangible
> qualities, are required. (*How to be a Top Secretary*, p. 150)

It is the etcetera which requires that the secretary be female, for it
includes those 'intangible qualities' and the performance of tasks which
cannot be job-defined for they are duties which every woman is expected
to perform by the very nature of her womanhood, a state of being
which she has spent most of her life perfecting — almost like an unpaid
apprenticeship. The secretary is expected to make coffee, run personal
errands, water plants, organise leaving/wedding/birthday presents, and
even sew on buttons for the boss. She is expected to be caring,
tactful, sensitive to *his* moods, patient, protective and tidy — in short
she is there to make his life easy and comfortable, protect him from
unwanted visitors, lie to cover for his mistakes and make him feel
important. Of course, these duties may be, and often are, a break in the
routine of typing and can be used as an excuse to leave the office for
half an hour, but at the same time they clearly reinforce the woman's
subservient role and act as a direct slap in the face for those women
who go into secretarial work with the expectation of a challenging
career.

**Control through class and race**

The problems faced by all women in the struggle for a decent, well
paid, possibly even interesting job are difficult to overcome, but if you
happen to be black and working-class then the hurdles you face are
almost insurmountable. Black women in Britain (as in all white
controlled societies) are concentrated in the worst jobs in terms of pay
and conditions of work (to say nothing of job satisfaction and promotion prospects). And even those with shorthand and typing qualifications have to confront racist discrimination by employers.

In the USA, where affirmative action legislation requires employers
with government contracts to make extra efforts to hire and promote
women and minorities (blacks and other ethnic groups), it is not
uncommon for black women to be put in the lowest paid jobs and then
located in a back room somewhere out of sight of clients and customers.
As offices in the USA are moving more quickly towards automation
than in this country, the numbers of lower skilled machine operating
jobs have increased, widening the gap between 'top' jobs performed by
whites and the low-level jobs — largely performed by blacks. As one
book on American office workers describes the situation:

> Racism is . . . clearly visible to anyone who walks through a big
> office company. Pretty, young, white women work as private
> secretaries in the carpeted offices of the new [city centre] buildings.
> Black clericals are mainly reserved for the key-punch room, the
> typing pool, or the data processing center across town — the routine,
> pressurized, low-paid jobs. (Jean Tepperman, *Not Servants, Not
> Machines: Office Workers Speak Out*, Beacon Press, 1976, p. 49)

In this country, some black women get so tired of the inevitable
prejudice which they encounter at interviews that they are forced to
resort to the less secure, although in some instances more highly paid,
practice of temping, but even this is no real solution. Despite the Race
Relations Act which was designed to prevent discrimination against
racial minorities, some temporary employment agencies permit the
most blatant racist discrimination on the part of their employer clients.
An ex-interviewer from a temporary agency had this to say:

> In some agencies, to my knowledge, if a client did not want
> coloured people, it was put down as 'no suntan' or 'no accents'
> wanted. I would say the agencies themselves in one way or another
> were breaking the law to keep clients or trying to make money
> because the whole object of agencies quite honestly is money,
> money, money. (BBC Radio 4, August 1977)

Another ex-agency worker suggested that the discrimination extended
to Irish women as well.
  While it is assumed that secretarial skills can enable working-class
girls to move 'up in the world' and into high-powered jobs, such
mobility depends, as I said before, less on technical skills, but rather
more on the individual's ability to adapt to a system of values which
completely devalues and negates her own background and culture. She
must first of all learn to manipulate and develop what are clearly
middle-class modes of femininity (those intangible qualities again) in
order to attain an air of gentility and blend in harmoniously with the
professionalism of office life.
  Apart from interaction with teachers and other professionals in
positions of authority, working-class girls will have had little close
personal contact with middle-class people by the time they leave
school, and start their first jobs. The first encounter can be quite a
shock as Susan describes:

> At the time of taking my first job I was from a working class
> background with little perception of the values and behaviour of
> other social classes. . . . The education I had received by the time
> I was 16 . . . was of a very limited nature, and the secondary modern

school I attended played a vital role in determining what kind of job I would obtain after leaving school. My last year of school was mainly concerned with acquiring shorthand and typing skills. . . . My first job as a junior shorthand typist at a chartered accountants professional office was when I first encountered a different class of people whom I integrated with because of the work we had in common. It was not just the chartered accountants that were from a middle class background, but also many of the secretaries, and I felt that they had an education and self-confidence which was lacking in myself. I was not equipped to answer at my interview such a question as to how much money I should receive and the lowly wage that I was paid was a consequence of this process of manipulation.

My work consisted of cleaning the vending machine, running errands and typing letters concerning firms that had gone bankrupt or into liquidation. Having not been given any background knowledge on factors relating to bankruptcy and liquidation I was completely disinterested in the work and approached it in a mechanical fashion. The different class background from myself that most of my superiors came from served to exacerbate the lowly position of my job, and although I did become very friendly with many of the people who worked there I could not overcome the superiority which emanated from them and they did not regard me as having the ability to talk on an intellectual level. (written statement)

Most offices, especially professional establishments, are imbued with middle-class values, values which are kept alive by the supposed middle-class nature of 'mental' work. This may once have been true, but is no longer an apt description of the type of routine, mundane nature of many of the clerical and secretarial jobs performed by women. Key-punching is the best example of the type of job which cannot easily be fitted into the category of 'mental' work and the same is true of the vast majority of typing jobs. Objectively, these jobs are comparable with routine, assembly-line factory work, but the aura of professionalism within which they are performed precludes their subjective comparison.

Faced with an apparent choice, the working-class girl can attempt the ascent of the hierarchy, or stay where she is. The top jobs will still go to the women who have the confidence and socially acceptable language and accent acquired through a middle- or upper-class background and education. Among these are women who have bypassed the lower rungs by taking a university degree and, finding they are unemployable, go on to take secretarial courses. Their university degree endows them automatically with a certain status, the assumption being that university education equals intelligence. The top jobs are reserved for these women who, however, discover perhaps more quickly that the ladder is short and the ceiling low.

### Where do you want it, love, under the table? Sexual harassment or flattery?

The 'intangible qualities' referred to earlier combine to make up a sexual and social stereotype. In other words, the secretary must 'look the part, act the part, and sound the part' — the part itself being difficult to define because it is rooted in common sense, class-specific ideas about femininity.

The old double standards about women's behaviour apply in the office as elsewhere in society. The secretary is expected to dress fashionably but with decorum; she is expected to exude an air of femininity and sensuality and yet not be overtly sexual. Women who become the object of men's sexual fantasies because of daring or sexually explicit clothing would be considered by these same men to lower the tone of the office. While they may joke and use explicitly sexual double meanings with the 'girls in the pool', their own secretaries, like their wives, must somehow mask their sexuality beneath a veil of madonna-like purity. At the same time, however, some women are forced to leave because of sexual overtures by their bosses and one woman I spoke to was fired because she refused to sleep with her boss.

While sexual encounters or office affairs are often based more in the imagination than in reality, almost every woman I've spoken to has experienced some form of sexual harassment. Harassment of this type takes many forms from simply being leered at, to being forced to listen to the sordid details of a man's sexual exploits, to actual physical assault, the former being perhaps more difficult to 'prove', as described by Carolyn:

> You know that men are flirting with you — they're being flirtatious and patronising and you're the little girl. It's the tone of voice in comparison to one speaking to male associates that irritates you — that's part of the reason why I hate office work . . . when you go down the hall, if there's a group of men who are meeting and you're the only woman walking down that hall, and you hear these little comments, right? They stop talking. There they are carrying on a conversation and you walk by and they stop talking and you hate it. You hate it so much and there's nothing you can do about it because they're not doing anything. . . . If they would do something, then you could come back with a good retort.

Sometimes they do do something. Marion's first day at a job i
Birmingham:

> I was introduced round the other directors and the main people in
> the company and I was taken down by two of the secretaries who
> were very pleased to have a reasonably attractive secretary to show
> around. And these other secretaries who I didn't actually mix with
> were into this sort of double conversation — they really enjoyed it!
> It must have kept them going for some reason. And this one guy I
> met, I was literally taken into the room, there were a couple of
> people there with him — a couple of guys he wanted to show off to
> and he shook my hand and said hello, what's your name and my
> name's so and so and then he says, 'Right, now we're acquainted,
> where do you want it — under the table or in the board room?' An
> that was my first day.

So how does one respond? Take the matter to an industrial tribunal an
complain of sexual harassment? How do you prove it? What abou
backing and support as an individual? Anyway, as in many rape tria
it's usually assumed to be the woman's fault — she's probabl
encouraged it by wearing provocative clothing. Besides, in the offic
it's part of the routine — just another joke to get through the day! Let
see how Marion dealt with it. What did she say?

> It's difficult to know what to say. That's the situation always.
> You've got to work with them, they can make things really difficul
> and also if you draw attention to the fact that you're disgusted by
> it or just didn't like it, it makes them do it even more. I just ignore
> them, that's the best reaction I've found, just ignore them.

Yes, but they won't go away and they can make things difficult. Wh
ruin a man's career for the sake of a secretary? Deny the allegatio
and close ranks. That's what Marion realised — she didn't have a leg t
stand on. Nor could she count on the support of other secretaries. A
she pointed out to me, when she first took over the job, the office wa
buzzing with stories about an affair her predecessor was alleged to ha
had with the tool room manager, stories spread by men and wome
alike in the office. She later found out the stories were untrue, ju
office gossip. As she said: 'Every job I've had I've found out later I ha
an affair with someone.'

On the other hand, it should also be emphasised that, taken on the
own, double meanings and sexually implicit conversations can be seen a
relatively harmless and are engaged in by women as well as men as on
of a number of distractions to get through the day with. I've see
several rising young executives blush bright red as a result of sexuall

explicit teasing by a group of women, an exercise which often grows directly from a feeling of solidarity and shared interests which, despite rivalry, often exists amongst women who work together in offices. However, physical sexual harassment by men is not harmless and reinforces very clearly the subordination of women.

### Loyalty and rivalry: divide and rule

The typical one to one boss/secretary relationship can only work as long as the secretary maintains a feeling of loyalty to her boss. If she does her work well, she receives flattery and can be made to feel indispensable. She complies and adapts. As all decisions are made by him, her individuality and personality are subordinated to his. He may be enlightened and give her some responsibility, but here her domain of decisions will probably be limited to choosing which type of coffee to buy or which colour flimsy to use for the correspondence file. He produces the ideas which she reproduces on paper. He commands, she obeys. If she sees him doing something wrong and suggests an alternative, this must be done with tact to allow him to assume it as his original idea. Or as the manual advises:

> You must understand your employer. Study him closely: tread warily during the first few weeks; get to know his likes and dislikes, his every mood. Find out the best time to interrupt him, if interrupt him you must. Gradually adjust your methods of working to fit in more easily with him. A lack of understanding of your employer will mar your success as a secretary. (S. Hardwick-Smith and B. Rowe, *The Private Secretary*, p. 13)

At the same time, however, stories abound of secretaries who actually do their boss's job without actually being paid for the added responsibility. This indeed would be impossible; to acknowledge such a situation would immediately explode the myth of the boss's superior intellect if it were found that a mere woman could do his job. One woman, for instance, found herself having to teach her boss's job to his successor. Despite the fact that it would have made more sense for the woman to take over the job, it was clearly felt that it should go to a man.

If the secretary complains, or becomes dissatisfied, or decides that she doesn't like her boss, then the relationship must break down and she must leave and find another job — such is the extent of job security in secretarial work.

Generally, an illusion of status within the hierarchy and the status she acquires from her employer's position within the company can be sufficient to guarantee her loyalty and hence isolation from other

women office workers. Her loyalties then are to management and t
company, but not to her co-workers. Rivalry between women
society generally is encouraged in the interests of men, and in t
working environment it serves the purpose of control. If women a
divided among themselves, there is little likelihood that they will co
bine and begin to make economic and other demands of management.

Of course, some women don't even consider 'promotion' a remo
possibility. Not because they aren't ambitious, but because they rec
nise the limitations of the career structure and, if they have childre
they are likely to have heavy domestic responsibilities which make
difficult to take on a demanding job. Having recognised that there
little satisfaction in the actual work they are doing, they look for oth
sources of satisfaction, such as the company of other women. Attemp
ing to ascend the ladder, for instance, does not present itself as a r
choice, because becoming someone's secretary involves exchangi
what can be a friendly cosy atmosphere with a group of women one c
relate to, for the isolation of an office with only a man for company
a man whose status in the company, whole cultural, social and econom
interests put him clearly out of reach as a confidant. It would be high
unlikely for a man to have the vaguest sympathetic understanding f
his secretary's personal problems and concerns.

The boss/secretary relationship is, then, dependent on loyalty, whe
the woman is urged and encouraged by the nature of the job to mai
tain a level of confidence and distance. The isolated nature of the j
means that women are divided from one another and less likely to thi
of unionisation. Age also divides. Older women react against 'tho
young kids who don't want to work because they're more interested
dressing up' and younger women resent 'those old biddies who thi
they own the place'. Of course, young women with no family comm
ments can afford to buy clothes and spend time and money on th
appearance, a luxury denied women with children. This type of rival
between women of different ages is maintained by the image of offic
as populated by 'pretty young things' vying for attention as the b
dressed, most attractive and popular with the men, and the faste
typist. In fact, in one job I had as a typist in an office with three oth
typists, I actually found myself listening to their typing and almo
unconsciously trying to type faster than any of them, until I realis
I was simply increasing the firm's output.

The 'frivolous' attitude which some older women attribute
younger ones has some basis in reality. If they are single and childle
it is possible for women to take a less than serious attitude towar
work, on the one hand because many do not see themselves as wag
workers for the rest of their lives, relying on the intervention of marria
and children to take them away from it all. On the other hand th
chances of changing jobs are greatly increased because many employe

prefer them to older women. Not only because they like to have their offices adorned by 'pretty young things' but because they can pay them less. In addition, when firms want to reduce their staffs by 'natural wastage' — a method which is gaining increasing respectability by firms wishing to introduce word processors — they can always rely on younger women leaving more frequently either to get married or have children.

A classic example of the way in which women are encouraged to compete and at the same time be exploited is in the area of salaries. Most firms discourage employees from discussing their salaries with colleagues. Others make it a condition of employment. To illustrate, I quote from my employment contract with a large chemical firm: 'Since questions of salary are handled with extreme confidence in this company, you will only discuss your salary with your immediate superior.' The process of asking for a raise is one which can cause extreme embarrassment and one which a woman I know preferred to avoid than have to admit that she couldn't survive on twenty-eight pounds a week (in 1979!). In the end, many women are forced to change jobs in order to get a salary increase. By keeping salaries secret, each individual employee can be led to assume she/he is earning more than everyone else. At the same time, there is the threat of not really wanting to know how much the others earn for fear of finding out someone doing the same job is earning more, an obvious indication that the other person is more highly regarded.

### Women, microprocessing technology, and unemployment

In 1974 there were 101,400 unemployed women. By February 1979 that figure had increased to 363,480, plus 32,060 women registered as seeking part-time work, but not claiming unemployment benefit — a figure which does not, therefore, register in unemployment statistics. In addition, many married women do not register at all as unemployed and according to the Department of Employment, they could number 175,000. Unemployment among women is a trend which is likely to increase, not only because of the decline in industries, such as textiles, clothing, and footwear, which have traditionally employed large numbers of women, but also as a direct result of cutbacks in public sector expenditure affecting education, the social services and the health service.

With two in five women workers employed in clerical and secretarial jobs, it is impossible to overstate the importance of office work to women — not in terms of job satisfaction or as an ideal job, but, in the climate of increased and increasing unemployment, as one of the few sectors of employment where women have been reasonably certain of getting jobs.

The purpose of introducing word processors and related office equipment is not to lighten the load of office workers, as is argued by manufacturers and employers, but to render more efficient what is and traditionally has been a costly and highly labour-intensive employment sector, i.e. it has relied on the employment of large numbers of people and rather less on machinery. Machinery, if cheap enough to install, can be more cost-effective than people, as is the case now with word processors. Their introduction may make some jobs more interesting and, of course, there is the novelty of working with a highly advanced piece of equipment, but for the majority who will be required to operate the machines, work will become more boring, routine and intensified, with none of the distractions usually offered in traditional office environments, such as the option to talk to workmates. Perhaps it would be more useful to allow a word processor operator to speak for herself. Carole worked for five years as a WP operator in the world's largest bank in San Francisco:

> CJ: Secretarial people didn't like the WPs because they already had the skills and the pay, but it was the novelty. You know, everybody was excited to learn this new thing that was going to help alleviate boredom and make life easier and then they found out that they really didn't do that at all — in fact they made it more boring.
> HD: Can you say why they made it more boring?
> CJ: Because people felt that they were plugged into machines, that they were appendages to machines rather than people performing functions with other people.
> HD: Is that true for the clerical and the secretarial workers?
> CJ: Yes, very much so. We used to have jokes about how we expected that soon they'd chain us to our desks and give us catheters so we'd never have to go the bathroom. And the thing is that once word processing or video display equipment is introduced, it's possible to keep track exactly of the amount of productivity each individual displays and set raises and evaluations accordingly. And people feel very pressured to get out their production. The standards are raised. When I first started at the bank the standards were 8,000 keystrokes an hour and when I left they were 12,000 over a five-year time period.

While job loss does not cause grave concern in the USA, the situation in Britain is quite different. Where word processors have been introduced, the result has been drastic reductions, in some cases by half, in the numbers of jobs available. These reductions have not been achieved simply by making people redundant — a move which would certainly cause conflict — but through the less conspicuous method of 'natural wastage'. When women leave on retirement, to get married, or have children, or, as in some cases, because managements exert pressure on them to leave by making life difficult at work, then those jobs are not filled. The ultimate impact is then felt mainly by school leavers who find they just do not have a job to go to where they can use their secretarial skills, or by women who plan to return to paid work when their children are older.

### Are unions the answer?

Many women would argue no. Unions have traditionally been male-dominated and at times openly hostile to women workers, even where they work alongside them. The whole union structure is very alienating to women, not just because the language and organisational procedure of union meetings is a completely masculine affair, but also because meetings are usually held in the evenings when women with children have other pressing responsibilities and when women without would rather go to a disco than sit on a hard chair in a cold hall in boredom.

In addition, white-collar workers often consider themselves above that type of activity, equating unionisation with industrial workers, preferring to negotiate with their employers as individuals. But as we've seen, individual negotiating is no guarantee against low pay, in fact it just reinforces it. Many firms have staff associations or special committees made up of personnel officials and departmental representatives which then meet to discuss grievances. But the types of grievances taken up remain at a level at which managements can readily agree to changes without threatening their profit levels. Some firms even resort to changing titles, one large company in the East Midlands now refers to all its workers as 'associates', giving them the impression that they have a real stake in the company with no improvement in wages.

The effect of staff associations and individual attention is to keep workers in ignorance of their true interests. Employers are extremely hostile to unionisation in offices, not just because outside negotiation would threaten the friendly family atmosphere of the firm, but because collective bargaining through the impersonal medium of a trade union on behalf of its members in the company would by its nature threaten managerial control.

Interestingly enough, it is in those organisations, such as local government and the public sector generally, where close working relationships have been almost totally replaced by the alienation of a bureaucratic structure, where unionisation among women office workers is strong.

**Conclusion**

I have tried, in the limited space available, to describe the nature
secretarial work, and to point towards the ways in which certa
features of the work act as constraints on unionisation. The vario
ways in which women are divided from one another along cla
race and age lines render them easier to control; such divisive tact
act as an obstacle to the perception of their common interests
workers which cross these barriers. Managements also encourage t
development of the feeling of indispensability on the part of individ
women workers, in the attempt to foster loyalty towards individ
bosses or departments and through them towards the company
organisation. A reward system is perpetuated which offers status
opposed to financial gain.

I have perhaps neglected to emphasise strongly enough the real feeli
of solidarity which exists among women office workers, especia
those sharing an office, perhaps because this feeling is rarely channel
into activities which challenge managerial control over such importa
issues as wages and the organisation of work.

The time has now come, however, when jobs in office work a
being threatened by automation. Given the fairly gloomy picture I ha
painted of the office, it appears contradictory that I should now
arguing the case for the defence of those jobs in the face of the chang
offered by automation. But if the choice is unemployment, then
seems to me sound economic sense to defend any job against no job
all.

Male-dominated unions will initially be concerned with defendi
the traditional rights of the male breadwinner. The idea that wome
place is in the home is still prevalent in the minds of many people a
in a period of high and increasing unemployment gains new credibili
And yet, many women are sole breadwinners. If unions do not ta
effective steps to defend women's jobs and demand the right to cont
the introduction of this new technology, and fight the likely result
unemployment amongst women, then women will have to move the
selves and begin to recognise their status as workers.

If women wish to preserve their hard-won rights to (albeit limite
financial independence, through paid employment, then the o
solution is collective organisation with other women — trade unions w
only cease to be male-dominated when women join and change the
from within to defend their interests as working women.

# 6 'Now that I'm married . . .'

*Dorothy Hobson*

I went to university when my son went to school. This chapter is based on work which I did talking to young women about their lives at home. One of the areas of their lives which they enjoyed most was radio and television. I am now looking at how these programmes are produced and explicitly at how women and their families understand and enjoy them.

> DH: 'Is being married or being a mother as you expected it would be?'
> Pat: 'I never really thought about it.'
> DH: 'Did you have any ideas about how it would be before you got married?'
> Pat: 'All a bed of roses! [laughs] They soon changed.'

This chapter is about young women at home with small children or babies and consists mainly of them talking about their lives now that they are married. They also talk about their lives at school and the period when they worked before they were married. Because the women are quite young, aged between nineteen and twenty-one, although one is a little older — twenty-eight — they all remember very clearly their feelings when they were at school and how they then thought about their future jobs and marriage and babies. What is clear when they are talking, is that there are certain choices which they made, which they would perhaps change if they were to make those choices now. What is important is the regret which they have for things which they have lost, particularly their best friends and the freedom to go out when they want to. Now that they are married with a husband and young children, they have to a certain extent, achieved what they wanted and what they were brought up to believe was the 'right thing for a girl to want', but now they find that they have lost some of the most enjoyable aspects of their lives. This is not to say that they are

101

unhappily married or that they regret getting married and having children, but rather that they feel that there should be *more* to their lives.

It is perhaps best to begin with a short description of who the women are and how I come to be writing about them. A couple of years ago I was involved in research which was concerned with talking to women at home with young children, about their lives now and how their present experiences were different from when they were younger — at school, or at work, before they had children. In fact, for some of them the ending of work happened at the same time as getting married and becoming mothers, for they had been pregnant when they had married and this, of course, had had a significant effect on their decision to get married. All of the women had been born in Birmingham, so from one point of view, they were lucky in that their families and often their husband's families were never too far away. Yet this seemed to make little difference to their chance to do things which they wanted to. Your mother may be willing to babysit for you to go out with your husband, but she may be less willing to sit for you to go out with your girl friend; not because she would necessarily disapprove, but because she may feel that it is unwise to encourage her daughter to do anything which might cause trouble between her daughter and her husband!

When they had been at work, the young women had jobs in shops, clerical or filing jobs in offices, or assembly work in factories. These had not always been the jobs which they had thought they might like to do when they were at school. Then, they had ambitions to be hair-dressers, nurses, secretaries, but they had forfeited those ambitions when they met their boy friends, often even before they left school. Since they had left work they were living in flats or houses and their lives had changed dramatically. Although they all lived on large council estates, they had few if any friends, and they all felt very isolated. Apart from the company of their children, they were often alone in their homes, without anyone to talk to, for long periods of the day and sometimes the evening. True, they were free to do their housework and shopping when they wanted to and did not have to 'obey a boss', as their husbands may be doing at work, but this freedom was at the expense of losing what was most important to them — the *company* of other people. I hope that this article will not be depressing to girls who, like the women I have talked to, may see marriage and a family as their future career. What I hope is that they may see the need to retain their friends and hold on to their own interests as well as seeing their future in terms of their marriage and family.

**School**

DH: Did you like school?
Linda: No [laughs] . No, I used to hate it.
DH: What did you specially hate about it?
Linda: It was being there — if you could have took the work home I would have been alright, but being there, people watching over you, you know, you couldn't do anything wrong.
DH: Was it, I mean, is the school strict?
Linda: No, not really no. Now I've left sometimes I wish I was back there.
DH: Why do you wish that?
Linda: I miss everybody, you know, we was all close in our form, there's a few live round here now, you know, by us, but it's not the same.

Linda's comments about school are similar to other women whom I talked to. Because school is now somewhat distanced from them, it is not the actual work of school which they talk about, nor the teachers, nor the day-to-day matters of school life, which may be what girls who are still at school would talk about; what she remembers and regrets is the *loss of her friends*. This theme continues when women talk about their experience of work — it is again their friends at work whom they miss. The women whom I talked to had all seen school as something to be 'got over' before they left to start work. Then work, in its turn, became something to be 'got over' before the real work of marriage came. Now they saw the business of bringing up their children as something to be 'got over' before they could return to work. It was as if they were always wanting to get the current part of their lives over in the hope that things would be better later on. Yet they looked back with happiness to the time when they were free to go out with their friends, before they married.

### Class and jobs

All the women I talked to were working-class, their parents had been working-class, their husbands had working-class jobs but most importantly, they had gone through the experience of school with their class and sex crucially affecting both their experience of school and the way in which they thought about their jobs when they left school. When they had left school they had all taken jobs which can be seen as typical for working-class girls. In the following extracts Anne is talking about her feelings when she was at school. She was not typical of the women I talked to because she had passed the 11-plus examination and gone to a girls' grammar school. However, far from giving her the opportunity to think she could move into a better job when she left school, she had spent her time at school feeling inferior to the other girls in her form and this has seemed to act against her and made her feel that she could not do the same school work as they could.

KEY TO TRANSCRIPTS

. . .    pause, also (pause)
( )    non-verbal communication e.g. (laughs)
[ ]    comments from the interviewer, e.g. [mm] , [yes]
(. . .) passage edited out

ANNE

D: Did you like it at school?
A: No, not really.
D: What didn't you like about it?

A: Er, they was a different class from me to be quite honest, [mm],
erm, they were all quite snobs (laughs) [yes], and I'm not, I've not
got a very good background, I'm the only one out of seven that went
to a grammar school and my mother couldn't afford to buy me all
the extra things that these other people had [yes], you know, I
mean they always had their hair done nice and, they have *everything*
in the school uniform, you know [mm], I just had to make do
[yes]. It made me miss school a lot. I just didn't fit in really [no].
D: When you left school did you have any idea about what you
were going to do?
A: Er, no. I always knew I'd end up in a factory because at school,
you know, 'Careers' — they always used to go on, 'You've gorra
find something to do.' But I hadn't got any idea. You know,
everybody else wanted to be nurses, and all these special things,
but I didn't feel I'd got the ability really. I didn't think that I
would pass any exams [mm], because you know, I just didn't try
anyway, so I thought, 'Well it's not worth me thinking of
anything else.'

Anne had felt so conscious of her working-class background, being
different from the other girls at school, that it had actually worked
against her and made her doubt her own abilities, even though she
realised now that she must have been as 'good' as the others when she
took the 11-plus exam and passed.

The other women in the study had all been to secondary modern
or comprehensive schools. In some cases they had had ambitions to
try to get more interesting jobs when they left school, but they had
eventually abandoned those ambitions and taken the conventional jobs
for working-class girls: in offices, shops or factories. Their experience of
comprehensive education had not made them have ambitions for jobs
which could be termed as middle class. Some of them had wanted to
become hairdressers or nurses, but even these ambitions had been lost
and they had in their own words 'ended up in an office' or as Anne
says 'I always knew I'd end up in a factory'. Often their parents had
tried to encourage them to stay on at school or had offered to pay for
them to do some training after they had left school. Betty talks about
the way she chose her job.

BETTY

D: Er, when you first started work, or before you started work
and you were at school, who decided what job you were going to
do? Was it mainly you or did your parents have very much to do
with it?
B: No, I think it was mainly me, 'cause me mum wanted me to go

in an office and I didn't want to, I wanted to go in a shop or
something. First of all I wanted to go into hairdressing and I was
doing that for a year before I left school, just on a Saturday,
[mm] , and then I thought, 'I don't really like it.' It was long hours
and I think the wages were only about £2.00 per week then. There
was awful long hours and I went off the idea and the shop I was
going to, me dad had to pay £100 for me to start anyway [yes] .
Well he was prepared to pay the £100 for me but then I thought,
'Well what if I changed me mind and I don't like it.' You know,
after I'd been there a bit. (. . .) So I didn't go in the hairdressers,
I got a job in town instead [mm] .

Although her father was willing to pay the fee for her to begin workin
in the hairdressers, she was worried that she may want more mone
when she was working and she also was worried that she might 'chang
her mind', after her father had paid.

A more common reason why the women I had talked to had change
their mind about any ambitions which they had for jobs after they ha
left school had been the crucial factor of meeting a boy, who in som
cases they had later married. The moment they started 'going steady' o
'courting' was the time when they changed their ambitions, or perhap
realised their real ambition, which was to get married. When she was a
school, Pat had ambitions to join the Air Force, but these were abar
doned when she met her future husband just before she left school.

PAT

D: Did you work when you left school?
P: Yes, I worked in, I was going to join, I had me heart set on
joining the Air Force but, er (laughs), I met me hubby and things
went from there.

It was as if her real 'career' was 'marriage and motherhood' and onc
she met the man she later married, there was no need to continue wit
her ambitions for an alternative 'career'. Pat had 'accepted' her futur
seemingly even before she left school.

D: Had you left school when you met him?
P: No, I was just sixteen when I met him and I was sitting my
exams and, er, I was sixteen and four days old when I met him.
(laughs)
D: So what job did you do then?
P: Well, I worked in a chemists, and then I worked in Curry's in
Martineau Way in town [yes] , as a stock control clerk, and then we

were married not long after that, while I was working there and he
was sent to Germany and I sort of went out there.

Pat's husband was in the army and she went abroad with him, but she
never realised her own ambition to join the Air Force.


## Leisure

> Lorna: I've got three friends, girls [mm] , one's getting married
> soon, but the other two they're still single, they still go out a lot,
> and *I miss all that* (laughs).

The loss of the freedom to go out with their girl friends, to do what
they want in their spare time, is the thing which the women in my
study missed the most. It is also the aspect of their lives before they
were married which they remember with most interest and enthusiasm.
Before they were married the women had gone out with their girl
friends to dances, discos, cinema, shopping for clothes and make-up
and generally done all the usual 'hobbies' of unmarried girls. What is
interesting about their understanding of what they did in their spare
time is that they did not think of these as 'hobbies'. Hobbies were
something active — collecting stamps, playing a sport, learning to play
an instrument — and these were certainly not things which they had
wanted to do. However, for their husbands they saw 'going to the
match' or 'going out with their mates' as spare time activities which
their husbands were free to do. In the following extracts the women
are talking about how they used to go out with their girl friends before
they were married.

LORNA

D: Before you, when you left school . . . what did you used to do
in your spare time then?
L: Oh, I used to go out a lot then.
D: How often was 'a lot'?
L: Well, I used to go out Fridays, Saturday, Sunday and Monday and
probably just round to friends the other nights. I was never in
(laughs).
D: When you did go out where did you used to go?
L: Oh, dancing or pictures, you know, up town.

As well as going out with their friends the women had spent time just
being with their girl friends and enjoying themselves.

LINDA

D: Did you have any hobbies before you were married, what did you used to do in your spare time then?

L: Well before I was married I went to night school, I think it was twice a week — erm typing, you know [yes], I enjoyed that . . . I really enjoyed that, it was only for a couple of hours a night. After I'd done that I'd usually go and sit with me friend till late at night and then go home.

D: If you went out with a girl friend, where did you go?

L: Oh, we went to the Locarno, Barbarella's, Oh, anywhere in town, you know. We'd take, say Saturday, we'd go out, we'd go to one place and then maybe another night we'd go to the pictures.

D: So how much roughly did you go out before you were married?

L: Er, we went out quite a lot, we went out Friday nights and Saturday nights. One night to the pictures and Saturday night to a disco and in the week we'd go to the pictures again, then we'd stay in. And then I'd got me typing, I think it was only a Monday night when I come to think of it, and if we did have an odd night we'd stay in, washing our hair (laughs). But it all changed when I went back with him [her boyfriend, now her husband] . I still had me night at typing, and me day in, and the rest of the time we was sitting in his mom's house or we'd go to the pictures.

What Linda shows in this extract is that although she went out with her girl friend, as soon as she went back with her boyfriend, she had to give up going out on her own and doing the things which she enjoyed. Other women talked of the fact that once they were 'courting' their boy friends would not go to dances or discos with them. They gave up both their spare-time activities and their girl friends. Now that they were married with young children, what the women would really have liked to have done was to go to the same discos with their old friends. Of course, none of them was able to go out dancing on their own because their husbands thought that they would only want to go to dances or discos to meet other men. However, this was not the reason why they wanted to go, it was simply for the pleasure of enjoying something which they had loved doing before they settled down to married life. It was clear from talking to the women, that they would have been better off if they had kept up their own interests when they had first started going out with their boyfriends and not abandoned both their girl friends and the interests, however limited they now felt that these had been.

One of the reasons why the women had given up their own spare time pleasures was linked with the start of 'going steady' and 'saving to get married'. It is assumed that the need for a home and family are something which only young women want and not an ambition of their boyfriends. Men seem to have 'gone along' with the idea of saving for marriage and they have been willing to stay at home listening to records or watching television at the home of their parents. The women have given up their own spare time activities, on the pretext of saving money, and the only time the couple have spent money has been when going to the cinema or going out for a drink. However, it seems that the men had still had their 'nightout' with their mates or their visits to the local football matches. This resulted in these women giving up their relationships with their girl friends and setting the pattern for their future, which in this case meant loneliness and feelings of resignation.


**Being married and being a mother**

D: Is being married or being a mother as you expected it would be?


LINDA

L: (Long pause) No, not really, it's hard (laughs).
D: How did you expect it would be?
L: I thought it would be easy and be fun, but it's not, no.


LORNA

L: It's harder than I thought it would be. Before when I went to work, it was easy. I come home and I could go out dancing on a night, and I'd never be tired, but now you get up in the morning, you do your housework, by the time six o'clock you're sitting on the settee, half asleep. I mean, he'll come home and if he said, 'Come on, we'll go dancing,' I don't think I could, I feel that tired.
D: So how did you expect it would be?
L: I don't know, I think I was sort of rushed into it and I didn't really think about it, 'cos I was four months pregnant before we got married and his mother wanted to rush. I didn't want to get married, I wanted to get married after she was born. Well, he didn't say nothing, he just stood there and his mother wanted us to get married and er, I didn't want to get married.


BETTY

D: So is your life how you expected it would be with the children and . . .
B: I s'pose it is really 'cause I never really thought about it much, about the children. I just thought I'd just carry on going to work

and that really.

D: Before you had the children how had you thought things would be?

B: Well I just thought it would be just like it was when I was single but I'd be married so I could please myself what I done y'know. We'd just sort of go on holiday together and that and things like that. Do just more or less what I wanted to do instead of having to get home at a certain time every night. [mm] I never really thought about having children and having to look after them and stop going to work. It never occurred to me (laughs).

All these accounts tell how the whole experience of 'being married' and 'being a mother', had come as a surprise to the women. They had been shocked to find how hard it was, particularly the whole business of childcare which they had found very difficult, especially caring for young babies. For some of them it had been an experience which had been forced upon them as they had been expecting their babies when they had married so they had not even had time to adjust to being married and being responsible for their husbands and homes. However, I do not want to create the impression that the young women I talked to were all desperately unhappy or regretting their marriage, for this was definitely not the case. Their feelings about everything were contradictory, for often the aspects of their lives which they found most enjoyable and gave them the most pleasure were at the same time the very things which restricted them. This was particularly the case when they talked about their children. This was often the most enjoyable aspect of their lives, but at the same time it was the reason why they could not go out to work or were not free to go out at night. However, they did see looking after their children as being very different from doing housework and it was certainly not boring even when it was hard work. What was clear when I was talking to the women was that they had thought of 'getting married' but not of 'being married' and the reality of their situation was now not as pleasant as they had thought it would be. Perhaps Anne sums up how many of the women felt about their lives when she says, 'No boring, just (. . .) I feel as though there should be something else.'

**What about the future?**

Perhaps the saddest part of the study which I made was the way that the women thought about their own futures. They were, after all, very young women and their lives stretched before them for many years. However, they could not see the possibility of any change in their situation, nor, indeed, did they think of themselves at all. Their own futures had been lost in their thinking about their children's futures. They worried about their children growing up and being happy without really considering their own happiness in the meantime. It was as if their own lives would be held in limbo until their babies were married in twenty years time! The following comments were typical:

> Pat: Well all I really think about is Michelle growing up and what she'll be like and what she'll be doing. But I don't really think about myself.
> Lorna: Well the only thing I worry about is getting old, just the one thing and worry about these growing up. You know, in this kind of world. Especially her, I mean, I sort of, I had a nice boyfriend, fiance, I mean, she could come up to anything couldn't she?

These women were themselves only nineteen and twenty, yet they thought about their children being married instead of the interim years for themselves. Other women suggested that they might have more babies even though they had told me that they were waiting for their children to go to school so that they could think about getting part-time work. What was clear, was that they realised that they had achieved their ambition to be married and 'settled down' and what they had to do was to come to terms with it. As Lorna, who had only been married for six months, said, 'Well, I suppose you get used to it in time, I suppose I will.'

I said at the beginning of this chapter that I did not want to present a depressing picture of marriage to young girls who see their future as being happily married with their own children. There is nothing wrong with those ideas as long as the romance of the whole situation does not blot out the reality which may result. If the words which the women spoke to me have had any impact in this chapter, I would like to think that they might make young girls determined not to follow exactly in the footsteps of the women I talked to. As I have tried to show, their greatest regrets had not been getting married and having their children, but giving up their own individuality much earlier in their relationships with their boyfriends. They had sacrificed their ideas or ambitions for jobs, their hobbies and their girl friends and after they had left work they had lost their companions from their jobs as well. It is important that girls should see themselves having the 'right' to good jobs and the opportunities to enjoy themselves as they wish and not to feel that as soon as they meet their boyfriends, they have to give up everything and conform to different standards once they start 'going steady'. If the women whom I talked to had retained their girl friends and still gone out with them before they married it would have been easier for them to continue to go out with them after they had married and become mothers. As I have said earlier, it was not that the women were unhappy or regretted getting married but rather that they felt that there should be 'something else' in their lives.

# 7 Just like a Jackie story

*Angela McRobbie*

Illustrated by *Rhonda Wilson*

For several years now I have been writing and researching on aspects of girls' lives; this article is taken from some work I did in 1977, and at present I am investigating girls' work: hairdressing, boutique work and office jobs.

It would be difficult to imagine an adolescent without magazines like *Jackie*. They are so much a part of the clutter of our everyday lives we barely notice them. On the newstands, under the school desk or in the privacy of the bedroom, their existence seems so natural that we take them for granted. Like 'Top of the Pops', *Jackie* is something of a national institution, a family affair. So familiar are we with its codes that we can, perhaps jokingly, make sense of our experiences in its terms. It sets the framework within which a whole range of adolescent themes and issues are dealt with. And the regularity of its appearance and its advice over the years means that few of us are likely to have been totally unaffected by it. Its romances become our romances, the feelings it portrays, our feelings, its jealousies, ours.

Without ever having purchased a copy, the chances are that most people could roughly describe its format, its front cover. And because mums and dads, brothers and sisters, regularly flick through its pages in their spare moments, it has an actual readership which far outstrips its already huge sales figures (approximately 600,000 weekly). This very familiarity lends it a cosiness, a kind of reliability. It's both modern (the models young and fashionable, the colours bright, the design 'trendy'), and unchanging. In fact, since it first appeared in the early 1960s, its layout and contents have remained almost the same. (Girl on cover, two picture stories, problem page, fashion/beauty feature and pop pin up.) The repetition of this pattern, year in, year out, means that the magazine comes to serve as a kind of symbolic landmark against which quite literally generations of girls can chart their adolescent biographies. *Jackie*'s success over the last sixteen years is bound up with the continuing attraction which its formula has for eleven- to fourteen-year-old girls. Any changes it makes are strictly minor and are only evident on close analysis of the magazine over a considerable span of time. What then *is* this image which provokes such popularity and loyalty amongst teenage girls, black and white, working-class and middle-class?

Photograph by
*Pam Bloor*

In fact, everything about *Jackie* is designed to capture the interests of its desired readership. *Jackie* is a modern (and therefore young) girl's name. It's short, snappy, and up to date, and so offers a point of immediate identification to its potential readers. Each week's cover displays this week's *Jackie* smiling out of the picture towards the passing girl, the reader. And in so far as the model looks smart (never sloppy), pretty (never plain), and cute (never aggressive), she also sets the limits to which the reader should aspire in terms of appearance. Yet hidden behind her smile is another sign, one of complicity about who the real focus of attention is. Along with the listed contents ('Will You Be His Dream Girl?'), the coyness and flirtiness of the model's expression leaves the reader in no doubt. The glance is *primarily* aimed at the handsome 'guy' who is just about to appear round the corner, just about to get off the next bus. In this way the cover graphically defines both its market and the consuming passions which seemingly characterise such a market.

From cover to cover, *Jackie* presents its readers with topics, subjects and sets of meanings. But because these meanings are so commonplace, because we, the readers are so used, already, to equating adolescence with problems, romance, and a whole string of insecurities, we lose track of them as constructs and as only one of a possible *range* of meanings. *Jackie* is so definitive about its dealing with youth and femininity, it's so authoritative (in the friendliest way), it implies ultimately that it's all 'sewn up', all dealt with here. This makes it difficult for readers to imagine alternatives.

What I want to suggest is that although the magazine does respond to the real needs, feelings and experiences of girls, the meanings it

makes available to them, and the means by which these experiences ar
to be made sense of, are both limited and limiting. Ostensibly, *Jackie*
along with the rest of the pop media, aims to entertain, to give pleasure
With magazines, this involves looking and reading, while with musi
obviously the emphasis is first on listening and then also on looking
But in both cases these actions are not as simple as they seem. The
also imply *ways* of looking, *ways* of listening. *Jackie* teaches us *how* t
look in both senses. How to find an attractive self-image is part an
parcel of learning how to look at *Jackie* and its view of the world
uncritically. In other words, *Jackie* presents its readers with relativel
closed sets of meanings.

My argument will not, however, be that the entire pop media i
therefore a bad thing, something ultimately to be done away with
Quite the opposite. Light reading and exciting listening are vital parts c
our social lives, I want to suggest here that these could be made *mor*
fulfilling, *more* exciting. Altogether they could embrace wider meaning
— as they stand right now, the commercial pop media encourages gir
to value themselves only in so far as they are valued by boys. Reade
and listeners alike are rarely encouraged to attach any importance t
relationships and friendships which are not romances. Apparentl
devoted to leisure and fun, their idea of fun, and especially *Jackie*'s,
almost wholly restricted to the neurotic search for a 'fella'. It is in thes
limited self-images, and the narrow possibilities they present, that th
brunt of my critique lies.

Yet such a critique does not imply that these messages are swallowe
whole. Although girls can 'live the *Jackie* dream', this does not nece
sarily mean they apply its wisdoms to their everyday lives in
mechanical fashion. Or, to put it another way, there is an unambiguou
space between what *Jackie* describes and prescribes, and what happer
in practice. Linked to this is the idea that *Jackie* cannot be held sole
responsible for the narrow and restricted lives many girls are forced t
lead. If girls end up in boring and unsatisfying jobs, and if, as an escar
they return to the home, to housework and child-rearing which turn
out to be even more unsatisfying (see Dorothy Hobson's chapter), th
is because a whole range of factors militate against them having an
alternative, against them having any confidence that they could then
selves play an active role in making things better. Ultimately the girl
'career' at home and in the workplace is determined by her social clas
her sex and her race. All of these possess a great deal more power tha
*Jackie* magazine, yet it is only when we see the way in which they a
played out, not alone, but alongside a whole range of institutions — i
the school, in the family, in leisure, and therefore *also* in *Jackie* th
we can begin to make sense of the way in which, in every aspect c
their social lives, women and girls are treated as inferior, incapable c
exercising control over their own lives. The confidence that *Jack*

encourages stretches little further than that needed to smile at the local heart-throb.

It's always difficult to be precise about the effect the media has. Their power inevitably works insidiously, obliquely. The social scientists who try to measure the effect of 'Starsky and Hutch' by placing children in front of the screen in laboratories fully equipped with sophisticated monitoring devices, and then continue over some period of time to observe their behaviour for its violence and aggression 'levels', impose a rigidity which simply is not applicable in terms of how people actually watch television or read magazines. They also fail to recognise that programmes like 'Starsky and Hutch' don't operate in a vacuum. Almost every other aspect of social life encourages little boys to be (within certain limits) violent, indeed a whole battery of 'professionals' are more worried if they don't show sufficient aggression.

Girls don't simply read the advice on the Cathy and Claire page one day and apply it the next. Like watching television, reading magazines is rarely an absolutely private affair. Both activities are carried out at least against the background noise of social situations. The television may be on in the living room while each member of the family is engaged in a different activity, none of which involves sitting 'glue eyed'. Likewise, the thirteen-year-old girl can have one eye on the television and the other on *Jackie*, at the same time as she is trying to finish her homework before her friend calls round to accompany her to the youth club.

The density and complexity of the social fabrics within which a magazine like *Jackie* is read is nicely summarised in the following incident. The 'powder room' in the Bullring Shopping Centre in Birmingham is a well-known place for girls who are 'wagging off' school to while away the afternoon. One day I came across a group of Asian girls dressed in a combination of satin trousers and school uniform, engrossed in a typical *Jackie* quiz. They each had a copy of the magazine, one girl was playing the role of quiz-mistress asking the questions round the group and keeping track of the marks: 'When he arrives late, in his sports car, to pick you up for a special date do you: (a) smile sweetly as though nothing had happened? (b) Sulk until he begs your forgiveness? (c) Make it clear you're not a girl who likes to be kept waiting?' and so on. . . . Every question and answer was greeted with gales of laughter and giggling. As a game, their enjoyment was indisputable, but it seems unlikely that the situation outlined bore very much relation to the romantic experience of the participants, or indeed that of any thirteen-year-old girls.

Not only can magazines like *Jackie* be experienced in ways which have little to do with the everyday lives of their readers, (as pure fantasy), they can also be used in ways which seem to run directly counter to their intended usage. For example, as lunch-time reading,

*Jackie* is quite legitimate, but during class it becomes an expression of boredom, a weapon against the authority of the teacher, a sign of discontent. In the home it can signal the desire for some privacy and in the youth club it's either a sure sign that there really is nothing else to do, or else it's a plea once again for autonomy from the interventions of youth leaders anxious to engage the girls in a game of basketball.

It is only by contextualising *Jackie* in this way that we can begin to make sense of it as a communication process. It is also important to view it in relation to all the other women's magazines which are equally familiar parts of our 'social furniture'. From the age of five onwards, girls are personified in a range of magazines. These chart their readers' lives chronologically and with such exactness they seem all the more natural. From *Mandy* and *Bunty* to *Jackie*, *19*, *Honey* and *Cosmopolitan*, from *Woman* and *Woman's Own* to *Good Housekeeping*, the 'real career for a woman is spelt out in such a way as to leave the reader in little doubt. After all, there are no male equivalents. For their light reading, men instead have hobby magazines — from fishing and car maintenance to pornography. The nearest any of these come to the home is Do-It-Yourself, and that's a strictly weekend affair.

Instead of having hobbies, instead of going fishing, learning to play the guitar, or even learning to swim or play tennis, the girl is encouraged to load all her eggs in the basket of romance and hope it pays off

It must be clear by now that the one concept which holds *Jackie* together, which gives it coherence, is romance. This finds its fullest expression in the picture stories and in the problems. But it is also there

in the fashion, beauty, and pop features — as the very reason it is worth dressing up or making up. In short it represents the prime sensibility which runs right through the magazine, the very framework through which all emotions are channelled. And linked to this is the idea that the only attachments worth forming are those with potential steadies and with future husbands. Closeness or commitment of any other kind doesn't find a place in the *Jackie* world. What's more, immersion in this culture of romance is synonymous with a blocking out of the real world and a retreat into the sphere of the senses, to the red roses, set smiles and secret signs of classic 'love'. Sweet Nothings!

Nowhere is this rigid adherence to the pattern of traditional true love more clearly expressed than in the picture stories. Rarely are there more than two characters and they tend to look quite different from the teenage girls who buy *Jackie*. They are older, glamorous and seem strangely old-fashioned. The girls wear heavy 1960s eye make-up, even mini-skirts, and the boys often look like James Bond figures! The usual explanation offered for this is that the artists who do the drawing are contracted as cheap labour from Southern Spain, they are sent the blocks with the story outline and they simply have to provide the visuals. The assumption then is that the figures are bound to look a little out-of-date. Not only is this assumption chauvinistic, it also fails to explain why a magazine purportedly for young teenagers should describe the emotions and passions of young adults who look ten years older than the readers. Why not, after all, have out-of-date schoolgirls? The answer to this is quite simply that, officially, thirteen-year-old girls, especially in school uniform, are not meant to engage in such passion, are not meant to display such maturity of emotion. By focusing on young people who look as though they left school some time ago, the *Jackie* editors are insuring themselves against criticism from the establishment (from Mrs Mary Whitehouse) that they may be leading young girls astray!

The typical plot follows a predictable path. A relationship is formed, threatened and then either consolidated or else tragically dissolved. As the story proceeds to a climax so the visuals rise to the occasion and express, with graphic detail, the moment when, arriving late at the party, the timid heroine finds *him* in the arms of *her* untrustworthy best friend; or else when *she*, learning of his infidelity, runs out in front of a passing car. This central image is larger and commands more space than all the other pictures around it. It spills out over its frame like a dramatic 'still' from a film clip and proclaims its horrible significance, the moment all girls dread. The stuffiness and claustrophobia of this seemingly pleasurable state (love) cannot be emphasised enough; it puts the girl in the position of relentless edginess, she's either waiting anxiously for him to appear or else nervously anticipating the day he might disappear. The entire social world that she inhabits is reduced to the sum of the romantic possibilities it throws up. Offices, car-parks, dentists' waiting rooms, supermarkets, and hospitals; all of these are stripped of their normal social functions and become instead surrogate marriage bureaux.

While some stories seem to be set in London, the majority provoke a sense of anonymity by giving no indication of locale. The characters speak a hip kind of language with no accent or regional inflection, and they have a slightly displaced quality about them. They have all left school, but work hovers invisibly in the background as a necessary time-filler between one evening and the next (or, at best, another potential breeding ground for romance). Recognisable social backgrounds are rare — the small town, equated with boredom, is signalled through the symbols of coffee bar and motorbike — the country is somewhere to escape from a broken romance, and the city is where 'it all happens'. But it's a city strangely bereft of population; there are no children, no old people, no mums and dads, no foreigners and no black teenagers. It's a world inhabited by rootless, classless, white young people whose sole objective in life seems to be the search for the right partner. For girls this means fighting to get him, fighting to keep him, and simultaneously trying to have some fun!

No story ever ends with two girls alone together enjoying themselves. A happy ending means a happy couple, a sad one, a single girl. Having eliminated the possibility of strong supportive relations between girls, between people of different ages, sexes, and colour, pure unadulterated 'love' is once again elevated to the dizzy heights. More seriously romance displaces and makes irrelevant sexuality and the very real problems it poses for girls. The implication is that boys' demands and girls' desires rarely go beyond the stage of the clinch. Male sexual aggression and exploitation are magically removed and boys themselves undergo a strange metamorphosis — they become as loving and caring as the girls (well almost — because they can always succumb to the temptation of the irresistible untrustworthy best friend). Although they may reveal more softness and emotion than we might expect, this does not imply a blurring of sex roles. While boys can *be* wild, exciting, zany — whilst they can even *be* footballers or pop stars girls simply *are* — loving, romantic, or else jealous, possessive, frightened. Ultimately what these stories have in common is a sense of deep-rooted fear — of losing or else of never finding your 'guy'.

It is precisely these fears which are explored and 'treated' in the problem page. If the picture stories deal with the fantastic and the melodramatic, then the problem page concerns itself with the opposite. In stark contrast with the bright and thus 'happy' colours of the rest of the magazine, the problem page is suitably set out in gloomy black and white, the colours of 'realism'. The Cathy and Claire page addresses itself to the day-to-day life of the readers. The intimacy of this relationship is expressed in the use of their first names. Cathy and Claire sound like sympathetic elder sisters rather than professional counsellors. (Older women's magazines usually include the full name of the agony columnist, thus lending her an air of authority and professionalism.)

The central point I want to make here is that although Cathy and Claire do undoubtedly respond to their readers' problems, to the whole battery of questions about best friends, boyfriends, pocket money and housework, they don't do so in purely 'clinical' terms. Advice is not like medicine, it deals with social relations rather than individual symptoms. This means that, once again, what girls are advised to do corresponds to looking at the world and the women's role in a certain way. And, as far as *Jackie* is concerned this involves sticking strictly to the *status quo*. Maybe it's easiest to demonstrate this by showing what the Cathy and Claire page never does. For example if a girl has a problem with an unreliable 'fella', the advice is invariably to let him go — only because she's bound to find a more suitable partner in the near future. (Not because it may be more fun to be single.) Unconventional behaviour is never encouraged and girls whose friends have a taste for 'freaky' clothes are advised to ditch them. Most vividly, this absence of *positive* advice is expressed in the letter from a girl whose problem was simple. She'd been invited to a wedding, was supposed to take a partner and didn't have one readily available.

It would undoubtedly be beyond the possibilities of the *Jackie* framework to suggest braving it out and going alone, even more unlikely would be the idea of bringing a girlfriend. Instead, the girl in question is advised to chat up some available boy: 'You could say something like, "I've been invited to this wedding and I've got to take a partner and I just don't know who to ask". Then you could look at him and smile sweetly.'

It could be argued that there is a real strand of 'common sense' in this reply. Social etiquette as it is makes it very difficult for people who are not in steady units to take part in everyday leisure. 'Spinsters' (a degrading term by any standards) and widows, are well acquainted with this problem; often they simply don't get invited to social occasions. They feel left out, a burden; other women feel obliged to get their husbands to offer to dance with them. Quite simply, in their failure they represent a threat. The worst that could happen. No wonder the girl in question is looking for advice. Her choices are few — the stigma of failure by going alone, the loneliness of not going and staying at home, or else the possibility of compromise, a friendly encounter with a suitable boy and the minimum risk of humiliation. If that's how things are then maybe Cathy and Claire take the most reasonable line. But the point is that if it's *so* bad then maybe things should change — and changing social customs and practices may not necessarily be any *more* painful than putting up with them. What if the boy declines, doesn't like weddings or already has a steady girlfriend in the next town? One thing is clear, boys aren't expected to suffer in the same way — going to a wedding alone is no indelible sign of stigma to them. Likewise, bachelors, far from being felt sorry for, are generally seen as possessing some kind of mystique — having avoided being 'caught' by a woman, they represent a challenge, and as such, at a wedding, have a choice of willing dance partners.

Once again we are faced here with the contradiction between *Jackie*'s ostensible commitment to fun and pleasure and the pain and suffering which seems to be so much part of the girl's (and woman's) life. It is as though, by way of compensation, we (the readers) have instead a series of glorious moments which make up for what goes in between. The *Jackie* world equates pure pleasure with those transitory moments (the clinch — and then he kissed me) so that the girl's life, present and future, is made sense of in terms of such scenes, the first kiss, the proposal, the wedding day, the birth of the first child, and by this time we are in the territory of *Woman's Own* and have successfully and smoothly negotiated the passage from adolescence to adulthood. As far as *Jackie* is concerned the emphasis on such moments solves some, but not all, problems. There is still the fundamental contradiction between momentary thrills and the fact that after all love is meant to last for ever. The effect of this tension is to increase the fears and insecurities of the girl, hence the continual uncertainty which taints even the most passionate of moments: 'Is this really forever?' 'Will this really last?' 'How can I know that he means it?' and so on. Moreover, it could be argued that in channelling all pleasure into these long-awaited moments *Jackie* is performing a highly conservative function. It both deflects interest away from the less exciting often boring and exploitative hours, weeks, even years, that go in between, and simultaneously devalues any other pleasures which do not promise undying commitment, marriage and security.

What this does mean, for certain, is that the women's sphere is unambiguously that of the emotions — they are equated with her life's project and as such she is expected to throw herself into them with complete abandon and commitment. The possibility of enjoying one-self out there in the real world or of struggling to make it more enjoyable; the possibility of working with men and women in a satisfying way and one which does not always depend on romance for its thrill — all of this is ruled out. These are terms in which *Jackie* strictly does not trade.

Possibly the only hobbies which are deemed truly suitable for *Jackie* readers are fashion and beauty. It is in these pursuits that their energies not expended on the actual pursuit of boys can be legitimately expressed. But even as hobbies, these interests display a strangely coercive edge. The thought of what happens if you don't wash your hair, shave under your arms, use deodorant, polish your nails and so on is so unspeakably unpleasant that the enjoyment normally equated with spare-time activities becomes blurred. In other words, fashion and beauty involve a set of routines which have more in common with housework than with playing tennis. They are feminine chores from which men and boys are more or less exempt. They depend on planning and forethought, they are time-consuming and often seem distinctly more like work than leisure. Although men and boys have become increasingly fashion-conscious in the last few years they are not expected to place such importance on their daily beauty rituals, the day-to-day 'reproduction' of their looks.

Two things complicate *Jackie*'s encouragement of these 'hobbies'. First, their readers are not earning a salary and therefore can't possibly afford to keep up with high fashion, or even buy a new mascara every other week. This means that *Jackie* must introduce its readers into the world of feminine consumption, simultaneously recognising the narrowness of their budget. Obviously there's no possibility of doing without make-up, without new clothes, so the answer is chainstore fashion and Woolworth's beauty! Pocket money and birthday money are to be channelled into these outlets rather than on records, books or towards a new sound system; indeed, girls are explicitly advised to borrow records from boyfriends allowing *all* their spare cash to be focused on feminine products. The second problem which confronts the *Jackie* team in relation to these products is their inherent 'puritanism', that is, the extent to which they associate the use of make-up and the wearing of 'flashy' clothes with immorality, with 'loose' sexual behaviour. The question then is to encourage the use of make-up, but not its over-use. And here discretion is the name of the game. The beauty features are littered with phrases like 'a touch of', 'a hint of', 'a trace of', 'a slight glow of' and so on. Instead of transforming girls into sexual goddesses like those who adorn the covers of *Cosmopolitan*, the aim is to gently improve on ('draw attention to your best features'), and emphasise the naturalness of young looks. These routines and beauty schedules are presented as necessary stages in securing a romantic future − even finding a job depends on them. The objective is to adopt a strategy which involves convincing the world, through the subtle use of make-up, that the reader is indeed a natural beauty. This is because men and boys, fathers, husbands, and employers, are united in their dislike of obviously artificial aids, they too prefer to think of their wives, daughters, girl-friends and employees as naturally 'lovely'. 'Most boyfriends (there are few exceptions) hate loads of make-up, they think it goes with a loud, brassy personality and are usually frightened off by a painted face. Ask the majority and they'll say they prefer natural looks and subtle make-up − so that's the way it has to be.'

This quote is the clearest expression of how the readers are taught to capitulate entirely to male-defined preferences. Beauty care is so closely linked to the general care of the body (no smoking and plenty of sleep) that girls are encouraged to equate relentless beauty 'work' with simply learning to look after themselves. Beauty becomes then more relevant as *education* than that which they receive in the school. It is like a vicious circle. First, they are pushed into prioritising marriage as a career — then informed that to ensure that this goes smoothly they must employ a whole battery of techniques, skills and ploys. *Jackie* fits into this as a friendly kind of text-book, a manual which works on the assumption that there are no real alternatives to this prescribed goal.

What's more, by doing her own washing, laundering, repairing, the girl is not only shifting some of the burden of household labour from her mother, but she is also introducing herself gradually into the sphere of what we call 'domestic labour', that work which is carried out day in, day out by women, but which is usually invisible, 'natural' Similarly, the *Jackie* emphasis on the regularity with which these beauty labours must be carried out is relentless. Just as the mother must make sure that meals are ready on the table every day, so must the girl always have a clean pair of tights, a freshly laundered skirt and well-manicured finger nails. Like housework, the chores are endless, but *Jackie* makes it palatable by setting it within the context of fun and pleasure: 'If you do have a problem with your hair, find out what it is and do something about it right away' or, 'When you're all alone you can have a great time making yourself up . . . trying out different hair styles and seeing what suits you best.'

Beautification is, then, the ideal 'hobby' for a girl. It relates both to the notion of securing a boyfriend and in its repetition it prefigures the housework which is the eventual outcome of love, romance and boy friends.

The adolescent girl truly is allowed no time off from her feminine work. Time not taken up with the active pursuit of her goal is to be invested in the maintenance and re-upholstery of the self. Only such commitment guarantees the desired effects — the expected rewards.

In contrast to the all-embracing world of beauty care, fashion in *Jackie* is a strictly secondary affair. This is partly because thirteen-year old girls are normally still dependent on parents for major items of clothing. The weekly fashion feature displays clothes that can be bought in well known chain-stores, even supermarkets. The reader is encouraged to plan her wardrobe according to her small budget, but this does not include making use of jumble sales or organising swaps with friends. Ideally, according to *Jackie*, the girl should possess pretty daytime clothes and something slightly more 'exotic' for special occasions. Quite often clothes have a symbolic significance attached to them — they're seen as objects bound to catch his attention and are remembered in this way. Thus, in recalling past 'happiness', the girl in question will frequently describe what she was wearing that night.

Fashion is never way-out, outlandish or freaky, it is never something created by any one, individual girl or even by a group of girls. Instead, it is a matter in blending in well with the background, looking nice without interrupting everyday life and 'sparkling' only in the evening. The idea that some girls could honestly have little or no interest in clothes is unimaginable, even more unlikely the possibility that girls could enjoy fashion without in any sense directing this interest at boys.

The problem in discussing fashion like this, however, is that it is difficult to avoid sounding goody-goody, anti-fashion, anti-fun, and anti-femininity. There are a number of possible ways of trying to overcome this difficulty. First, it can be shown that there is little fun in simply following *Jackie* fashion blindly and that looking conventional can be synonymous with being conventional, not always the most desirable self-image for young people. Second, that anyway the *Jackie* promises are hollow, the most beautiful of dresses doesn't guarantee that its wearer will indeed be most popular, most sought-after and so on. And third, that *Jackie* clothes are quite often obstacles to fun. Clean, pretty, fragile clothes restrict their wearers' freedom, and having fun can mean getting dirty, looking untidy and disregarding such details as perfectly styled hair, clean nails and carefully applied mascara.

However, the most trenchant criticism that can be held against *Jackie* with regard to style is the way in which girls are denied any choice in the self-images created through style. Neither experimentation nor originality is encouraged. Again and again the readers are referred back to the men and boys whose approval is so desperately sought.

All of these points raise the question of the meaning of style and fashion. Historically women's clothes and fashion have been designed by men so, not surprisingly, they tend to reflect male ideas about how women should look, act, and be. Altogether the emphasis has been on transforming women into objects rather than allowing them to be normal active human beings. Stiletto heels, for example, make walking, never mind running, a feat in itself; but more than this, *symbolically* they represent women's dependent fragile status. They summon up all sort of ideas about male chivalry, female bondage; they have an immediate and unambiguous resonance as sexual signs.

As a result, it would be difficult to imagine feminists adopting such a style, but just because we reject such oppressive images doesn't mean we all choose our footwear in Clarkes. If, as a sociologist claimed recently, 'we speak through our clothes', then it is almost certain that our choice of clothes will make some kind of public statements about the way we see our own role and the way we want to challenge traditional conceptions of femininity. Similarly, the super-sophisticated elegant shop assistant is saying through *her* clothes that she's happy (for the moment) to go along with the status quo, even though her feet are killing her, and the punk girl in her parodying of what nice girls should look like, in her symbolic undermining of femininity, is also saying something about male-defined style. As Poly Styrene put it in 1976, 'O Bondage Up Yours'; not exactly the sort of thing girls are supposed to say, and it's interesting that to date *Jackie* has hardly commented on the existence of punk as a popular style and subculture. Instead, the magazine settles for mainstream, chain-store style. This is presented to the readers as what style is about and, needless to say, the fashion and dress of Asian and Afro-Caribbean girls is treated as though it doesn't exist. White style *is* style and the elaborate outfits of young immigrant girls goes unnoticed.

The astonishing thing about the way pop music is presented in *Jackie* is that the music is silenced and in its place the reader is offered the 'star'. As a kind of necessary by-product, the music simply provides the rationale which grants the star his place inside the pages of *Jackie* but once there it is quickly forgotten. As the 'creative energy', even the 'genius' behind the 'hit single' record or latest album, the emphasis is on him and, of course, on his masculinity. Although female stars are mentioned in passing, the pin-ups are without exception male. The enjoyment which music provides girls with, particularly for dancing, is dismissed out of hand as unworthy of comment. Pop music *is*, then, pinups, the likes and dislikes, the latest news from the star himself. Once again the emphasis is on the visuals and the pop features carry remarkably little writing apart from a range of 'snippets' (for example, 'Hot Gossip' where the readers are told about Rod's new car, Abba's planned film, or Kate Bush's latest release, new house, boyfriend, etc.). But these pieces of information would be of little meaning without the accompanying photograph, the purpose of which is to print indelibly in the minds of the readers a series of images, faces, most of which are understood primarily in terms of attractiveness, beauty or 'good looks'. As far as male pin-ups are concerned, their main role is symbolic. Designed quite literally to be pinned up, the girl is implicitly positioned as looker, viewer, admirer, and in so far as the poster is normally placed on the bedroom wall, above the girl's bed, it looks forward to the day when the girl can translate her fantasies into reality, and sleep with the boy who bears an uncanny resemblance to ... Bob Geldof, Paul McCartney, ... In this instance, staring dreamily up at the boy/poster she is passive and waiting. Just as she waits to be asked to dance by a boy; just as she waits to be asked out on a date; and later waits to be proposed to; so she looks up at the picture with passive longing. This kind of image is one we are so familiar with right across the popular media. A recent cinema advert for a certain kind of perfume shows a teenage girl dozing off to sleep. In her dreams she is at the disco. Sud denly the singer, microphone in hands, leaves the stage, crosses the room and picks her out from the swaying mass of dancing girls; the perfume has done its work, and the other girls stare enviously.

But the pop star, to be comprehensible in terms of romance, must be more than just a handsome object, just as real-life boys should be more than just a pretty face. He has to be personalised, given a personality and so the way he is presented is in terms of his friendliness, his cute cheekiness or his boy-next-door-like qualities. All of which serves to make him more recognisable, more real as the desired object in the girl's romantic landscape. He is shown relaxing at home with his mum and dad ('pop stars are not all rebels, drug-takers, and drop-outs, in fact they're not so different from you or I'), even on holiday with his wife ('what's more, pop stars can even be good husbands, being in the rock world doesn't *necessarily* mean having a different girl every night'). In short, when they are personalised in this way their images serve to respectabilise the pop world and thus make it more palatable for *Jackie* readers who, it is assumed, are conventional, ordinary, and adhere to conservative values. Basically, the stars are made to look like 'nice boys'. I'm not suggesting here that the world of male rock stars with their drugs, groupies, and fast cars, present an unconventional alternative and therefore an improvement on traditional stay-at-home values. Ultimately there isn't much to choose between them, in each case the girl or woman is dependent, oppressed and exploited, possibly only marginally more as groupie than as wife, mother, or adoring fan.

The best way, once again, of clarifying this point is to spell out in more detail what *Jackie* pop features don't say, don't include, don't consider. First of all, they concentrate on mainstream show-biz pop music, they are only interested in commercial pop and rarely show pictures of new wave or more experimental bands. The assumption being that girls are inherently less adventurous than boys and that this is reflected in their musical taste. Second, they carry no reviews of pop records or LPs. This means that the girl is encouraged only to like it or dislike it. She is provided with no idea that music can carry different meanings, that it can be created with highly complex instruments, that it can represent new departures or that it can simply follow familiar well-tested formulae. Nor is she involved in a discussion about how music can express different emotions, how it can call to mind with astonishing accuracy past situations, 'forgotten moments'. Instead, it simply *is*, and as long as girls equate pop only with the latest single by Abba then *Jackie* has nothing to worry about. The pop industry (like the fashion and cosmetic industry) have their sales guaranteed, no disruptive values are being expressed and girls are still, for the moment, happy to go along with the *status quo*.

In a similar vein, though perhaps by this stage not surprisingly, girls are provided with no information about how to set up a band, nor are

they encouraged to learn to play an instrument. Genius of the type re
resented by the pin-ups, is, it seems, something that one is born wi
and something that girls seem to be born without. The idea of lear
ing and working is ignored and the old rags-to-riches story takes i
place. What *Jackie* reader doesn't know that David Essex used to be
London barrow boy, or that Sting of The Police used to be a teache
Linked to this is the idea that the only conceivable motive for playi
in a band is to become rich and famous, just like Rod Stewart. Playi
for pleasure, not profits, is yet again outside the *Jackie* scheme
things.

What then can be said about *Jackie*? The ferocity of my critique,
must admit, has increased in the course of writing this article. But the
seems little point to conclude by merely cataloguing its sins. *Jack*
will continue to attract a huge readership each week, not because
furnishes its readers with any positive self-image, not because it encou
ages them to value themselves and each other, but because it offers i
exclusive attention to an already powerless group, to a group whi
attracts little public attention and which is already, from an early ag
systematically denied any real sense of identity, creativity, or contr
*Jackie* merely does in a friendly, intimate way what has been quiet
assumed throughout its readers' short careers. And as long as this grov
can be nourished with their weekly dose of feminine culture, noboc
really need worry. Girls, after all, tend not to pop pills, drink ther
selves stupid or engage in running battles with the police on Bright
beach. Not that encouragement to participate in such rituals would re
resent a step forward, far from it. What *is* needed, however, is an alt
native mode of communication, one where the readers would have t
power to express their feelings, their demands, their desires. One whe
the publishers and owners don't have a vested interest in maintaini
huge profit margins for themselves as well as for those industries o
which commercial magazines depend for advertising revenue. As tr
book goes to press, the possibility of launching such a magazine is cu
rently being discussed by a group of women and girls in London. I
aptly called *Shocking Pink*!

# 8 Resistances and responses:

## the experiences of black girls in Britain

*Valerie Amos* and *Pratibha Parmar*

In this chapter we seek to examine some of the problems that black women face. The chapters in this book cover many different aspects of young women's sexuality, but we have in one chapter to address as many general issues as we can. Many of you may feel that this is tokenism, but we decided that it was important to use the space to say something positive about black women's struggles rather than be invisible yet again.[1]

### Afro-Asian unity

There are several reasons for writing jointly about the lives and exper- iences of Asian and Afro Caribbean girls in Britain. First, most existing literature which seeks to articulate the experience of black girls begins from a racist standpoint, denying *the autonomy of black culture* and trying instead to integrate the experience of black people into more general discussions about life in Britain. On the other hand, token attempts have been made within feminist writing to include material on black girls but this serves only to add 'cross-cultural' spice to predomin- antly ethnocentric work. By this, we mean material written from and about the dominant culture, i.e. British culture, which ignores the existence of other cultures in the society. We feel strongly that there is a need for black women to write about their experience of living in Britain, but at the same time the particularity of a black woman's experience should be made visible not only in black writings, but within the context of more general writings on education, leisure, sexuality, family life *and other aspects of institutional racism* which impinge directly on the lives of black women. Thus we do not look into the black community for the answers to the problems we face as a result of racist practices in this country, we look to the structures and institu- tions which function in that racist manner.

Secondly, we would like to explain what we mean when we talk about black girls and black women. We use the term black to refer to the two main groups of black people in this country, namely those people who came originally from India, Pakistan, Bangladesh, many via East Africa and those people who have their origins in Africa or who as a result of slavery now have their immediate origins in a number of Caribbean countries. We are aware that many differences exist in the cultures, languages and religions not only between the Afro/Caribbean and Asian communities, but also within these two groups. We do not see our cultural differences as operating antagonistically because we recognise the autonomy of our separate cultures. By working together we have developed a common understanding of our oppression and from this basis we build our solidarity. The black struggle is a political one and it is important that we fight our oppression together.

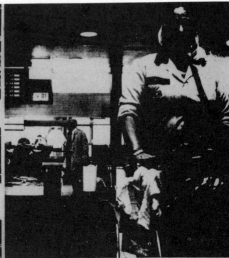

Rajput windows and the ethereal voice of the sitar.
Murals of the legends of Krishna and silks and brocades from Rajasthan.
A glimpse of India on your way to New York.

**AIR-INDIA**

Ash trays and the extensive dirty floors of the airport.
The arrivals and departure board of Heathrow and the overalls from Acme.
A glimpse of exploitation on your way to New York.

**IMMIGRANT-LABOUR**

This is what the Organisation of Women of Asian and African Descent have to say:[2]

> despite the ethnic and cultural differences between these two groups (Asian and Afro/Caribbean), we do not distinguish between them unless it is necessary to refer specifically to one or other of the two groups, as it will be occasionally. This is because our joint historical experience as victims of colonialism, and our

present experience as second class citizens in a racist society have created firm bonds between us which are more significant to us than any differences which may exist. (*Black Women in Britain Speak Out*, OWAAD, 1979)

Our basic aim in this chapter is to challenge some of the myths and stereotypes that exist not only about black girls but about black people generally. Given the limitations of being a token chapter, it is difficult to cover as many areas of black girls' experiences as we would like. Consequently, we have touched on a few general areas, giving some idea of the issues involved rather than anything more in depth or detailed. Having explained the basis and importance of Afro/Asian unity, we then look at some of the existing attitudes to black people and through our criticisms of these approaches we outline our perspective which places a primary importance on an examination of racism, and the ways in which racism structures and determines black girls' life-experiences. We then go on to examine some of the racist and sexist stereotypes that exist about black women. In our final section, 'Action and reaction' we look at the areas of employment and education and very briefly outline the struggles that black women have taken on in these spheres. In our conclusion we look at the positive growth of an autonomous black women's movement and also critically evaluate some of the reasons for black women's absence in the white women's movement.

## Racism – our starting point

In the last few years there have been an increasing number of individuals and organisations which have been taking a keen interest in black youth in British society. The reasons behind this interest are as varied as the individuals and organisations who share it. Sociologists, journalists, social workers, teachers, community/youth workers, police, the schools and other institutions of the state have produced between them a vast amount of literature on black youth and their 'cultural conflicts', 'identity crises' and 'generational conflicts'.

Like other literature on the black community, material on black girls has started off from the premise that they are a problem for themselves, for their parents and for white society, more particularly for white teachers, social workers and the police force.

*Our cultural norms and values* have been seen as responsible for bad housing, overcrowded schools and unemployment amongst other social ills. By adopting such a perspective, white academics and practitioners in the so-called 'helping and caring' professions have shifted the blame from the nature of the society we live in on to our religion, culture and communities.

The following quotes from some white social workers illustrate th╕
above point quite clearly:[3]

Most of my ethnic minority clients have child-care or mental health
problems — because these are areas of conflict with our own *culture*

Particularly with the West Indians, there are problems with tee╕
age girls. Their *culture* is so different and the girls want mo╕
freedom.

I do a lot of work with adolescents — West Indians are particularly
good at being caught by the police. It has a lot to do with police dis
cretion, i.e. West Indian *culture* is to stand around the street corner
and the police book them.

We need to be more flexible in our assessments — e.g. West Indian
family discipline/marital expectations among Asian families. We
could assess the situation as being disharmonious, but it is *culturally* how husbands address their wives or treat them.
*The Views of Social Workers on Multi-Racial Areas*, CRE,
April 1977.

The problem then is us, our cultures, and the solution is seen as res╕
ing on the degree to which we are prepared to integrate, to accept whi╕
cultural values. By this they mean that if only Afro/Caribbean an╕
Asian people would behave like whites, dress like them, eat like them
have the same family size as them, and speak like them, that is adop
white English cultural habits, then they would find it easier to ignor
the fact that they are black and there would be no problem of ra╕
in Britain.
      For example, some more telling quotes from white social worker╕

I try to get minorities to understand the different values and parts
of behaviour so that they fit in better.

They require more help with simple things like hygiene, child-car╕
health, more advice on family planning, more help for the women
who are unhappy and isolated, more classes to learn English.

Some more liberal-minded workers have been forced to recognis╕
through the independent activities of black people that there is a legit
mate reason for resistance to integration and assimilation. As blac╕
people, we do not need to be 'taught' white culture, we already have╕
culture and it is the denial of our culture by white people which is on╕
source of the problem. These social workers, therefore, feel that if, ╕

whites, they understand the black community's cultures and languages better, then they might not experience so many problems in working with them. Further quotes to illustrate the above point:

> It is a question of different scales of values — one has to let a West Indian do things which one would not expect a white person to do — it is a matter of understanding their culture.

> I don't think we have changed our method of work although I think we should do. One always questions the conventional approach to ethnic groups, we try to avoid recognising publicy that they are different. We should look at other ways of dealing with this, to study the different cultures or take them into account.

From aiming for integration to being tolerant about 'their cultures' is part of the same process of racism. White workers have to recognise that most people in the black communities do not particularly want to be assimilated, nor do we want to be tolerated. We have every right to be here.

Our starting point, then, is that Britain is a racist society and it is racism which needs to be looked at, not multi-racialism, multi-culturalism, identity crises or other spurious notions which serve only to evade and/or deflect from the real issues.

Furthermore, any adequate account of the situation of black girls in Britain has to begin with the premise that their day-to-day experiences are determined by three crucial factors — race, class and sex/gender.

For instance, if we take the factor of race, then it has to be said that the situation of black girls cannot be isolated from that of the rest of the black community, as they are equally affected by bad housing conditions, unemployment, or employment in low-paid non-unionised sweat shops and factories, by a racist police force, by racist attacks on the streets and in schools, and racist immigration laws.

The area of racist immigration laws has a double disadvantage for black girls, particularly Asian girls.

On 14th November 1979 the Tory government published their white paper proposals for revision of the immigration rules. These proposals, which are now law, are aimed at reducing immigration of Asian males. One of the ways in which they have attempted to do this is by taking away the right of Asian girls who either were not born in Britain or one of whose parents was not born here, to decide whom to marry. For example, if an Asian girl has lived in Britain most of her life, gone to school here and grown up here, then married a man in India and wanted to live with him in Britain, she could not do this.

The government has taken it upon itself to decide who black women should marry.

Below are some views on this legislation of some Asian girls who have either lived in Britain most of their lives or who were born here.

ON IMMIGRATION
(sixteen- to eighteen-year olds)

They are making too much out of arranged marriages and using it for their own purpose. We have to realise that. (Abida)

It's for us, the girls and our families, to work out our problems and issues of marriage and it's not for the government to decide or to take a stand and say 'Oh, Asian marriages don't work out so we won't allow them'. (Daxa)

The government doesn't really give a damn as long as there are no more black faces; they don't really mind who does what with their lives. (Surjit)

The main point is really to stop black immigration and nought else. And the next thing they will say is 'go home, we have no more use for you'. (Daxa)

You mean to tell me that once we come here, have our homes here and we work here and our life is here and everything else, and then they turn around and say 'go back to your jungle, we don't want you here'. (Abida)

What we are saying is that we have the right to decide where we live, where we get married, who with and when and not have the government tell us. (Surjit)

The girls are saying that they belong here. Britain is their home and they have every right to be here. But why is it that we came here in the first place and settled here?

## We are here, because you were there

To understand the situation of Afro-Caribbean and Asian people in Britain today, we have to first look at the forces and motivations behind our migration here in the historical context of British imperialism. What has been termed the 'Third World' has always been a source of cheap labour to countries like Britain and the other Western industrialised nations and in Britain's case this was a relationship based on the political and economic exploitation of her colonies. The West

Indian islands and the Asian sub-continent present a classic example of this exploitation, which benefits the developed nation and hinders the development of the exploited nation.

A common misconception held by a majority of British people is that relations between themselves and the peoples of the Caribbean or the Indian sub-continent only began when the first black immigrants came to Britain in the late 1940s and early 1950s.[4]

> These poor, benighted people, for reasons which the British some-
> times find it hard to bring to mind, picked themselves up out of
> their villages and plantations and quite uninvited made this long,
> strange and apparently unpredictable journey to the doors of British
> industry — which as you know, out of the goodness of their hearts,
> gave them jobs. (Stuart Hall)

This is what the British people like to believe. But, of course, Britain's relations with the peoples of the Caribbean and the Indian sub-continent did not begin in the 1940s. For centuries, Britain ruled our countries and systematically perverted their economies for her own ends. The Indian sub-continent was used to produce the cotton, tea, jute, and other raw materials needed by Britain for her own industrial develop-ment. India's own textile industry was destroyed so that Britain could export her own cotton goods both to India and to other British colonies. Land policies destroyed many traditional agricultural and home craft industries such as weaving and spinning and this created widespread migration of peasants from the villages to the cities. Tremendous hardship and suffering was imposed on the Indian peoples as Britain continued to exploit and ignore their needs so that her own economic requirements could be fulfilled.

Britain's material prosperity and dominance was founded in the seventeenth century on the slave trade and the plantation system. After the abolition of slavery, no industrial development which would serve the needs of the people was allowed to take place in the Carib-bean. The natural resources of the Caribbean, sugar, bananas, cocoa, bauxite, etc., were sucked out for the requirements of British industry.

The inevitable result for the people both in the Indian sub-continent and the Caribbean was mass poverty and unemployment while the wealth acquired through conquest, colonisation and trade continued to enrich the British nation.

Even after independence the situation in these less developed coun-tries did not improve because the economic relationship remained the same. They were dependent on the colonial powers for the capital required to regenerate and redevelop their economies. There was little investment in these areas and widespread poverty and massive unemployment led to large-scale migration to the 'developed' nations

in search of jobs. The period of the 1950s and 1960s was one of migration to Britain. The British economy was in a state of growth and there
were a number of job vacancies which needed to be filled particularly
in the non-growth sectors of industry. These jobs were characterised by
low pay and bad working conditions and they were the jobs which
white workers refused to do.

British people have been led to believe that we came here to take
away their jobs, their homes, to overcrowd their schools and to 'swamp'
their culture. What is conveniently forgotten and deliberately missed
out from the teaching of British history is that we were, in fact, invited
to come here and promised a better life in a country where the streets
were apparently 'paved with gold'. This whole idea of the wealth and
richness of Britain wasn't conjured up by us, but was deliberately
perpetuated by particular British interests to encourage us to come to
Britain and help rebuild its economy after the Second World War. For
example, in the Caribbean, direct recruitment centres were set up by
the National Health Service, by London Transport and the British
Hotels and Restaurants Association. In India, Pakistan, and Bangladesh
managers for textile firms were sent out to recruit workers directly for
their mills in the Midlands and in Yorkshire and in many cases they
paid for the fares for workers to come here. The case of East African
Asians is slightly different. The East African Asians were mostly small
shop-owners, clerks in the government services and bankers. Most of
them had migrated from the Indian states of Gujerat and Punjab to
East Africa. A large section of them had originally gone as bonded
labourers in the 1890s. They were the minority group which the British
had brought in from India to serve as intermediaries between themselves, the white colonialists, and the indigenous, exploited African
population. On the whole, the Indians did the smaller jobs which the
Europeans could not be bothered with. For example, they became
traders, merchants or petty officials. The following account of how one
man travelled to Africa illustrates the situation very vividly and it also
shows the hardship that thousands of other men and women like him
had to endure.

> In 1932 life in India was hard and of little hope to us. Colonialism
> still existed and it was because of this that I started thinking about
> migrating. I knew that in the late nineteenth century the British
> colonialists had trained the Indians to be soldiers and transferred
> them to places like the West Indies and East Africa. Soon after that
> the great migration period of India started; the peoples went to work
> as labourers on the railways, or they went to work the machinery or
> they started to trade. Some even went to farm the land.

He describes the conditions on board the ship bound for Africa:

There were no decent toilet facilities on the deck so the whole place started stinking. Those who had paid for better conditions complained to the official, who ignored everything except delivering this load of people to its destination. So we were spat at. We could do nothing but whitewash the deck wherever it was not covered by mattresses or luggage. We tried our best to keep clean but our efforts were in vain and fever broke out. There were few doctors on the lower deck and the other doctors were too proud or insufficiently equipped and could do nothing. Death had broken into the ship and was carrying away soul after soul. As soon as someone died, the Captain called a squad who put the body in a jute bag, weighed it down with heavy rocks, then over it went. It was a formidable sight.

This experience of migration from the Asian sub-continent to Africa is not dissimilar to the experience of African people during the slave period. Africans were brutalised, beaten and degraded before being herded together like cattle and shipped from the West African coast to America, the West Indian islands and Latin America. The slaves serviced the plantation economies of the American South and the Caribbean and the loss of human life was immeasurable. After the abolition of slavery *indentured labourers* from India were transported to some parts of South America and the Caribbean and later to East Africa *to service the requirements of British capital*. Black people were treated as human cargo, their function was to secure a profit for British capitalist enterprise. Britain developed a particular relationship with her colonies, a relationship based on exploitation.

East African Asians came to Britain around 1966. In 1967 the Kenyatta Government in Kenya, who had introduced the Africanisation policies, granted only temporary residence to those British Asians who had not opted for Kenyan citizenship at the time of Kenyan Independence in 1963.

The only viable alternative for the British Asians was to come to Britain. In 1965 and 1966, when they were not subject to any immigration control, 6,000 Asians with British citizenship came to Britain.

But the British government at the time (which was Labour) was acutely aware of all those other British Asians and Africans all around the world, whom she had used to develop her imperial colonies. Therefore, keen to stop their mass entry into Britain, they moved very swiftly to try and control this new source of immigration to Britain. They did this by altering the legal rights of entry through the 1968 Immigration Act. The British Asians were redefined by this Act as Commonwealth Citizens and since the Commonwealth citizens were subject to *the voucher system*, the British Asians in Kenya would also be liable to this procedure for entry into the United Kingdom. The only distinction was that they would be allocated special vouchers as distinct from work vouchers.

A voucher system was first introduced through the Commonwealth Immigration Act of 1962. This act distinguished two kinds of citizens of the United Kingdom and Colonies by dividing British passport-holders, whose passport had been issued by the British government, from those UK citizens whose passport had been, or could be, issued by a Colonial government. The latter category were no longer free to enter the UK to take employment unless a voucher was obtained first. A limited number of these vouchers, which differentiated between skilled and unskilled work, were issued to Commonwealth countries each year, although after 1965 only 8,500 in total were available and in that year vouchers for unskilled jobs were withdrawn completely.

This system established that immigration of heads of household from the black Commonwealth was geared to the requirements of the British economy. 'It was also a system which took discrimination out of the market place and gave it the sanction of the State. It made racism respectable and clinical by institutionalizing it.'[5]

Furthermore, vouchers for Kenyan Asians were only issued to heads of households, normally males, for themselves and certain categories of dependants. Here the dependent status of Asian women was made very clear. Women holding British passports had great difficulty in proving that they were heads of households. Widowed, divorced, deserted women and those women with British passports whose husbands were non-British citizens came into this group.

The problem of sexist discriminatory immigration laws is still continuing and further restrictions are being placed on black women's rights. A report was published in 1978 of the Parliamentary Select Committee on Race Relations and Immigration. This committee, which was composed of representatives from all the parties in the House of Commons, recommended that the government attack the right of our dependants in our countries of origin to join us here, and at the same time, allow the police to step up their harassment of our communities in the search for so-called illegal immigrants.

But one of the most serious threats posed by the report is to the future of black families and black culture. One of the recommendations of the report was that children over twelve years old born abroad to those settled here will not be allowed to join their parents. This kind of legislation has caused great bitterness because of the way in which it breaks up black families.[6]

> Usha: I have two children in India. I can't see any reason for them not to be allowed to come and join their mother. They are being looked after by my mother. That's why I am working, to save enough money to bring them all over here. I have a wish to look after them ourselves. The government has to take notice of our customs. If I don't bring my mother here, she will be on her own

with no one to look after her. Everyone should be able to bring their families and close relatives here.

In this section we have tried to establish a historical continuity: of who black people are, how we came to Britain, under what circumstances and what has been happening since we have been here. As one woman said:[7]

They ruled and looted our countries for many years and took most of our wealth away. And now we come and live here and work hard, they start going on about us taking away their houses and their jobs. What do they think they were doing when they came to our countries? (P. Parmar, 'Asian Women Stand Firm' in *Bradford Black*, Bradford Black Collective, May/June 1978)

### Black female stereotypes

So what's it like for a black girl growing up in England today? There are lots of pressures, of course, to be this or to be that. In a sense black girls fall outside the stereotypical images which bombard white women every day of their lives. These images relate to all aspects of life, e.g. the family, where unreal images of family life are portrayed on television, particularly in advertisements. The most important area, however, is that of sexuality – the whole way in which girls and women are pressured to see themselves (especially) in relation to other people, particularly men. Girls aren't expected to think for themselves – all this is supposed to be for the male to do. Women aren't expected to think, to have ideas, to be creative. Girls have little or no opportunity to break out of this vicious circle because the only things open to them are marriage or work in a tedious monotonous job which is often described by career officers in glowing terms. Girls, then, don't have any *real choice* and for black girls the problems they face because of their colour worsens the situation.

Why is it that the images of the family presented in the media have so little relevance to the family situation of the majority of black women in this country? It all stems from the ways in which black people are perceived in this society. Black family life is seen as being in some way peculiar and different, and this difference means that the black family has no status, particularly in relation to the way in which the white, nuclear family structure is seen. Black family life can't be described or explained in those terms so it has to be denigrated.

Black women are seen and represented in a particular way by white society. The stereotypes differ for the Afro/Caribbean and the Asian communities, but despite the difference in the stereotypes the racism underlying them is the same. Women of Asian origin range from being seen as sexually exotic creatures, full of 'Eastern promise', to being seen as completely dominated by their menfolk, oppressed wives and mothers who have little or nothing to say in relation to their families.

The images seem very far removed from the reality of life as lived by so many women in the Asian community. Working in sweat shops, as a number of them do, for low pay in overcrowded conditions. Facing constant harassment, not only on the street, physically, but also culturally, with attacks and abuse which attempt to degrade and denigrate their way of life. The criticisms of family life are again based on a number of 'common sense' images of what family life in the Asian community is supposed to be all about. Asian people are said to live in overcrowded conditions, eat different food, wear different clothes and even speak a different language. All these things present a threat to what are seen as the dominant values of white society because Asians don't want to mesh in, they maintain their cultural traditions as far as that is possible, looking to each other for the strength and support they require to cope with living in a racist society.

In the Afro/Caribbean community stereotypes also exist but as mentioned before they are different. Women of Afro/Caribbean origin have long been outside Western definitions of beauty. In sexual terms, they are perceived as 'prostitutes'. They have children outside the marriage relationship and in a number of cases do not even aspire to marriage. They are also seen as 'caring' women — personifying mother-hood and domesticity. The image here is of the black Mamma or nurse ruling the kitchen or nursery with an 'iron glove'. But there is another, even more familiar, stereotype that we would like to examine and challenge. One which is often used as a means of demonstrating the so-called 'backwardness' of black culture; the myth of arranged marriages.

### The myth of arranged marriages

The practice of arranged marriages is most frequently used as an explanation for the oppression of Asian girls. It is one area which has received frequent sensational news headlines in the papers and many television programmes have been made about it. Most of this coverage has given a distorted and false picture of the tradition and practice of arranged marriages. The overall stereotypical image is that of Asian girls caught between two cultures, her parents' culture and the culture of her white English peers. Asian girls are said to see their white friends at school or work going out to discos and films and 'choosing' their own boyfriends and potential husbands, while they (the poor Asian girls) are forced into a marriage with someone who is usually twice their age, someone who doesn't understand the English romantic etiquette like white men do and, of course, someone whom they have never seen until the actual wedding ceremony. Asian girls are said to have absolutely no 'freedom' to partake in the choosing of their husbands while white English girls have all the 'freedom' they want or need. If Asian girls had the same degree of so-called 'choice' about their marriage then it would help to create a more integrated society. Invariably, it's the parents with their archaic ideas who are seen as stopping this integration into white British society.

The stereotype that we have outlined might seem a little crude, but these are the ideas and attitudes which are dominant amongst most white people.

Nothing, however, could be further from the reality. This kind of gross generalisation has led to many myths about the practice of arranged marriages (we are not denying that arranged marriages are oppressive, but marriage as practised in white British culture is also oppressive).

What we want to challenge is the illusion that white girls have a great deal of choice about whom they marry. The reality is that, in the majority of cases, if they marry they will marry boys from a similar class background, in the same region or geographical area.

For example, what chance does a white working-class girl who has left school at sixteen with a few or no CSE's and is working in a factory or doing a typing course, have of meeting up with and marrying a white middle-class boy who has been to the local grammar school, then university, and is professionally employed. Not only is there not much chance of these two every marrying, but there's not much chance of them ever even meeting.

So 'choice', 'arrangement' and 'freedom' are all relative concepts and often it is people's class which determines whom they meet, and whom they marry, more than any romantic or idealistic notions of falling in love with 'Mr Right' who happens to fatefully cross your path.

For Asian girls, the amount of choice they have over whom they marry varies a lot from one Asian community to another, and from one Asian family to another. Some parents are more strict than others, just like some white English parents exercise more control over their children than others.

The following discussion between three fifteen-year-old Asian girls shows many similarities in their experiences of staying out late, etc. with that of their white peers. It also shows the closeness of some girls and their parents and destroys the myth of the Asian parents who keep their daughters locked up and chained in their rooms.

Kamaljit: I've known this boy for about two years now. We aren't thinking of getting married yet but if I was to tell my parents about

it they would agree because he is my religion. Besides, all my sisters
have married who they wanted to, so I don't see why they should
refuse me. My mum knows this boy and she doesn't mind, but if he
was English I think she would mind. I don't know how she would
react. She wouldn't go angry, but she would tell me not to see him.
Then it would be up to me to decide whether to see him or not. But
I am the sort who can't leave a family but can leave a boy.

Yasmin: My brother is going out with an English girl and both my
parents have seen them together and they don't say anything about
it. But when they see me with a lad they always tell me off. My
brother can stop out all night and they don't let me stop out even
until midnight. Boys get more privileges than girls.

Rekha: My parents are all right because they let my sisters and I go
anywhere we want to and come back when we like too. They are
the same with my brother. It's all right as long as they know where
we are going and who we are with.

Talking about going out in the evening:

Kamaljit: I love the disco's and the parties. My friend and I go to a
disco together. . . . We go about 8 and come back at 2 a.m. My mum
says it's all right as long as I go with a friend.

Rekha: Since I have grown up in England I have been brought up to
expect all these things. I like them, and if I went back to Africa I
would like it but I would miss all the disco's and fashions. My
parents like the clothes I wear.

Yasmin: My parents don't like pop music and when I wear a dress
which is a bit low they usually tell me off for wearing it.

Talking about who they can discuss boyfriends, etc. with at home:

Rekha: I can talk about a few things to my mum, about friends
but I don't think I would talk about boyfriends. I can talk about
boys generally to my sisters, but not saying I am going out with one.

Kamaljit: I am always telling my parents about my boyfriend. He
is Indian and he comes to the house. My mother doesn't mind as
long as I tell her everything. But I only tell my personal problems
to my best friend. But my parents are broad-minded and they understand.

Rekha: My mother understands. I don't tell my father. There was this Indian boy going with me and she found out. I went on seeing him and she knew and didn't even tell my father.

One of the things the above discussion shows is that the problems Asian girls experience *vis-à-vis* their parents are often very similar to white English girls even though their difficulties are caused by different factors. The generalisations made about Asian parents forcing their daughters into arranged marriages gives a distorted picture of Asian cultural practices and ignores the positive and constructive relationship most girls have with their parents.

Photograph by
*Pratibha Parmar*

As we have said, there are many pressures on black girls growing up in England to fit into one stereotyped image or another. We have tried to show what some of these pressures are and also what the myths are about their lives, particularly in the area of sexuality, but there are also pressures of a different sort for black girls at work, at school and on the streets.

### Action and reaction

The exploitation of black female labour is often overlooked because so many employment statistics and reports focus on the employment situation as it affects black men, especially as it is often assumed that black women have greater access to employment opportunities. What are these opportunities then?

Black women of Asian origin have had to come to terms with whole new spheres of experience, particularly in the area of employment, and they have had to redefine their many roles. Their economic situation makes it important for black women to work and they have to work in order to supplement the family wage. The Grunwick dispute was an example of the way in which black workers defied management and asserted their right to engage in trade union activity. The relationship of women especially black women, to trade union activity has traditionally been one of indifference because unions have consistently ignored the needs of black female workers. Many women work because they have to, but the man in the family is still regarded by many as the main wage earner. This situation is changing because so many black women are now the sole wage earners in their families. Increasingly, black women have become active in trade union disputes and the militant position taken by them has helped to shatter a number of illusions held about women and work and has also gone some way to dispelling some of the stereotypical images of black women mentioned earlier.

The Grunwick dispute is perhaps the most well-known example of the way in which black women have been fighting back. A number of black women challenged the authority of the State and the agents of state power, the police, in a confrontation which lasted for several months. This is how one worker describes the conditions at Grunwick's: 'They treat us like animals here. . . . We had to get permission to go to the toilet. It was a sort of rule of terror. In this day and age the treatment we got was worse than in Roots.' (*Race Today*, 1977) These women won an important victory. By refusing to be intimidated by the management of the firm, they and their supporters showed the importance of a unified struggle by black people.

Black women have also been at the forefront of nursing disputes throughout the 1970s agitating for better pay, better working conditions and shorter hours. Nursing is seen as a caring profession suitable for women.[9]

No woman is more identified with service work than black women. . . . The relationship between the black woman and nursing of other people's children and other people's husbands and wives, dates from before any National Health Service. Whether working in hospitals as auxiliaries, SEN, or SRN, in the head of the black nurse from the Caribbean is the echo of slavery, in the head of the Asian nurse is the servitude to Sahib and Memsahibs. (*Race Today*, August 1974)

Black women today no longer believe the myths about nursing: that nursing is a vocation that gives them dignity and responsibility. They have come to realise they are exploited as much in hospitals as they are in factories, laundries and sweat shops. A number of racist practices operate within the hospital hierarchy. Initially black nurses are channelled into doing the SEN course, a course which cannot lead to promotion, rather than SRN. As one nurse said: [10]

> When you are interviewed they ask you if you want to do the course in two years or three, and all of us said we would like to do the two year course. It's only when you get here that you realise that if you do two years, you will be an SEN. (*Race Today*, August 1974)

Black nurses also complain that in a number of instances the practical teaching, help and advice they should get on the wards, white nurses are not prepared to give them. Black nurses have responded to the racism they face in these situations by organising strikes, work-to-rules and other forms of resistance.

Schools are another area where black girls have experienced racism not only from some white teachers and heads but also from their white peers. Asian girls are often picked on for the way they dress or for the food they eat.

> Mumtaz: I have been called things like Paki and wog ever since I came to this school and ever since I moved into this area. I have got used to it now. People are a bit more friendly now.

> Nisha: I think this school is better than most because at schools like E . . . or T . . . . the Indians sit on one side and the English on the other. They call each other names and almost every day there's a fight. The girl next door goes to T . . . and she says I am different from other Indians, but I don't know how she means. She says that they smell. I think she's a bit stupid.

> Rita: I get hurt by what they say, but I know they are just being stupid. They don't know what they are saying. They are only saying it because they are frightened of our culture and because they don't really understand it, I think if they know a bit more they might understand.

It's not only in schools that girls come under racist attacks, but also in their homes and on the streets.

> Gulshan: It's worse where I live, because we are the only Indian family. Our next door neighbours are all right, but the people living further away call us names. 'Go back where you came from', 'wog',

'Paki', 'We are the National Front' and all the rest. I just ignore them.

Many girls fight back.

> Nisha: If somebody calls me Paki I would go to them and kick them in the teeth. I don't often get called names, just about once a year, and then I get really angry and hit them. If somebody said that to me I would say 'Pink ice cream'. There are some English people in our country and we don't go around calling them names.

There are many racist practices in schools and in education generally that we have not mentioned. For example, bussing of black children into other areas, racist curriculum, the dumping of black children in educationally subnormal schools and biased intelligence tests. A more recent form of racist practice is the growing use of disruptive units or 'sin-bins' as they are commonly called. A high percentage of children in educationally subnormal schools or remedial units are West Indian. And if there is no room in these places then black children are suspended from schools on the quiet. All these are attempts by the authorities to try and control black children, make them passive and discipline them for the lowest paid and dirtiest jobs on the market.

As can be seen, no areas of black people's lives are untouched by the racism of British society. But despite these attempts to stereotype, control and demoralise them, black people have put up resistances and fought to gain control over their lives.

## Conclusion

We would like to conclude by stating what we see as the importance of the growth and development of a black women's movement in Britain. We have tried to show a number of the ways in which racism limits and circumscribes the lives of black girls in Britain. We have tried to present that experience as it is lived. Racism, however, is not the only oppression a black woman faces. She is also oppressed in class terms, as part of the working class, and in gender terms, because she is a woman.

Existing political organisations cannot always incorporate all these struggles and although we feel that as black women we should organise with other black people against the racism in this society, and as part of the working class we should organise around the issues of work and non-work, and as women we should organise with other women, as black women we also need to organise separately around the issues that are particular to our experiences as black women, experiences which come out of the triple oppression we face.

Most girls have a distorted image of what the Women's Liberation Movement is all about and what organising in a women's movement means. The only contact they may have with the ideas of women's liberation is through television or maybe through what men say about it. Black girls see the movement as dominated by white, middle-class women who in many cases fail to recognise the specific and complex nature of black women's oppression. For these reasons black girls feel they have nothing in common with a movement which doesn't even realise they exist.

It is all very well for white women to demand equal pay and abortion on demand but equal pay with whom, the other black women working in the overcrowded sweat shop or in the hot laundry or working as auxiliary nurses and cleaners? In asking for abortions on demand, white women are failing to recognise what contraception and abortion *mean* to black women. It may mean being sterilised without your knowledge or consent, it means black women being used as guinea pigs in experiments for new drugs, it means contraceptives like depo provera which have numerous side effects being used on black women, but not on white women. A number of women also fail to understand and recognise the importance placed by black women on having children. Having a child is sometimes the only way in which a black girl can show that she has some control over herself. It may be the only thing she *wants* that she can *have*.

The main issue here is the gap which exists between the experience of black women who face racism every day in addition to their oppression in class and gender terms and white women who are afraid to confront their own racism. White women fail to understand a number of the cultural traditions which exist in the black community and the important part they play in our growth and development as black women. They simply label practices they do not understand as oppressive and although there are some issues which we need to fight together as women, white women need to come to terms with the fact that they are part and parcel of a racist system, they are oppressors and as such are distanced from a number of the problems which black women confront every day.[11]

Despite the tremendous pressures on black women living in Britain, the militant action that many have taken has destroyed the illusion of the passive or apathetic black woman. In this chapter we have challenged the many myths that exist about black women and in so doing have shown the strength of black womanhood. As black sisters we all have to be involved in re-creating our own history, constantly questioning and fighting attempts which are made to oppress us. We should be organising wherever we are, at school, work, home or in the community, and in this way demonstrate the importance of our struggle.

## Notes

1 We are both members of the Race and Politics Group at the Centre for Contemporary Cultural Studies, Birmingham University. This group is currently working on a book entitled 'White Power, Black Struggle — Britain in the 1970's' to be published by Hutchinsons. Some of the issues touched on in this article will be developed more fully in that book. Other members of the group are: H. Carby, B. Findlay, P. Gilroy, A. Green, S. Jones, E. Lawrence, J. Solomos and R. Wilson.

2 *Black Women in Britain — Speak Out*, Organisation of Women of Asian and African Descent, 1979.

3 *The Views of Social Workers in Multi-Racial Areas*, Commission for Racial Equality, April 1977.

4 Stuart Hall, 'Racism and Reaction', in *Five Views of Multi-Racial Britain* Commission for Racial Equality.

5 *Our Lives — Young People's Autobiographies,* Inner London Education Authority.

6 A. Sivanandan, 'Race, Class and the State', *The Black Experience in Britain,* Institute of Race Relations, 1976.

7 Parmar, P.: 'Asian Women Stand Firm', *Bradford Black*, May/June 1978, The Bradford Black Collective.

8 *Ibid.*

9 *Race Today*, 1977, Race Today Collective.

10 *Race Today*, 1974.

11 *Ibid.*

Photograph by
*Pam Bloor*

150

Photograph by
*Pam Bloor*

Photograph by
*Pam Bloor*

152

Photograph by
*Pam Bloor*

# Part II

# Making changes

# 9 Romance and sexuality:

## between the devil and the deep blue sea?

*Myra Connell, Tricia Davis, Sue McIntosh,
Mandy Root*

Illustrated by *Charlotte Tucker*

We think we should say something about who we are and why we've
tried to write this chapter. We're four women, in our twenties and
thirties, who are studying aspects of women's lives (young and middle-
aged), but want our work to be useful. We work (some of the time)
together, and we know each other fairly well, but we have developed
a lot of our ideas in the context of the Women's Movement generally,
not just with each other. We come from different backgrounds, and
we've been to a range of schools (secondary modern, grammar, private),
and we're all white. This is very important, we think, for this article.
We have tried to think about experience other than our own, but this
has been easier in relation to class than to race. The reason we've left
questions of race alone is that we know so little about the way in which
girls experience sexuality in cultures other than ours. Indian girls, for
instance, probably vary in their experiences depending on the regional
and religious traditions in their families. Living in Britain provides
another set of conditions and values, and many conflicts. It would be
presumptuous of us to try and talk about this as white women. However, we're not all that happy about having separate chapters on West
Indian and Asian girls either — this implies that they are totally separate
and different — which is, of course, untrue. Perhaps all we can say is
that this is an imperfect solution.

The way we wrote this was to discuss ideas with friends, other
students, teenage girls, and each other, look at magazines and books,
and gradually work out themes. We also spent an evening with a tape
recorder and some drink, discussing our own teenage sexuality and
'romantic' experiences, accompanied by a lot of laughter and vul-
garity! We know we represent different generations of teenage (each
one only spans seven years, after all), so we haven't taken ourselves
as proof of anything. But it was interesting to find that we did have
many experiences in common — groping with boys in cars or cinemas,
going to dances and discos, finding that the image of the knight on a
white horse and the maiden in distress was hard to maintain in the face

ROMANCE-
A
TALE OF
CHIVALRY

ANY
FICTITIOUS
AND
WONDERFUL
TALE

WHICH
PASSES
BEYOND
THE
LIMITS
OF
ORDINARY
LIFE.

of reality, and wondering whether loving men was worth the effort and if not what were the alternatives.

We also think we need to say something about our own sexual orientations and choices. We have had different experiences — relating to men, and to women. Sometimes this has been monogamous (meaning full commitment to one person only), sometimes not. We have all found it difficult to question what we do sexually, but have chosen to do that rather than accept the restriction of *not* questioning it. This connects to our reasons for writing this. As feminists, we think that female sexuality is still very little discussed, and certainly not in a way that copes with the physical, emotional, social and political levels that we feel it operates at. We think of our teenage (and our current lives!) as a period of tremendous confusion, in the face of a conspiracy of silence on what really goes on about sex, emotions and relationships. So, although this chapter has nearly driven us mad at times, and we are very aware of its inadequacies, we hope it at least helps to start the discussion.

**Romantic stories: 'I love you with all my heart'**

'I think I understand now what Mama . . . meant when she told me only to . . . give myself to . . . a man I loved with . . . all my heart.'

'You love me like that?' the Earl asked.

'I love you with all my heart . . . my body . . . and my soul. I love you with . . . all of me. And I want you to tell me how I can give you . . . all of myself.'

She reached up her arms as she spoke to put them round his neck and draw his head down to hers.

'My darling, my love, my wife!'

His lips, passionate, insistent, demanding, held her captive, she felt his hands touching her, his heart pounding against hers.

Then Syringa knew that he lifted her towards the stars and there was nothing in the whole universe save themselves and their love.

This is the last scene of a romantic novel by Barbara Cartland. We've begun with it because although Barbara Cartland probably appeals more to older women, we think that the extract contains several ideas that are typical of countless other romantic stories in novels, magazines and films. These romantic ideas have had a definite place in our lives, and not just as something we have read and enjoyed in an escapist way. Romance has seeped into our real lives, and coloured the way we feel about the emotional and sexual relationships we have had. We don't know whether it has the same place in your life as it has in ours — every group of young women will see and use romance in a

A LOVE AFFAIR

ESPECIALLY ANY AFFAIR

INVOLVING A MARRIAGE

BETWEEN DIFFERENT

SOCIAL CLASSES

different way; but we think it is unlikely that you could be a girl in this society and not be touched in some way by romance.

So what are these ideas that are typical of romance?

Romance, first of all, is something that is supposed to happen *to* you, something that only fate can bring about. In the stories girls aren't supposed to go out and find relationships, they're supposed to wait passively for the boy to make the first move.

Second, in romantic fiction the woman is supposed to be totally ignorant about sex. Syringa spends the whole book absolutely unaware that her feelings for the earl have anything to do with sex. Even in this scene where, safely married, they have got into bed together, she doesn't know at all what she's supposed to do. Furthermore, she expects him to be able to teach her. With typically hesitant speech she says: 'I want you . . . to tell me . . . how I can give you . . . myself', and then 'he lifted her . . . towards the stars'. There are two points to make about this: one is that there is a double standard in operation; allowing, expecting and needing him to have had some sexual experience (and in fact we have seen him earlier in the book, moving in a sated kind of way among 'loose women' who have been 'throwing themselves at him'), while insisting that *she* must be virginal. And second, it seems rather odd to imagine that a man should know more about a woman's sexuality than she does herself. In our experience, men find women's sexual needs quite difficult to understand, needing lots of explanation.

Which brings us on to the next point. Syringa's first sexual experience is set to be magical. It's going to be tremendously exciting and absolutely successful. Our culture is full of grand images about sex making the earth move. It may be overwhelming at times; but those times are quite unlikely to include the first one. We want to suggest that the way sex is seen in romantic fiction implies that it's something mystical and magical, whereas in fact we think it is something that needs to be learnt about and looked at openly, and which gets better with practice.

'There was nothing in the whole universe save themselves and their love.' Love, in romantic fiction, excludes everything else, particularly for the woman. True love (which isn't usually clearly analysed as a feeling, but is magically recognised) is always for ever and always in the end leads to marriage. Again, in our experience, love often lasts a very short time, and the kind of passionate sexual feeling that by tradition blinds you to everything else is by no means the only or ideal reason for choosing someone to marry. Love typically causes confusion, not clear thinking. 'How do you know when you're in love?' asked one of the girls we worked with; and then answers, 'I'm moody, miserable and confused.'

Often also, in romantic fiction, the moment of falling in love with a man, or of realising that that has happened, involves some association

AN IMAGINATIVE LIE TO TALK EXTRAVAG- ANTLY OR WITH AN INFUSION OF FICTION

TO LIE

TO BUILD CASTLES IN THE AIR.

FROM THE DEFINITION OF ROMANCE, FROM CHAMBERS 20TH CENTURY DICTIONARY.

with violence. It is as if the only man who can awaken the woman's sexuality, who can get over the feeling in her that sex is something nasty that nice girls don't do, is one who can master her, dominate her, force her into it. Syringa realises she loves the earl when, mistakenly thinking that she has been 'loose', he kisses her brutally. Then, after he has flung himself out of the room, 'his face contorted into the visage of a devil', she

> put a trembling hand to her lips, and as she did so, as she felt them bruised and painful to her own touch, she knew she loved him!
> This was love, this streak of fire that had swept through her even as he had held her so roughly in his arms and kissed her so brutally!
> It was almost like a blinding light to realise that what she had felt for him all along was not the affection of a friend but the love of a woman for a man! (pp. 157-8)

Many of the ideas about love that are in this novel are, as we have said, also to be found in more modern magazines and comics. Girls may now be allowed to have some interest in and knowledge about sex; but a distinction is still made between nice girls and girls who 'go too far'; and it is the boys whose wants and needs dominate: the girls adapt to them rather than the other way round, even to the extent of altering their bodies by dieting and cosmetics in order to match the boy's standard. Sex in fiction is still something magical and more powerful than anything else, and once the girl has got her boy, as the story ends with the wonderful kiss, we are left with the impression that all the problems are now solved, that having found a partner means peace and security – maybe true to some extent, but not in every case and not in the sense that life will no longer involve any difficulties. The trouble is that although women know that many marriages that began with a couple in love end in divorce, we still keep the romantic notion alive in our heads that for us it will be different, we'll be the exception to the rule. And the fiction's constant concentration on love, to the exclusion of work and other relationships, implies relentlessly that love, meaning relationships with boys, is the most important thing in girls' lives.

What we want to do in this chapter is to bring into question some of the romantic ideas about love and sexuality. Most commonly in our society, love, sex, and marriage are expected to go together. You can't, or shouldn't, have sex without love, it's usually said; love ideally leads to marriage which lasts for ever; sex and/or love between people of the same sex is ignored or laughed at or seen as a passing phase.

We ourselves haven't experienced these things in the way that most people are expected to. We've had sexual experiences which have not led to marriage and have not been about love, though they have been

IT BEGINS
WHEN
YOU
SINK
INTO
HIS ARMS

positive and good; not all our sexual experience has been with men. As we've talked about it, both in working on this chapter and previously in our experience in the women's movement, we've realised that many other women feel the same sort of conflict between what it's supposed to be like and what it really feels like.

The rest of this chapter is in four sections. First we look at how women's sexuality is represented in advertising and then at the way in which women are talked about in sex manuals. Our argument will be that in both of these, femininity means passivity and subservience to men. After that we look at some of the differences between these representations and women's actual experience; and in the last section we discuss some of the possible alternatives to a whole-hearted accep-tance of romance.

### Advertising — from the girls next door to the liberated lady

Mass media advertising is, for most of us, a constant part of our daily lives and images of women in advertisements play an important role in telling us what femininity is supposed to be. Wherever we go, in the streets, the cinema, the underground, even at home, we're confronted with a barrage of supposedly glamorous images of women. Their purpose, it seems, is to sell us the products which will remove our 'imperfections' so that we too can be glamorous.

There is nothing wrong, of course, in wanting to feel good about the way we look. Experimenting with different images of ourselves can be an important part of self-discovery, and fun too. But showing women as wanting to feel good about ourselves for ourselves is not what mass media advertising is about. For a start, advertisements imply that we should all look alike. They also assume that looking good means look-ing good for men, and that feeling good means knowing that men admire you. Sometimes this is expressed in very obvious ways. If you look carefully at advertisements you'll find that a common theme is the 'glamorous woman' with one or two men in tow. The message which is put across loudly and clearly is that product X — anything from a brand of drink to a particular perfume — will increase 'sex appeal' and, therefore, the chances of being loved by men.

Men don't even have to be present in the advertisements though. We see ourselves, and women in advertisements are seen, through the eyes of real or potential *men*. This is a more difficult point to make, but John Berger has put it very well in a book called *Ways of Seeing*. He writes:

According to usage and convention, which are at last being ques-tioned but have by no means been overcome, the social presence of

AND ENDS ○ ○ ○ ○ ○ ○ WITH YOUR ARMS IN HIS SINK.

woman is different in kind from that of a man. A man's presence is dependent upon the promise of power which it embodies. By contrast a woman's presence expresses her own attitude to herself and defines what can and cannot be done to her. . . . Men act, women appear.

In other words, the male body seems to mean power because being masculine in our society is about being powerful. The female body in our society has totally different connotations. It comes across as passive and available. This can be seen more clearly, perhaps, if the figure of a woman in an advertisement is changed into a man. The meaning of the advertisement is transformed. It often becomes meaningless and ridiculous. Because of the different meanings attached to the male and female body, advertisements selling male cosmetics, on the whole, avoid using the male body and simply suggest it, either through props or with the help of the phallic symbolism of packaging. If a man does appear in the advertisement, the 'sales appeal' is built on a different set of assumptions to those used to sell products to women. A current (1980) advertisement for male cosmetics, for example, shows the range of male toiletries and cosmetics. In the background is a framed photo of a man in a dinner jacket. On one arm is a glamorous woman. His other arm shields his face from a photographer. The caption reads: 'It's not just the way he looks that makes him what he is.' Clearly, masculinity is about doing, being 'somebody'. The man who buys this particular brand of cosmetics buys them *because* of who he is. Many advertisements selling cosmetics to women, on the other hand, suggest that women buy cosmetics in order to *become* somebody. She is often shown as nothing more than a collection of products. 'Dress by X, stockings by Y, hair by Z.'

So the sexuality of women, while it seems much more assertive in advertisements than in romantic fiction, is just as dependent upon the presence of a man or the ability to get a man. Sex is still something *done* to a woman. The goal is to be irresistible, not confident enough to take initiative oneself. In advertisements, too, because the product is presented as the solution to every problem, the sexually desirable image is the answer to all problems. Advertisements tell us that with product Y we will be loved, and therefore able to love ourselves. What more could any woman want?

The answer to that is — quite a bit — and, over the past few years, advertising has changed in response to changes in women's lives. A new image has been added, and smiling out at us from the pages of women's magazines we now see not only 'the femme fatale', 'the girl next door', 'the sleeping beauty', but also 'the liberated lady'. She works, she has her own bank account and steps out into the world with a confident smile on her face. Looking at this new image more carefully, though, we find that it's only expressing a new variation on what is basically the old definition of femininity. What is stressed in the 'liberated lady' image is not that women do paid work, let alone that their work is usually underpaid and low status. The statement made is that paid work gives a woman the spending power to increase her value as a sexually desirable object. She can, for example, buy that bright red sports car and drive off with the wind spreading her blonde hair conveniently out behind her. An alternative message is that even whilst working women remain sexually desirable to men, and that this is much more important than whether she likes her job, how much she gets paid and so on. Not only does her nail varnish not chip, but it is her make-up, not her, which in the words of one advertisement, 'works an eight hour day.'

**Sex manuals: science makes sex respectable**

Although the idea of sex manuals is as old as the hills, there has been a boom in them since the 1960s, and particularly since the so-called 'sexual revolution' and the dawning of 'permissiveness'. But it was the Kinsey Report, published in Britain in 1953 as *Sexual Behavior in the Human Female*, which really marked the beginning of this trend. The report was based on information collected from 8,000 women and although it recognised that for a whole complex of reasons women weren't as likely as men to seek out sexual experience, it did none the less assert on paper that women could enjoy sex and gave this assertion scientific status. During the 1950s and 1960s many books on sexuality were produced which took up this theme of women's ability to enjoy sex. In fact, sexual enjoyment for women, as long as it was within marriage, became not just a right but a duty. And in this sense it was a double-edged discovery. Women were suddenly being encouraged from almost every direction to have more sex. Without going into it in more detail, it is possible to interpret this as an attempt to stabilise the family in society, by servicing, to an even greater extent, *men's* sexual needs. And so, underlying this 'progressive' recognition was a very clear idea about how and where such sexuality was to be expressed.

The arrival of the pill as a method of contraception in the mid-1960s increased the belief that women are now as sexually free as men and those of us who grew up during the 1960s and 1970s have become used to being told that we live in a 'permissive society'; that whether we approve or not, sex and love need no longer be linked together; and that technique, not feeling, is the key to good sexual experience. The large number of sex manuals appearing in bookshops seems convincing evidence in support of these arguments. We want to ask, though, how far the sex manuals do get away from old definitions of sexuality like those offered in romantic fiction and whether the break that some of them make between sex and romantic love really offers anything for women?

On the positive side, sex manuals have contributed to more openness about sex and 'sexual problems' and have continued to emphasise, as they did in the 1950s, that women can enjoy sex, which is at least something. Certainly in *our* mothers' generation this was not widely accepted.

At the same time, the underlying assumptions of many of these manuals have created false definitions of what the problems are and, therefore, have led to limited solutions. This is true of even the more helpful ones. *The New Sex Therapy* by Helen Singer Kaplan (Penguin, 1978), for example, describes a sexual therapy which involves activities like touching and caressing a sexual partner without pressure to perform sexually. This emphasis on general sensuality is perhaps particularly important for us as women. Kaplan doesn't simply assume that romantic love leads to sexual fulfilment, she also shows how social factors affect our sexual responses. She points out, for example, that a woman's failure to have an orgasm may be due to over-anxiety about pleasing a partner and that this anxiety is caused by the stress in our society on women's dependence on men. On the other hand, the book assumes that sexuality is solely something that happens between heterosexual couples rather than part of a person's general relationship to herself which can be expressed in many different ways and in different relationships. A woman, in other words, need not be innocent but, just as in romantic fiction, she is seen to need a man to complete her sexual identity.

In many other sex manuals the heterosexual couple is even more clearly accepted as a norm. Robert Chartham in *Advice to Women* (Tandem, 1971) describes both homosexuality and masturbation as 'poor substitutes'. In fact, Chartham sees the correct place for the expression of sexuality as being in marriage. But not only does he assume that heterosexuality in marriage is the norm, he also sees male sexuality as the standard against which all sexuality is judged. In Chartham's view, if a sexual relationship is not satisfactory then it is the woman who has to change. She has to become a more active sexual partner in order to prevent the man from going off in search of sexual satisfaction elsewhere. There is no indication that the *woman* might do this if *her* needs are not met, for, according to Chartham, women' sexuality is linked to her emotions. Men, on the other hand, are more concerned with the physical experience of sex, and therefore, 'by nature' are polygamous. In Chartham's book it might not be the man who teaches the woman about sexuality, as in the romantic novels. But it is still the man whose sexuality and sexual satisfaction is at the centre of the relationship.

Almost all sex manuals use the format of the expert on sexuality giving advice. Women's own experience is used to illustrate points rather than to make them. This form, in itself, tends to distort our view of female sexuality, obscuring its relationship to other aspects of our lives and implying a standard which each woman should measure up to. As Shere Hite puts it, in her Introduction to *The Hite Report*:

> Women have never been asked how they felt about sex. Researchers looking for statistical 'norms' have asked all the wrong questions for all the wrong reasons — and often wound up telling women how they should feel, rather than asking them how they do feel. Female sexuality has been seen essentially as a response to male sexuality. There has rarely been any acknowledgement that female sexuality might have a complex nature of its own which would be more than just a logical counterpart of (what we think of as) male sexuality.

*The Joys of Sex* by Alex Comfort doesn't adopt this formula of the expert giving good advice and, although edited by the expert (in the form of Dr Comfort), it is supposedly written by an anonymous married couple. It starts from the assumption that sex is fun, rather than that its readers have problems, and it manages to avoid making sexuality and emotions seem like one and the same thing, but only by avoiding the emotions altogether. Sexuality in *The Joys of Sex* is a series of fantasy games. Although the woman partner joins in these games, underlying the fantasies (which have names like Burglar and Maiden, Master and Slave, Sultan and Concubine), is the very clear assumption that not only is women's sexuality complementary to men's but it is actually subservient to it. The old myth, used in so many romantic novels, that women need to be swept off their feet, reappears in a thinly veiled and rather nasty disguise.

**Real life romance**

One thing is clear. The images of women created in romantic novels, in advertisements, and, indeed, in sex manuals, are miles away from the ways in which most women live their lives. This section of the chapter attempts to answer some questions about the way in which women really experience romance. What is the secret of its success? How can we account for its almost universal popularity, especially when most women know in advance that its pleasures pass so quickly, and that it's so clearly linked with the days, months, and years of drudgery which follow it? Is it that women and girls are simply fatalistic about the quality of life they expect and so welcome romance as a brief happy interlude — with open arms? Or do they see it as symbolising the high

THE PRINCESS HAS NEVER SEEN ANYONE SPINNING, AND ASKS IF SHE MIGHT TRY. NO SOONER HAS SHE TAKEN THE DISTAFF IN HER HAND, THAN A SPLINTER GETS UNDER HER FINGERNAIL, AND SHE DIES. HER FATHER LEAVES TALIA'S BODY IN THE PALACE, AND ABANDONS IT FOR EVER. SOME TIME LATER A KING IS HUNTING IN THE FOREST, FINDS THE PALACE, AND EXPLORES IT. HE IS ASTONISHED TO FIND IT DESERTED EXCEPT FOR THE PRINCESS WHOM HE TAKES TO BE ASLEEP. HE CANNOT ROUSE HER, YET FALLS IN LOVE WITH HER INSENSIBLE BODY. HE RAPES HER, LEAVES HER, AND FORGETS HER. NINE MONTHS LATER TALIA GIVES BIRTH TO TWINS, WHO FEED AT THEIR MOTHER'S BREAST. ONE OF THE INFANTS MISTAKENLY SUCKS THE FINGER THAT WAS PRICKED, AND DRAWS OUT THE SPLINTER, RESTORING TALIA TO LIFE. SOME WHILE LATER, WHILST HUNTING AGAIN, THE KING RECOLLECTS HIS ADVENTURE, REVISITS THE PALACE, AND REMAINS SEVERAL DAYS WITH THE PRINCESS.

"SHE'D BE BETTER OFF WITH A FROG!"

FROM A SEVENTEENTH-CENTURY NEAPOLITAN STORY.

points of their emotional lives — the joy of which is necessarily offset by the pain, hardship, self-sacrifice, and hard work that follows it?

It would be easy to argue that women have no choice; that the power of the media and its obsession with romance; that commercial pressures to buy romance objects (engagement rings, mementoes, wedding dresses and so on) and that institutional expectations (at school and in work) — all of these make it hard for women to avoid romance — it is so deeply embedded into the very fabric of their lives. The problem with this is, however, that women don't just blindly do as they are told by the media — nor do they automatically obey all the rules of romance. The way in which they do accept it, use it and experience it — is part of a complex social process — romance 'keys into' various aspects of women's lives and connects up with their subordination in a far from simple way. In this section we will try to make sense of these processes.

The most basic way in which romance operates is *materially* and this is particularly true for working-class girls and women. In other words, it relates to the very way in which women are forced to make a living, to survive economically and to 'make ends meet'. Let's put it this way. Women and girls are faced with dull uninteresting jobs, with little chance of good training, never mind promotion, and rarely if ever are they encouraged into the kinds of *collective* activity necessary to change this situation. It is not surprising, then, that most girls opt for the most easily available *individual* solution. Boy, romance, sports car, lazy weekend. In this context, girls are exercising a kind of limited choice; maybe they're just making the best of a bad deal, but there are none the less certain forms of action involved. Romance doesn't magically just happen. Rather, it's the result of unconscious choices, social pressures, and girls' and women's attempts to escape the boredom of everyday life. The problem is that while dreams and fantasies play important, necessary and pleasurable roles in our mental lives, they don't themselves promise any concrete solutions — and when they overtake reality they become stifling and oppressive.

Romance represents, then, a rational expression of, and response to, material and economic subordination. With wages never likely to cover the whole cost of their daily living expenses (rent or mortgage, food and bills, leisure and childminder), girls and young women must exploit their own 'natural' resources and thereby make sure that they are not lacking in romantic opportunity. There is more to romance than finance, but economics are a built-in component in all romantic relationships. If girls weren't aware of all these factors, they might well not pursue romance with the speed that they do. (My best friend at school used to refuse to reply to the letters from her boyfriend at boarding school — unless he included the stamps in his letters.)

This material element underlying most romantic attachments,

though basic, is not, however, its most prominent characteristic. This is rather its capacity to give pleasure to its participants. So what exactly are its pleasure-giving properties? Obviously its role in shaping dreams, escapes and fantasies is crucial here. But when it comes to everyday reality the picture isn't quite so clear. What we want to suggest is that girls and women can use romance to transform the more crudely *sexual* relationships offered to them by boys and men and make them more palatable for female consumption. That is, romance stresses all-over sensuality and gentleness rather than straightforward genital sex, it demands softness rather than aggression, sensitivity rather than 'screwing'. On top of this, girls' 'right' to romance means that they can demand that boys go through at least some of its motions to prove their commitment and this in turn works as a kind of lever in the power game in which in every other way they are disadvantaged from the start.

And so, to the extent that romance does satisfy some of the girls' and women's sexual needs, to the extent that it tips the balance of power slightly in their favour, and to the extent that it replaces tough, even brutal, sexual practices with softer more fragile ones, it can be seen to represent some sort of attempt to impose a more desirable set of images in the field of adolescent sexuality than those which are purely male defined.

In pointing to this active, negotiating role we are not, however, salvaging romance altogether. We are not saying that because women inject humanising elements into male sexuality in the guise of romance that this is the solution. Our aim is not to redeem it, but to put it in a real context. To put it in its social setting and watch how it works. And the first thing that should be said is that it's not *all* a matter of coincidence (bus-stop, wet day, she's there, I say 'Please share my umbrella' . . . that sort of thing). As a social fact, romance is subjected to all sorts of conventions and constraints. The most obvious of these is that boys and men make the first move, propose, buy the engagement ring and so on. But there are other less tangible factors in operation. Romances aren't embarked upon with just anyone and most girls go out with boys from the same racial background and social class and locality as themselves. They go to the clubs, pubs and disco's where they are likely to meet the same sort of boys as themselves, 'a nice type', as their mothers might put it, and all sorts of difficulties arise when this invisible set of conventions is broken. A 'no-gooder' is usually used to refer to a boy of lower social class just as 'a good catch' refers typically to somebody of slightly higher class. For a whole complex of reasons, most parents want their daughters to marry someone 'like ourselves'. So romance isn't quite a matter of fate; heiresses marrying dustmen, Cinderellas marrying princes are still the exception, never the rule.

Likewise, romantic encounters demand a lot of girls and women. Not only *being* in the right place at the right time but also *looking* 'just right'. The handsome boy at the local cafe may be able to get away with dirty jeans and greasy hair, but within romantic conventions girls must always be looking their best. As far as we are concerned the energy which girls are expected to put into the pursuit of romance is misplaced, to say the least. Girls are certainly not all shrinking violets, most know what they are looking for in a boyfriend and know how to try and find him . . . what we want to question is not the goal in itself but the amount of time and energy that must be invested in the search.

We have already described the way in which romance can be used as a kind of pleasurable counter to reality — a hope for a better life — a vision of partnerships based on caring, loving, and sharing, and not on him going out every night to the pub, to football on Saturdays and to his mum's on Sundays. Our suggestion is, then, that sometimes girls live out romance as a kind of antidote to their real lives, to what is, in fact, the boringness of going steady, of kissing in the back seat of his car and of listening to his tales of magnificence on the football field. What girls often do is inject a strong dose of melodrama and excitement into these liaisons and thereby make their own leisure (and school and work) more thrilling. A recent film by a German woman film director Petra Haffer, portrayed this process with great clarity. In *Madness. Life is all Madness*, the sixteen-year-old heroine finds her *Jackie*-type boyfriend but then when she gets disillusioned about his charm and passion she invents all sorts of roles for herself to play.

First, she imagines she is pregnant, then that she is abandoned by her hero, and then as an Ophelia, a great tragic heroine, she sits in class white-faced (lots of make-up) and red-eyed. She stays in every night waiting for his car to pull up outside the door and when it doesn't her drama is complete. Eventually she gets tired of this particular piece of theatricals and finds a new role. She plays hard to get, won't get into his car as he stops for her on her way home from school and jumps on the bus giving him a new independent wave! The pleasure which 'Karen Q.' derived from her romantic encounter lay much more in the dramatics which she wove around it and then related to her schoolfriends, than in the real thing.

But if romance can function as a fabrication — an embroidering on reality it can also provide a negative kind of pleasure — at least it's an improvement on the stage that went before. A real romance for most girls is an altogether better deal than a one-night-stand, a quick grope on the way home from the youth club and the fear of getting a bad name, which usually accompanies such adventures. The *fun* from being single has a lot more to do with *girlfriends* and *best friends* than with close encounters with the opposite sex, and when pressurised into conforming and finding a steady, most girls welcome *at least* the escape that this represents from the cattlemarket atmosphere which characterises the disco and even the pub. Unfortunately, in opting for a more settled 'loving' relationship with one boy, they are usually forced into abandoning their girlfriends and doing without the pleasure of hanging around with them, as Dorothy Hobson vividly illustrates in her chapter. What it comes to, in our society, is one or the other; you can't have your cake and eat it. A steady means no more flirting and fooling around with girlfriends at the disco, but it also means the end of more brutal exploitation by boys. It depends on fidelity, but insures against sexual abuse. Put so bluntly, it begins to sound like blackmail. Romance operates as a guarantee against loneliness, isolation and 'failure'. If all the girls in the class have a steady and go out in couples then joining the gang and finding someone who is understanding, friendly, sexy and so on, can be a relief, and in this sense maybe romance can seem like the end of the problem. With the security of her boyfriend, the girl need no longer worry about getting home late from the disco or the party; she need not fear the sexual danger which is involved in one-night stands; and, knowing that he will look after her, she can even drink more than her usual Babycham. In other words she can sit back and relax. Yet another kind of 'social contract' is in operation.

Hopefully we haven't totally demolished romance as a worthwhile pastime. It certainly hasn't been our aim to invalidate *all* close personal relationships with boys. And in so far as romance can mean warmth, sharing and fun, either as real experience or as fantasy, then maybe it's not such a bad deal. What we hope we *have* clarified are the disproportionate demands it makes on girls and the disappointment which it can result in. It's not that romance is a great conspiracy which allows girls some (strictly limited) fun; rather that it's difficult for girls to think of friendship or of sexuality with boys in anything other than romantic terms. And the terms invariably place women and girls in a subordinate role. If really understanding, loving, sensitive boys are so thin on the ground then maybe it's time we reassess the value of the search, maybe it's time we focused our energies elsewhere. In the next section we are going to look at some of the ways in which it is possible to step outside of romance and to challenge the conventions which surround it. Not just by making them more bearable, but by really doing something else, by refusing to follow the conventions. What we are saying next is that there can come a point where women can choose to reject romance because it ceases to be worthwhile negotiating compromises and it becomes worthwhile to break with it.

### Alternatives to romance. 'I've Got All My Life to Live!'

By now you may feel we are spoiling things by talking about them. On the other hand, if you've got this far maybe some of it makes

sense. But does it spoil things to talk about them? Talking realistically about romance doesn't necessarily mean removing the fun and excitement from the usual romantic scenarios — the first date, getting to know each other, going to the movies and so on. But it does open the way for overcoming some of its unambiguous pitfalls. In fact, talking with friends, attempting to separate out feelings of emotion from those of desire, finding ways of being frank with boyfriends and men about contraception, love-making, and the need for 'space' — most of all being realistic about the limits of romance, means you can in a sense have the best of both worlds — the fun and excitement without the unrealistic decisions that can result from relying on it uncritically.

First, we think that knowing more about love and sex than romance offers means that you can have a more honest relationship with your own self, and your body. You can admit that women have sexual feelings but, because of years of tradition, know very little about them and feel inhibited. You can quite easily experiment with your body, enjoy it, get to know it without the pressure to please anyone else. You can look in the mirror at your naked self; not through the eyes of men. Some women have tried exploring their bodies in small groups, with other women they trust, or with a close woman friend. Others would rather do it alone. It is important to be able to touch your body and learn what's exciting for you. Masturbation is a word that has strange connotations and is usually used anyway to refer to boys, but girls and women have just as much right to this kind of pleasure as men and boys and it's not just a question of getting to know your own body either. It is also important to get to know yourself, to find out what you are like, what you want and how you want to change. Girls are often brought up to please others, to look nice, to be a good daughter or to please boys. It takes a lot of courage to break through that and face what you really want for yourself, it can be quite scary, almost like daring yourself to take charge of what's going on, what's happening to you. You can feel or be made to feel selfish, but it's not selfish to work out what you want, it's a way of being honest and it's sometimes hard work. If your friends are doing that too then you've got a much more solid basis for friendship — you're starting off being open with each other instead of playing games 'I don't mind if you don't mind.' 'Suit yourself.' 'See if I care.' They can often be ways of getting other people to make decisions for you, and women have traditionally been encouraged into going along with this.

Just talking with close friends can be a way of exploring some of these things, so can spending time on your own. There is nothing wrong with choosing to spend an evening on your own. Sometimes keeping a diary can help — it's a way of talking to yourself and keeping track of your state (and changes) of mind. It's also private and privacy is not only valuable but well worth fighting for — like no one opening your letters — or the right to some space in your own home — if not physical space then some time when you won't be disturbed. Going out for a walk can be a way of getting this space. Or taking a bus ride. After all how can you find out about yourself if you're never alone?

Another question is boys. You may have been brought up to please others, but they've probably been brought up to be 'masculine', tough, self-sufficient and independent, free to decide how they want to enjoy themselves. In a group, boys invariably end up taking over and dominating and girls become the 'also-rans', a sort of audience for the boys. This is crazy, girls have just as much right to a good time as boys, why should they always provide an unofficial fan club?

One good thing about friendship groups is that you can get to know boys in an ordinary way, without the tramlines of romance. If you only think about boys in a sexual sense then it can be hard to get to know them as friends. There's such pressure put on all girls to get into a steady relationship with a boy as soon as possible. But that's a kind of tyranny and can prevent you from having boys as friends. After all it is possible to enjoy being with someone, talking, or doing things, without wanting an emotional or sexual commitment. Boys too get pressures put on them to see all girls as either potential girlfriends or 'nothing' and parents are sometimes the worst offenders here, making too much out of 'normal' friendships — they need this spelling out to them!

Of course, the best thing about friends is best friends. This book is full of tributes to them and those of us writing this know how important they are. You can almost map out your childhood and adolescence in terms of your best friends and what you did and talked about and felt. However, we don't want to imply that women never have problems between themselves. That, of course, is not true. But somehow these difficulties do seem easier to discuss openly and overcome, though this doesn't mean that *all* women automatically feel warm towards and want to befriend *all* other women. Indeed, what attracts' us to our friends is a mysterious process which we can't begin to dissect here.

We've talked so far about getting to know your body, your self and about making friends. We'll go on now to look at alternatives to the love 'n' romance number! Extending honesty to our bodies, our friendships and love, and generally to relationships with other people, can be hard, especially when feelings like these are always changing. Women can also be made to feel guilty about what is seen as self-centredness. But this is only because we have been brought up to believe that only by pleasing others can we ourselves find fulfilment or happiness. This goes along with the conventional idea of personal satisfaction through others — husbands, children, and family — and particularly through the institution of marriage. It's as though women are meant to be the emotional sponges to soak up other people's tensions and make them feel good. That's supposed to make us feel good. No wonder it's so hard for us to assert our needs, make our demands. We are always scared of hurting someone. But if we break through that image of ourselves and demand pleasure for ourselves, demand the right to be taken seriously, then we are cutting loose from that old idea of passive femininity. An example! One of us was both flattered and slightly uneasy about being asked out on a date by a male lecturer. She recognised the in-built inequality between their roles and didn't want to be the 'student' he happened to 'fancy'. After discussing it with friends she rang him up giving an alternative place and time that suited her. More generally, things like phoning or asking out are important, they show who is taking the initiative and the more equal a role girls play in these, the better will they be equipped for a more equal relationship. And this goes for the external *and* the internal dimensions of any 'romance'.

The way in which boys dominate in their behaviour also repeats itself in the way they talk. Who, for example, does the most talking? Who does most of the listening and sympathising? Who states their opinions most frankly? Is it possible to disagree, have an argument or discussion from a different position? Do you find you don't know what you think or feel when you are with him because it depends so much on him?

Who initiates touching and sex? And who makes their needs felt more easily? 'Am I just responding to his needs being the sort of partner I think he wants, guessing what that is; not beginning or finishing what I feel because it might make demands on him?' Sex tends to be an unquestioned idea. You do it, but it's not clear what this means. Often it seems to mean satisfying men. But are we satisfied or do we not dare try to answer that question honestly? Learning how to initiate and be active sexually with someone else is difficult, but the benefit of doing so is obvious, we can extend ourselves physically and emotionally, we can choose to make things happen. The main point, of course, is that we deserve enjoyment of our sexuality — everyone does. But it's also true that being honest about how we feel, admitting it, *does* mean a more open relationship, and one based less on dreams or guesswork and more on real knowledge and feelings about each other.

There are three other questions we want to address ourselves to in this part of the section. Lesbianism, multiple relationships, and celibacy. A lesbian is a woman who chooses to have sexual relationships only with other women. Although some of us writing this piece do have relationships with women as well as men, none of us are openly gay with all the social consequences that this involves. But we do know that people are not just born with a ready-made sexuality. Because we know that we learn our sexuality and that at some point women choose to become lesbian, we think it's right to raise the issue as one we all have to consider.

Lesbianism has been treated variously as a sickness, an impossibility, or a sin, so our conventional view of it tends to be negative and fearful. There are no laws against it because many men don't, or didn't, believe it exists. But women have been loving each other for centuries, sometimes sexually, sometimes not. This society expects everyone to be exclusively heterosexual and the conventional image of the lesbian is of someone who is ugly, strident, and unhappy. Girls' magazines sometimes publish letters from girls who think they may be lesbians, who have sexual feelings about girl friends or women teachers; the answer is usually along the lines of that given by Cathy and Claire in *Jackie*, 17 November 1979: 'At the moment you do seem to have a crush on Sheila and at your age that is perfectly natural. Attraction for boys will no doubt come in time too.' This attitude says that lesbianism is a phase that many girls go through and all but the unfortunate few come out into safe heterosexuality. In fact, it says more about the society that holds this view than it does about lesbianism itself. If our right to be sexual for ourselves, to express our sexuality in the way we want to without it being defined for us in relation to men, is worth fighting for, then lesbianism must be seen as a positive and possible choice. Lesbian feelings are not something we should all ignore in the hope that they will go away and leave us in peace as 'normal' women. They can, instead, make us question our own and everyone else's assumptions that we are automatically heterosexual for ever and ever.

Apart from this brief comment on lesbianism, the main focus of this article has been on relationships with boys. But we all know that initial passionate feelings change. After the first flush of desire is over, expecting total fulfilment from one person, especially for a long time, even twenty or thirty years, is unlikely, unrealistic. One way of coping with this — with the fact that although love and commitment to someone may grow sexual passion often doesn't — is to attempt to have relationships with more than one person openly. This means overcoming possessiveness and jealousy, that is, controlling and limiting someone else, and taking out your own insecurities on that person. This is hard, but it is possible; trust can build up as well as the opportunity of loving people without being smothered or without smothering. If this is made clear from the start, then a whole career of 'problems' can be, if not solved, at least aired, anticipated and accepted. At the same time, it is important that no one pushes you into doing what you don't want. Because men have always had more freedom to 'sleep around', they can find it easier to get into multiple relationships of this sort and can make women who don't want to feel guilty. They may have to be forced to discuss their feelings, and yours. You also need to be able to distinguish between genuine attempts to be open, and a situation where you're being manipulated or exploited. And you need to know in yourself whether any reservations you have are due to valid suspicion or a sort of conservatism. It's certainly impossible to try sorting this out on your own, and you need to talk to close women friends about it. While it's important to try to break down old, restrictive ways of relating to people, it is crucial not to be exploited.

It is precisely the smothering aspects of romance, wanting complete access to someone, that can end up its most oppressive feature. Lovers either think they own you and have the right to dictate what you can do, or else each partner becomes so thoroughly familiar with all the idiosyncrasies of the other that there is no room left for fun or exploration.

All of this doesn't mean you absolutely *have* to have relationships. But the availability of the pill and ideas of permissiveness have encouraged women to have sex, or sexual friendships often when they *don't* really want to. Right through their lives women are made to feel that they must have a man in tow to qualify as socially acceptable. But choosing to be on your own is not only really important *between* relationships, it is also a valid alternative in its own right. Women who have been in relationships and then choose to be celibate (i.e. not to have sexual relationships) often find they feel more in control of their own lives, deciding what to do and when to do it without immediately wondering how that will affect their partner. Men can drain off a lot of emotional energy from women and it can be very positive to be able to use that energy in relationships in general. In fact, women have been living independently in this way for years, but it still needs stressing as a viable alternative. That's not to say there are no problems about being on your own. You can be made to feel odd or un-sexual and sometimes you can genuinely feel the need for a close emotional relationship that's also physical. But it is also possible to be warm and close with friends without necessarily 'having sex' with them, and to enjoy the emotional contact without any strings being attached. Single, independent women, for instance, may choose to live alone or with friends, to have occasional affairs or to have children without combining that with living with or loving a particular partner. When you are a teenager you need to feel free to develop your emotional life at your own pace, without feeling you *must* have a boyfriend or that you *must* have sex and seeing celibacy as a real alternative can take the pressure off.

These ways of changing are just some of those we have encountered and there isn't room to talk more about them. At the end of the chapter we give the names of some other books that might help. What we want to do, finally, is to point to the things which make changing your life easier — once again friends, but also families and the question of 'free space'.

The first thing is friends. It is really difficult to change the way we relate without support from women friends. Discussing it all, thinking it through, talking about what's happened, what we've tried to do, what others are like, is very important. Girls and women have always done this, in a way. But if we combine this with the attempt to *change* the way we think about, and experience ourselves and other people, then this can be a real support. We've found that trying to change on our own is very discouraging and lonely. It can also mean that (especially if you're challenging, or rejecting, men) you can be thought weird, a slag, or whatever, even by other women — and you may come to take on those ideas about yourself out of lack of support from other people. But if a group of friends are trying to change together it's different; you don't feel unique or odd. And you can give each other strength to keep going, or in *your* turn reject a boy who can't cope with your demands. It's really good to feel strong against those 'normal' definitions of what's right!

Another thing that helps in this process of change is independent living conditions. It is hard enough to change — radically anyway, but it's even harder when surrounded by families, though, of course, it has been done. Parents often can't believe you're adult, and anyway they grew up themselves in surroundings where sex may not have been discussed except as something naughty (i.e. dirty) or clinical (i.e. clean). If it's possible to live away from home while you're single, it gives you a right to independence that parents have to accept. Sharing a house with friends, where each has their own room and you share kitchen, bathroom, and living-room, for instance, means both company and independence. The main problem is, of course, money. Many people don't earn enough to live away from home — in fact, employers often employ young people, especially women, exactly *because* they know they can pay low wages and expect parents to keep them for a low cost. But then there is the problem of getting a job at all — in many places this is exceedingly difficult with current high unemployment.

So it may be impossible to leave home even if you want to. At least this means you have to face your parents and try to change them, to some extent. Moving out can mean they don't get directly challenged, but go on thinking of you in the old way. You can also get support from, and support, sisters in the family and develop alternative ideas with them. In the past living at home has often meant being desperate to get married to get away, which is very understandable but it does mean escaping one man's house to live in another's! And the high divorce rate amongst young marrieds bears ample test to this. It's probably better to leave home and *live* with rather than *marry* someone, that way the same expectations of permanency, respectability, and probably children, would not be made, and if the relationship ends, the fuss and expense of divorce would be avoided and also the over-involvement of parents.

This means, too, that the decision about having children — whether or when to have them and under what conditions — is made, to some extent, independently of the decision about who to live with, and the need to leave home. Sometimes one way of leaving home and getting married is to become pregnant, but all this amounts to is escaping one oppressive situation by jumping into another, and this is certainly unfair to the baby who is being used as a power lever in a conflict in which it has no power whatsoever. Children, rightly, make a lot of demands and the decision to have them must take into account the needs of both mother and child. If living away from home is kept separate from the question of who to have relationships with, and when to have children, then these choices, when taken, will be positive ones. And the presence of children will be more realistically planned and looked forward to.

There are other problems about changing your way of life. Families are certainly one and we think you have to decide how long it is worth going on trying to change them, there may come a point when it is better if you can just cut your losses and establish an independent life. On the other hand, some of us have found that our families, especially our mothers and sisters, give us support and are willing to understand the way we want to live our lives and even question their own lives too. Another set of problems stems from the attitudes of boys. Some boys change easily, others cannot cope at all, or start taking it out on you. It probably depends partly on how the women in *their* families see themselves, and are treated. But of course, the wider society is sexist, dominated by men and masculine ideas, and this is reflected in jobs, schools, families, politics, newspapers, television, films, music. So most boys participate in that culture, and try to prove themselves 'men' in those terms. So you're likely to find them resistant to ideas of changing; you will need to have stamina! But most of all you will need to have friends. If your ideas are not just yours but those of your friends too, boys are in a much weaker position to ridicule or ignore what you demand. If *your* culture is strong enough, *they* can feel foolish for objecting. It is also true that boys may ridicule what they don't understand or haven't coped with between themselves — masculine 'togetherness' can be very threatening and competitive for individual boys. So getting a boy to understand and support what you're doing may be a long job. Again this is something that you may have to decide how much energy it's worth putting into.

Other problems relate to our own ambivalence about changing ourselves. We may find the struggle tiring, or not be entirely convinced we are right. Also, of course, our emotions have been formed over a large number of years, and though we don't believe in ideas of unchanging 'human nature', those emotions at times do feel pretty fixed. How do we change jealousy, for instance, or timidity? While we don't wish to deny the strength of these problems, it *is* true that support from women friends can help overcome them, or even prevent them arising. It's best, we've found, to admit them and then try and change — it's false to pretend to be perfect.

However, despite the problems, we personally feel good about the changes we have managed to make, and are still trying to make. This is not because of some abstract ideal, but because we're learning to be self-determining women who know what we want (more or less, anyway) and won't subordinate that to what men might want. We do have a greater sense of personal strength than we used to, we feel more adult, we have closer relationships with each other and other people. We're not so interested in doing 'what's right' or 'what's nice'; we're more interested in being and developing ourselves, and in changing the possibilities for other women, too. We're not saying we haven't got problems, but we do know we're getting stronger!

## Some other books to read

Unfortunately, we haven't got enough space to provide a comprehensive run-down on all those questions usually associated with sex education or 'the facts of life'. Instead, we're including a short list of those books we feel might be most useful. These are as follows:

Philips, Angela and Rakusen, Jill, eds, *Our Bodies Our Selves*, Pelican, 1980. Comprehensive and written in an open friendly tone, this British version of the original American edition provides an account of all aspects of our sexual lives, our health and our relationships. A necessary handbook!

Cousins, Jane, *Make it Happy*, Virago, 1978. Sub-titled 'What Sex is all about'. Especially good on contraception, pregnancy, abortion, childbirth, health, V.D. and the law.

Hite, Shere, *The Hite Report*, Summit Books, 1976. This is an American study of what 3,000 women of all ages said about how they experienced their sexuality (not what the experts told them they felt). It's very interesting and shows the importance to women of the clitoris for sexual pleasure, rather than the vagina.

# A NOTE ON LESBIAN SEXUALITY

*Trisha McCabe and Sharon K.*
Illustrated by *Charlotte Tucker*

We decided to write a separate piece on lesbian sexuality for two reasons. First of all, because when people write about sex and sexuality they usually mean (although they usually don't say so) heterosexual sex and heterosexuality. The authors of the previous article are careful not to make this assumption, but nevertheless it will probably be read in this way. In common sense sex *is* heterosexual. Second, it's not possible in our society for different sexualities to exist side by side in any simple way. Although we know that a very large percentage of the population is homosexual (some estimates are at least one in five people) that doesn't mean that everyone can happily choose whichever sexuality suits them and just get on with being themselves! Heterosexuality and homosexuality don't have the same status; our society is dominantly heterosexual and therefore being heterosexual is seen as normal. So what does that make us?

For lesbians, the position is even worse than for gay men. Some people even doubt whether we exist! We're surrounded by a culture – the mass media, education (and, of course, 'sex' education), families social life — which is exclusively heterosexual. We all understand heterosexuality, it's not something we learn about in a formal way it's just 'there', normal, obvious. We're not supposed to question it to make a choice about our sexuality; we're not even supposed to *have* a choice! You just *are* heterosexual — at least until you prove otherwise. Innocent until proved guilty?

Being a lesbian is seen as a problem. Being heterosexual isn't. The preceding chapter questions what sexuality is, makes romance and sex a problematic area of our lives, something to think about, question choose. It makes a nice change from only gay sexuality being seen as a problem, but isn't it funny how, on the whole, heterosexuality is something people have problems *with* but homosexuality and lesbianism are problems in themselves, problems *per se*.

Young women who have never had sexual experiences are assumed to be heterosexual. You don't actually have to *do* anything to be

heterosexual. Even if you've never done it, you know what 'it' is everyone, gay or straight, more or less understands what heterosexual sex involves, if only in its most stereotyped form. But how many heterosexual women understand lesbians? And why not? It seems odd to us, considering that women obviously have the capacity to understand other women's emotional and sexual needs. Otherwise, how on earth do we ever figure out our own? If we don't feel comfortable with our own bodies it's because we're taught to be sexual only for men, not for ourselves or other women. Which may be why so many women ask what do lesbians do in bed? No one ever asks what heterosexuals do in bed!

The only explanation we can come up with for this odd phenomenon — odd because how on earth do girls know what male sexuality is about and yet know next to nothing about female sexuality — is that all that everything, and everyone, from school books and teachers to magazines and workmates, ever talks about is heterosexual sex.

Given that most young women don't know much about lesbian sexuality, and yet seem frightened of or disgusted by this thing they don't understand, we thought that the best thing to do was to write a piece each about our own experience and ideas. They're very different in some ways — but then, contrary to popular opinion, we're not all the same, though we share similar problems. Just like heterosexual women.

### Sharon — one young lesbian's experience[1]

Many heterosexual women tend to think that lesbians are 'dirty'. have found this in my working and social life; whenever a lesbian is mentioned in conversation, the majority of women seem to be disgusted with the thought of it. You can't really blame them, though as society in all aspects has made them think this way.

Things can be very difficult for lesbians — in my job I have to lie about my social life. I have to use men's names to disguise those of women because if I were to say I was having a relationship with a woman the majority of the people I work with would just freak out. I find it extremely hard as I have to think every time I speak. I get so scared that something will slip out one day at work and the outcome would be unbearable to think about. I could just imagine all the girl I work with — they would just find me disgusting and even if I tried to explain it would make no difference. As exaggerated as this account may sound, it is completely true.

My family life is just the same and I feel awful about hiding my true identity from my parents. They are divorced and I live with my father who I have a very loving relationship with and would not like to hurt

Telling my dad just could never be as I know he wouldn't understand and therefore it would really hurt him. I did feel that maybe because I lived away from my mother I could approach her; I knew I had to confide in one of my parents. My mother being more open-minded, I thought it would work. I approached her very coolly. She was going on, as mothers do, about me settling down and getting myself a nice boyfriend so I just said, 'Mom, I'm gay'. At first it didn't sink in so I said it again.

'Do you sleep with women?' 'Have you ever been in love with a woman?' These were the sort of questions she threw at me. I felt so humiliated. If I was heterosexual and said, 'Mom, I'm going out with a fella' there would be no questions about my sex life. I am still the same person whether I'm gay or heterosexual. I just lost all my confidence and went to bed and cried myself to sleep. The next day I was so afraid to face my mother; we went shopping and the way I reacted was so stupid! When we went into a shop I was scared to look at a woman in case she thought I fancied her. Scared to look at a newspaper in case she thought I was eyeing up women. Then later came the accusations I knew she was going to throw at me.

'It's my fault, you're from a broken home.' 'You need a psychiatrist, you've been hurt by someone in the past.' I was so hurt; she made me feel as if there was something mentally wrong with me. I was so scared that she would bump into my dad because I was sure she would tell him, so I gave her some silly story about a phase I had gone through and now I was going out with a boy and everything was all right. Which brought me back to square one.

From this it may seem that lesbians have a rough time, but we have a wonderful time too. Maybe if I were older the situation with my parents wouldn't be so terrifying. Being a teenager I tend to feel less secure, maybe because I do not have much money and I rely on my father in more ways than one. But since I have come out of myself more I have met a lot of other lesbian women who are really great. We get on so well and have a really good time. If any of my friends or I have emotional or domestic problems we talk to each other and it is so nice to have people who are the same as me who are sincere and caring. I always feel a lot better once I've talked to them. Don't misunderstand what I'm saying, I have many straight friends too, but how can I talk to them about things when they either don't know I'm gay or, being straight, they can't really see the problems we face as lesbians?

I found, even before I let myself admit I was gay, that going out with my straight friends was too heterosexual for me; they, like everyone else, assumed that everyone is heterosexual. I remember when I was seventeen, my friends used to go on about their boyfriends and I really wanted to tell my best friend that I was gay because I was so

confused about what I could do. I knew about things like Gay Switch
board, but I didn't have the guts to contact them. So I told her I had
friend who was gay and she didn't know what to do. My friend totall
ignored what I said, so I just forgot it.

In contrast, with the lesbian women I know we go out in groups
as well as with lovers, and this makes me feel good because I can b
myself and that's what it's all about.

Many people say 'what do you get from a woman?' You canno
explain this, you just know. Being a woman I know what anothe
woman is like and likes, emotionally and physically. Women are a lo
more loving than men, in my experience. I can say this quite honestly
when I have slept with a man I felt like some sex object. They seeme
to have no interest in how you feel, they are always passing commen
about women's bodies, and what they would like to do to them. A
long as a man reaches his climax it does not matter how a woman feels
Many women who are heterosexual may find this absurd. If they enjo
sleeping with men, maybe they have found one who isn't as bad as that

One thing that really annoys me about straight women is that the
tend to think that if you're a lesbian you're going to attack them o
something. This is obviously not true. We have our likes and dislike
too — just because a woman is heterosexual, no one thinks she's goin
to go round jumping on every man she sees! Really, when people thin
that they're saying that we are going to behave like men, just becaus
we're lesbians! As for men, how many of them get off on just the ide
of women together? They feel that even when we say we're lesbian w
*still* belong to them. This is not true; we care about women, and w
only belong to ourselves.

### Trisha — different yet the same

Sharon's experience is in ways very different from mine. And in som
ways the same. I'm older than her so maybe taken more seriously
though sometimes I'm not so sure; people still think I might 'grow ou
of it'. I've also lived away from home for several years, which I thin
helps in the sense that my parents accept that my life is my own an
they won't interfere. I do have problems at work where, in lots o
situations, it's impossible to come out as a lesbian because peopl
would be horrified. Especially when working with young people, al
gay people have to counter the suspicion that they are out to corrup
those young people. Yet heterosexual workers aren't assumed to b
sexually interested in young people of the opposite sex. This is anothe
version of the 'watch out or they'll jump on you' theory. I do ge
support from my mother and sisters in particular, and my family'
acceptance of my sexuality is very important to me. In many ways i

makes up for the prejudice and ignorance I encounter in other people. I feel that my family has accepted my choices in every area of my life, and so have responded to my lesbianism in a relatively positive way. Big issues can be resolved, in my experience, if you and your family have achieved mutual respect. But being able to be myself with my family is different from the experience of most lesbians I know, so I think I'm very lucky.

But the point that we both want to stress is that our lesbianism isn't a problem to us, we see it as a very positive thing about ourselves and feel strongly that lesbianism and homosexuality should be presented to young people (and older ones) as viable forms of sexuality. The problem is actually other people, and society's attitudes in general, not us.

At the same time, we hope it's clear that lesbians aren't all the same, and have different experiences. My views are personal to me, and while my experience as a lesbian is obviously similar to other women, I don't expect every lesbian to agree with what I say, or feel exactly the same way I do. Our sexuality isn't the only thing that defines us; straight people seem to find this difficult to understand. They tend to have very stereotyped ideas about what 'a lesbian' is and forget that lesbians are secretaries, shop assistants, teachers, social workers, students, factory workers, not to mention being mothers or grandmothers, doing the shopping at the local supermarket, cooking the tea or delivering your post. Everywhere and everything, in fact. The problem is that women are defined in relation to sexuality: the most important thing you can know about anyone in our society is whether they're male or female. But if you don't fit into society's expectations of what women are — interested in men, marriage, etc. and available to men — then you're expected to be completely different from everyone else. Gay people are often treated as if we're a separate species!

This is clearest in the issue of lesbian mothers. Some people actually see being a lesbian and a mother as a contradiction — as if lesbians are so completely different from other women they can't possibly be interested in, have, want or care about children. But it's also to do with the idea that we are just 'born that way' (so everyone else is just 'born normal'?). Many women do go through heterosexual experiences, marriage or motherhood before discovering their lesbianism and choosing to relate sexually to women. Others choose to have children and bring them up with other women. Importantly, lesbian mothers often lose their children *simply because they're lesbians*. Their sexuality is seen as disqualifying them from motherhood (you didn't know there was a sexual 'means test' for mothers, did you?).

But having said that our sexuality isn't a total definition of us as people, I also have to say that being a lesbian is one of the things I

like most about myself. It's linked to every area of my life; I don't
stop being a lesbian when I get out of bed and go to work, shopping
or anything else. I don't put up with men making demands on me, or
comments about me, because I don't have to put up with it at home.
I don't just prioritise women sexually, but in every other way too.
Being a lesbian is a whole way of life for me, it doesn't stop or start.
Sexual relationships are part of that life, not separate from it. Lovers
are friends and sometimes friends are more important than lovers.
What is sex anyway? It's not something concentrated in your genitals
that bursts out every so often, it's not something reserved for after dark
in the privacy of your own home! Your sexuality is part of you, and
sexuality can be part of a relationship, but it's not separate and it's
not everything.

Being a lesbian to me means that I can be independent, no one can
tell me what to do, I make my own decisions. It also means caring for
other women, liking women, loving women. To do that I have to like
myself. You don't often hear women say what they like about themselves, it's always what they don't like; which bits are the 'wrong'
shape, what doesn't look right, what we do wrong. It sounds big
headed to say that you like yourself, but I don't really care; women
should be big-headed, we're nice people! Women have a lot of strength
and I've only found out about some of them since I came out. Not
having to put someone else first all the time means that you have the
space to find out things about yourself — the bad and the good. I've
stopped putting myself down so I don't like anyone else doing it to
me. And lesbians are put down a lot. We've tried to counteract some
of that prejudice, but this note is very limited. It would take more than
a whole book! Why do heterosexual people feel so outraged at the
mention of lesbianism? Why do they feel threatened, insecure, moral-
istic? What is so terrible about saying there is an alternative sexuality
to theirs? What's so wrong about having a choice? Maybe the people
who read this book, the teachers, parents, and the girls, will welcome
this opportunity to raise the issue, are genuinely concerned about
young gay people, won't bat an eyelid. Maybe pigs will fly.

We know that a woman does not need to have a man. We know that a child does not need to have a father. We know that no one needs to have the same lover for the rest of their life. . . . We know we don't have to make love unless we want to. We know our lovers because we know ourselves. We know that we can and will understand and control our own bodies. We know that most of what we've been told about sex and about women is a tissue of lies. We know we're not freaks. We know we're beautiful, sensitive, sensual and womanly. We know that women have always loved women, and that we'll go on doing it for ever. Angela Stewart-Park and Jules Cassidy *We're Here. Conversations with lesbian women*, (Quartet Books, 1977)

NOTE

1 Sharon can't use her full name here, because the risk to her job and her family life would be too great. A heterosexual teenager would be able to take the full credit for her work.

# 10 Learning to be a girl:

## girls, schools and the work of the Sheffield Education Group

*Anne Strong*

I have been working with Sheffield Women and Education group since 1977, and during that time we have done various talks, organised a travelling exhibition and written a pamphlet. We are also writing non sexist children's books with funding from the Equal Opportunities commission. I teach in further education and have practical experience in trying to teach sixteen-year-old apprentices the basics of women's studies! I also teach groups of girls. This chapter is based in part on my research into sex roles in children's literature. It is also linked to my experience as an active feminist and socialist.

Until recently, very little was written about how girls fare in our education system, what they learn in schools, and how they are treated differently, and generally do less well in schools than boys. The issue of class and schooling has been raised, Paul Willis's work (*Learning to Labour, 1977*), analysed the way in which working-class pupils (in his study they were all boys) have limited expectations and job choice because they are working-class. The boys themselves felt that the school regarded them differently, they complained that the career advice which the middle-class boys received was different as they would eventually go on to college, whereas they the working-class boys were destined for the local factory. In our society being born into a working class or a. middle class background has a great effect on future job chances and lifestyle.

However, another important factor — that of being male or female has until recently been overlooked. Education for girls has always been seen differently from that of boys; it has been argued that girls need a different education from boys as the boys would eventually go on to become the breadwinners whereas the girls would in most cases, go on to run a home and look after a family. Girls therefore did not need as long or as good an education as boys. These arguments still apply today in many cases, despite the fact that many

women are now equal or sole wage earners in their families. Recent high unemployment has led to calls for married women to give up their jobs to unemployed men who, it is felt, 'need' them more. These notions about women's work being secondary are still found in many areas of education as this chapter will later show. Other arguments which have been used in the past against educating girls have focused on 'women's nature' — it was felt that too much mental stimulation was bad for girls' health, and subjects such as maths and physics were too taxing for a girl's brain.

Sheffield Women and Education group are one of the groups throughout the country who are concerned with the education girls receive. Since 1976 we have been looking at different areas of education from a girl's point of view. We have looked at careers advice, subject choice, and other areas, finding out why girls in general do less well academically, and how the school reinforces ideas of male and female behaviour. In the way that Paul Willis pointed out that being working-class affected educational success, we wanted to show that being a girl also meant losing out in education. Some of our work has been concerned with making the links between sex, race and class, e.g. middle-class girls do better than working-class girls in general, and black girls tend to do less well than both. Classroom practice — what is actually taught to girls in schools, and how it is taught — has also been important for us. We are not only concerned with the subjects taught to girls, but the way in which the classroom operates to present girls with a picture of what a typical girl or a typical boy is. We refer to this as the 'hidden curriculum' — the school not only teaches girls formal subjects but behaviour as well — how to be female.

We know that education does not exist separately from the other institutions in our society that teach us how to be female — girls are very much influenced by families, friends, magazines and television. Similarly the jobs and roles girls are channelled towards are a result of the economic and political system we live under — until we change a capitalist society that needs women to do free child-care and housework and low paid jobs then we are only scratching the surface. There are important things that we can do to help make things better for girls now, and a list of suggestions for action appears at the end of this article.

The work we have done has been with parents, teachers and girls themselves. We have written and produced a pamphlet and written articles for magazines outlining our ideas. Local radio has also been useful for publicising meetings and conferences which we have held. Through girls themselves, parents and teaching unions, we have put together a picture of what schooling for girls is like today, and how it is changing.

### Wnat school used to be like?

> We try to educate girls into becoming imitation men and as a result we are wasting and frustrating their qualities of womanhood at great expense to the community, . . . . . . . . in addition to their needs as individuals our girls should be educated in terms of their main social function which is to make for themselves, their children and their husbands a secure and comfortable home and to be mothers. (Newsom Report, 1963)

Newsom wrote these remarks almost twenty years ago so maybe we ought to presume that things have changed. Certainly the history of education shows that the main idea was that girls were to be good wives and mothers. In fact, the entry of girls into full-time state education has been relatively recent. Before the 1870 Education Act made schooling available and compulsory for all children up to the age of ten years, schooling was done on a voluntary basis. This meant that most middle-class boys attended their public schools or had tutors, some middle-class girls attended boarding school or had governesses and most working-class children had little or no formal education at all. The kinds of tutoring that middle-class girls had was often more aimed at preparing them to be suitable 'catches' for some young man rather than being designed to further their knowledge. A girl was still not considered to need to know very much about the world, unless it was the world of decorum or household management. Many working-class children went to the local Sunday school as their only form of education, which was more concerned with teaching them how to behave and instilling 'morals' into them than actual knowledge. After all, they wouldn't use any real education anyway as the boys were destined for the factories in many cases and the girls the factories or shops and eventually the home.

Girls' education has been said to be dependent on three things; their social class, the demand for labour, and the prevailing notions of 'femininity' — what it is to be a girl. Rosemary Deem says that it wasn't the realisation that girls were entitled to an education that led to Acts such as the 1870 one, but rather that changes in the economy made it necessary for there to be a larger and better educated labour force. It was the new capitalist employers, e.g. the mill-owners in the North, who felt that education would provide a better and more reliable workforce. Girls of the working class weren't seen as delicate flowers like their middle-class sisters when it came to them working at the mill; the same notions of frail womanhood were lost in the need for profit.

So although the 1870 Act did provide formal access to school for girls, they didn't really benefit by it in large numbers. Some working-class girls were needed in the home, either to work in some form of home industry or to look after smaller children while their parents both worked. Many parents couldn't see the point of their girls being educated; they were never going to use it after all! They need not have worried; in fact, the education that most girls received at the time was much more centred on domestic tasks than on the arts or sciences. Suitable subjects for middle-class girls may have included 'a little French' or 'the arts' (nothing too taxing), but for working-class girls the emphasis was very much on how to run an efficient and frugal home. This idea that the home was the girl's future was summed up by Elizabeth Sewell in 1865 when she said that 'the aim of education is to fit the child for the position in life which they are hereafter to occupy. Boys are to be sent out into the world, to mingle with the bad and the good, to govern and direct. The school is the type of life they are hereafter to lead. Girls are to dwell in quiet homes, to exercise a noiseless influence, to be submissive and retiring.'

But in an age of mass poverty and overcrowding working-class girls found it difficult to live up to this shrinking violet image. None the less, they were still expected to benefit from this new education by learning how to provide a neat and tidy home, a home which would entice the menfolk away from the evils of the public house. Because of this, housecraft and needlework formed the main part of their education. Grants were given to schools to provide these courses for girls to do. The idea that girls might study the arts or languages was still seen as a waste of time.

The Hadow Report of 1926 even suggests that it was only the influence of girls in their home and family that kept the nation together. 'They [girls] should be shown that on the efficient care and management of the home depend the health, happiness and prosperity of the nation.' Elizabeth Sewell was convinced that the sorts of subjects that boys were beginning to do wouldn't possibly do for girls. She stated that, 'Her health would break down under the effort, and health is the obstacle which even under the most favourable circumstances must stand in the way of a girl acquiring the intellectual strength which at this age is so invaluable to a boy.'

Again this argument applied to middle-class girls more than working-class girls; compulsory education for girls often meant them doing housecraft at school as well as at home in the evening. The argument about girls' health is interesting as it is still used in many cases today. Girls' periods are often cited as the reason why girls behave in certain ways 'at certains times of the month'. They might be more clumsy at that time in the lab, or just moody and absent-minded in class. A 'Family Circle' booklet called *For Growing Boys* contains a picture of a school room with a girl as the central character staring into space and looking decidedly glum, the boy is told that this is due to her period which may make her 'uncomfortable or a little moody' — not conducive to good school work.

The argument that girls weren't capable of hard work, was in fact proved wrong by the school itself. Sue Sharpe points out that the report on the 'Difference in curricula between the sexes in secondary school' noted the overpressure of work on girls by physical and mental strain — the amount of housecraft they did at school was often phenomenal. The report also noted the strain on women teachers actually teaching the subjects.

At the beginning of the First World War, then, the education of girls was still based to a large extent on their future roles as housewives and mothers. But changes were beginning to occur, particularly in the field of higher education for girls. The advent of the war was a turning point for women in that they were needed to enter the hitherto male world of work. They only entered the war work late in the day and were often under the supervision of men, but it did represent for some women the move away from a career in the home. In the early 1920s middle-class girls began to have more scope in the world of paid work, entering professions such as teaching, secretarial work and nursing. This led to demands for a fairer deal in the education system

for girls and young women. The following is a quote from a book written about fiction in the two world wars which shows the new life many middle-class girls were beginning to lead. Rosalie, the character has been to boarding school and now:

> She's left the school! She's living in a splendid house in Pilchester Square looking for a post!
>     She's found a post! She's private secretary to Mr Simcox!
> She's left the splendid house in Pilchester Square! She's living an independent life! She's going to Mr Simcox's office, HER office, every day, just like a man! She's living on her own salary in a boarding house in Bayswater!

Unfortunately, Rosalie is from then on depicted as changing her character due to work, she becomes embittered, but then the idea was still very strong that women might not after all find true happiness in work. That was to be found in marriage. Very few women were encouraged to view their lives in terms of independence and a career. Education still laid official emphasis on girls' future training as wives and mothers.

Education reports well into this century have stressed the 'need' for girls' education to be linked to the home and the family particularly at times when the national economy is in a crisis or slump. After the Second World War, when again women had worked in large numbers, came a re-emergence of all the old theories of maternal deprivation. Women going out to work, it was (and still is) argued, would lead to their children growing up unstable, neurotic and goodness knows what else. Housework must be seen by women as an important job, one that could benefit the country and ensure healthy, happy children.

In the *Education of Girls* (1948), John Newsom argued that girls who were unenthusiastic about housework needed all the more a good domestic education to make them aware how important that work was. He argued that the economy needed the education of girls to be based on the home, after all they do this well and shouldn't regard this unpaid and low status work as inferior to men's work.

The ideas of Newsom and others then provided the basis on which education for girls entered the period of the 1960s. The introduction of the comprehensive system was meant to reduce inequalities in the school system by offering equal access to good state education for all. But if we actually look at the education of most girls today, do they get their equal share of access to subjects, equipment and resources? Do girls get as good a deal out of the system as boys?

## Girls and schooling today

Reforms such as the Sex Discrimination Act of 1975 have, it is argued, opened the path to equality for women. The Act has the capacity to cover the area of education, if girls are discriminated against in the school system then they can make a case under the Act. Even if we accept that the Act may provide formal equality for girls within the system, the fact remains that girls still do different subjects from boys and still do less well academically in general. Research carried out into subject choice shows that strict ideas on 'girls' ' and 'boys' ' subjects still exists. It is also presumed that girls' interests within a subject will be different from boys'. As a Sheffield history teacher remarked to his mixed class, 'This year's course should have something to interest everyone as it has battles and wars for the boys, and dress and food for the girls.'

A quote from *Spare Rib* also outlines this feeling that girls' interests will be different, 'In an art lesson once the (female) teacher said "To-day we are going to draw aeroplanes. The ladies (sic) may like to draw birds instead." I drew an aeroplane.' The ideas behind those statements — the reasons why the teachers felt that girls and boys would have different interests is what I want to deal with next. To do this, the whole way in which girls are taught in schools, from primary to further education, needs to be looked at. As this book is aimed at older pupils, many of the examples from primary school may no longer seem important, but they are part of the way in which the total education system, right from the start teaches girls to be girls. I'm sure they are still probably familiar to most of us; they still are to me.

### Primary school

By the time children enter the school at the age of five they have already begun to learn appropriate behaviour for their sex from their parents, grandparents, etc. Can you remember being told 'It's not ladylike to climb on things' or 'Don't mess up that dress, sit quietly' while the boys in the family were told 'Big boys don't cry' or 'Boys don't play with dolls'? Parents have ideas of what a 'real lad' or 'a proper little lady' is. Girls are allowed to be tomboys while they are young, but boys aren't really allowed to be 'cissies.' When the child gets to school they may find that the teachers too treat boys and girls very differently. There are still some schools whose structure differentiates between boys and girls, e.g. separate boys' and girls' playgrounds. We were told of one school where the divide was a painted yellow line across the yard which the children crossed at their peril! Teachers will say that girls and boys don't want to play together, or boys play too 'rough' for the little girls. Can you remember 'boys' tables' and 'girls' tables' in the classroom? Teachers will point out that it is difficult to get the boys and girls to sit together, but this is understandable when a favourite threat to boys who are misbehaving is 'I'll sit you with the girls.' A fate worse than death apparently!

Another area in the primary school that is often sex-typed is, in fact, play. Play forms a large part of children's lives when they are young; they are learning how to play roles. So what roles do girls learn in the primary school? Teachers will expect boys and girls to play with certain toys and become worried if they don't. How many teachers are happy to let their small boys dress up in frocks from the dressing-up box, to play with the dolls or the Wendy House? Yet small boys often do like to dress up, and why shouldn't they learn how to 'hold baby.' If we examine the advertising for toys, they are certainly sold as sex-specific toys. 'Boys' ' toys are the guns, boats, trains, building toysets. Girls' toys are the dolls' prams, paints, cookery sets, etc. At Christmas in many infant schools the toys 'from Santa' are wrapped in blue and pink paper to ensure that no girl gets a gun or no boy gets a bracelet! It is presumed that boys and girls at play are interested in totally different things. If a girl or boy steps over the line, it may be cause for concern; why should a boy be interested in a dolly and the dressing-up box unless something is 'wrong'?

Similar patterns can be traced right through primary education.

The infant school schemes most widely used are the ones that depict the boys playing with friends, climbing, riding a bike, making decisions, telling little sister what to do, and playing at being 'daddy'. The 'little' sister on the other hand is told what to do, rides a small bike, plays with dolls, prams, in the Wendy house making tea for brother and his friends and playing at being 'mummy'. Mothers and fathers in the schemes are also shown in traditional men's and women's roles. Dad goes out to work, drives a car, does the garden, makes decisions and reads the paper. Mum on the other hand is shown as a housewife, making beds, cleaning, cooking, looking after the children and the house.

These images are not even a true reflection of society. Many women do go out to work, do drive cars, dig the garden and make decisions, all these are not only done by men. Some men do look after children and do the shopping, but not in most reading schemes. In *One, two, three and away* the boys are engaged in an adventure in a boat which sails off down the river. The girl, Jennifer, appears only briefly in the story, and then only as a spectator, she takes no active part in the adventure or the rescue. It simply says 'Jennifer was with them.' On many occasions in reading schemes the girls are shown as passively watching the boys, following their lead.

A reading scheme in common use in schools is 'Ladybird'. They have actually of late begun to look at their books and produce less stereotyped images which needs encouraging. Unfortunately, their actual learning to read scheme is guilty of very stereotyped images of women and girls. Here is a quote from the scheme. 'Jane likes to help mummy. She wants to make cakes like mummy. "Yes I will be mummy and get the tea" says Jane. "I like to get the tea." Peter helps Daddy to make a big fire. "I like this work" says Peter.'

### 'I'm not having girls in my metalwork room': girls in secondary education

Some schools have a common curriculum up until the end of the second or third year. Before this everyone does science, cookery, etc. But even in schools that have this common approach the picture changes when it comes to exam subject choice. The fact that teachers share certain assumptions about male and female roles does mean that they will encourage girls and boys to do particular subjects.

Work done by women in Manchester pointed out that the whole image of a scientist for example is seen as the wrong image for girls: 'For adolescent girls, anxious to be recognised as feminine, the image of the scientist is unlikely to be appealing as it conflicts with society's ideal of womanhood.' What they mean is that the scientist is supposed to be cold and realistic, whereas girls are supposed to be more emotional and led by feelings.

Many schools do offer all subjects now to girls and boys to comply with the law, but there are still all sorts of pressures on girls to do traditional subjects, not least that they want a job at the end of it. After all, secretarial subjects are still more likely to get a girl a job at the moment than technical subjects where jobs are short.

Eileen Byrne has produced figures that show that while schools offer subjects to both sexes, barriers do deter girls and boys from doing non-traditional things. For example, Department of Education and Science statistics showed that in the case of physics in secondary school the figures were as follows:

*Percentage of pupils being offered access to subject*

|         | Single-sex schools | | Mixed schools | |
|---------|------|-------|------|-------|
|         | Boys | Girls | Boys | Girls |
| Physics | 85   | 62    | 91   | 75    |

while the percentage of pupils actually taking the subject was much lower for girls.

*Percentage actually taking subject*

|         | Single-sex schools | | Mixed schools | |
|---------|------|-------|------|-------|
|         | Boys | Girls | Boys | Girls |
| Physics | 51   | 14    | 47   | 11    |

It isn't enough, then, for schools to offer formal equality; positive discrimination to get girls to do 'boys' subjects' is needed as well as lots of support from sympathetic and feminist teachers.

## Girls and further education

An article in *Spare Rib* recently also pointed out that even when girls do manage to make it to college or university they are still treated differently from the men. Many complained of the patronising attitudes of the male tutors who still didn't feel that the 'girls'' work was on a par with the 'men's' even though they had the same qualifications.

Similarly girls who go on after school to technical or further education college will find that the attitudes they came across at school still apply there. In further education or technical colleges, girls still predominate in catering or secretarial work, whilst most of the engineers are boys. In my technical college some floors, i.e. the engineering and science departments, only have men's toilets on them while other floors, i.e. business studies and catering, only have girls' toilets on them.

Girls who decide to do apprenticeships at technical colleges find that the attitudes of most male teachers (or lecturers) are far from encouraging. They may well find themselves the only girl on the course, which presents problems. A girl painting/decorating apprentice in a further education college in South Yorkshire said, 'Well it's hard, you have to do things better than them, if I do something wrong, you know, mess something up, then I think they'll laugh at me, I think it's because I'm a girl.' This feeling that in order to do well the girls had to be careful all the time was very strong. Any mistakes by the boys were just mistakes any one could make, but if a girl did it, then it was further proof that girls couldn't really cope with it.

### Sheffield Women's Film Co-op

Sheffield Women's Film Co-op have produced a film about a girl who wants to be a motor mechanic. The film deals with the problems 'Pat' has, with the careers teacher and advisor who is helpful but eventually persuades Pat to take a job in the 'Parts' Department, rather than a garage workshop. The film shows the reactions of Pat's dad — 'That's no job for a girl' — and mum, and the reactions of her friends 'You wont be able to wear nail polish' and 'Tha'll get all muck down finger nails' being typical. In fact, her friends think the pay must be 'dead good' to induce Pat to do it. No one really understands why a good-looking girl like Pat wants a dirty job like that. In the end Pat does give in, no one will give her an apprenticeship so she does end up working in Parts — behind the garage giving out exhaust pipes, etc. to the mechanics. Not really what Pat originally wanted.

### What can we do about it?

Sheffield Women and Education have been working around ways of emphasising the role of girls in education and doing something about it. The growth of the Women's Liberation Movement over the past ten years has made ideas of women's equality more public, and some progress has been made. It's not only a question of differences in girls' and boys' education. The education of middle-class girls, especially in private education, is still very different from that which working-class girls are offered. In general their job choice is wider and more will go on to further education. Often the facilities at middle-class schools are better — this raises the question of single sex education. Some feminists argue that girls do better in girls' schools. Certainly in my single-sex school girls doing well in science was seen as normal as there were no boys to compare with, or to provide the idea that it wasn't really for girls. But do they solve the problem? Perhaps a better solution is to suggest single sex provision in subjects for girls/boys new to the academic area.

Another distinction needs to be made between black and white girls at school. Recent reports have pointed out the differences between black and white pupils' achievements and certainly black girls do less well in the academic and job market than white. The whole question of sex is bound up with class society and yet it is impossible to completely solve it purely within the terms of class. We need a total change in society to resolve all these inequalities. But there are positive things to be done. Here are some of the suggestions from Sheffield Women and Education.

### What teachers can do

1 Raise the issue in the unions.
2 Make changes in lessons and at school.
3 Organise women teachers' groups — it's difficult to make changes on your own.

### What girls can do

1 Organise a girls' group — the same thing applies.
2 Complain to teachers about their language and attitudes — preferably as a group!
3 Invite speakers in to put a different point of view — *Spare Rib* often has ideas, and so have local women's groups.
4 Use what literature, magazines, films, etc. you can get hold of — such as the Sheffield Women and Film Co-op's *Jobs for the Girls* or 'Building your Future' video by Women in Manual Trades, if you don't get good careers advice. Make them sit up and listen!

### Useful contacts

1 *Spare Rib*: monthly women's liberation magazine, 27, Clerkenwell Close, London, EC1.
2 Sheffield Women's Film Co-op: for *Jobs for the Girls* — available for schools to hire; c/o 34, Psalter Lane, Sheffield, S11.
3 Women in Manual Trades: helpful for girls intending to do non-traditional jobs. South of England: c/o Jessica Datta, 40, Dale St, London, W4. North of England: c/o Tess McMahon, 51, Hirst St,

Burnley, Lancs. Scotland: c/o Joan McLelland, 20, Stanley Rd, New-haven, Edinburgh.

4  Young Women's Magazine Group: c/o Paula Frampton, 4, Essex Rd, London W3.

5  G.I.S.T. — Girls into Science and Technology: c/o 9a, Didsbury Park, Didsbury, Manchester.

6  C.A.S.S.O.E. — Campaign Against Sexism and Sexual Oppression in Education: c/o Liz Wynton, 17, Lymington Rd, London, NW6.

7  Women and Education Newsletter: c/o 14, St. Brendans Rd, Manchester, 20.

And last but not least:

8  Sheffield Women and Education: c/o 29, Parkers Rd, Sheffield 10.

# 11 Working with girls:

write a song and make a record about it! [1]

*Monika Savier*

Translated by *Patricia Harbord*

In West Germany as in England, feminist youth work with girls is a relatively new field. The following article portrays the practical and the political problems of setting up a girls' group in a youth club (in this case in West Berlin). The author *MONIKA SAVIER* has been working on girls' projects for several years and has written many articles on this subject. I have translated the article in order to add an international perspective to this book. I have been involved in youth work in West Germany as a vacation job and am at present about to begin an MA in European Cultural History at the University of Warwick.

Patricia Harbord

Tina Müller emptied her pigeon-hole in the office, tore the label with her name on it from the edge of the shelf — she couldn't remove the feminist symbol which the girls had scribbled next to it in biro — then she picked up her guitar, which stood in the corner, and moved towards Hans, who was sitting watching her. She handed over her keys and said, 'I learnt a lot from your mistakes, so really I ought to be grateful to you. So long!'

She had worked in this youth club for two years. At first she had been a probationer, and afterwards she had stayed on because a permanent full-time post for a youth-worker had become vacant, and she got on well with the men and women who were her colleagues.

When, at the end of her probationary training period in the youth club, she decided to accept the post as a youth worker, she announced quite spontaneously during the final discussion with the team that in future she wanted to concern herself more with the problems of the girls at the club. She met with no opposition whatsoever from the team of youth workers — on the contrary, her colleagues, both male and female, all declared themselves well-disposed towards the idea. But one of the women in the team said, 'I've been thinking about that,

199

Photograph by
*Pam Bloor*

too, but I didn't expect you, of all people, to bring it up before I did!'
Tina Müller was startled; she hadn't wanted to compete with this
woman and had the feeling that this was a bad start for a girls' group.

In the following week Tina Müller began to rush about like a whirl-
wind. She got out her address book and leafed through it to find the
addresses of women she knew from her training course or from
women's bars and who she imagined might already have given some
thought to the problems of doing youth work with girls. She made
phone calls and appointments, was given tips about what she could
read and began to realise how naively she had set out into this field.
Gradually she began to sense that she had to sort out for herself just
what she was hoping to achieve, and that she had to prove to the team
that she could 'succeed' in establishing some kind of rapport with the
girls. She realised that this thing she had just started out on had a great
deal to do with her as a person, and that it was going to demand greater
emotional involvement on her part.

Full of determination, Tina had 'working with girls' put on the
agenda at the next meeting of the team. 'Is it a quick one, can we deal
with it under "organisational"?' asked Heiner, whose turn it was to
take the minutes.

Tina was startled. Though she knew she couldn't say very much
about it yet, the girls' group really wasn't an organisational problem.
She gulped. Heiner just sat back and waited. 'Hey, I wasn't trying to

Photograph by
*Pam Bloor*

reduce your problem to a question of organisation, Tina,' said Heiner amicably. Tina couldn't bring herself to look at him, she hated his condescending friendliness. How dare he say it was her problem? What did he really know about it?

Then she pulled herself together and returned his friendly gaze. 'Yes, you're right, I'd say the girls' group is initially an organisational problem, well, rooms and so on. . . .'

'Right, then let's start with that right away, at least we've finally got something new to talk about around here,' said Elke, who had become deputy leader a few months ago. Tina knew Elke was looking for new ideas and new approaches to her work, but she didn't have complete confidence in her, for she had never known Elke to tackle anything which wasn't guaranteed to impress the men in the team. If she had occasionally put forward ideas of her own and stood up for them, if she had taken the risk of being more detached in her dealings with the others, the men, she certainly wouldn't have been accepted by them into their little intellectual circle.

Elke spoke, jolting her from her thoughts. 'I'd be very surprised if you could get the girls interested in anything other than the boys. If you can succeed in doing that, then finding a room certainly isn't going to be a problem. For instance, you could go into the music room once a week and talk there.'

'I don't know yet if talking to the girls is going to be the best way of getting something started, but it's great to have a room for the group, anyway. I'll print a notice for the girls, and speak to them individually as well. The girls like the music room anyway, it's comfortable, and the boys hardly ever go in there, because there's never anything going on in there,' said Tina.

'Did I get you right, Tina, you did mean that the boys can go into the room while the group's in there, didn't you?' asked Hans, the leader of the team, who had been appointed to the post by the local council.

'Why do you ask?' replied Tina evasively. 'Well, you know, I've heard from other clubs about girls' groups, I think it's a trend which has to reach every club sooner or later, and now it's arrived here, but, thank heavens, I've already had a chance to think it all over in depth. Well, all I wanted to say is that every colleague I've spoken to said that the boys aren't prepared to stand for being shut out of one of the rooms, so they try to get in anyway, and when they start trying the odd door gets broken down now and again. . . .' Hans laughed at his own casual manner — 'and you know how much money we may still have to spend on repairs this year, so I think we'd better just leave the door open right from the start, Tina,' he added, turning to her and giving her a friendly smile.

'How are the girls supposed to talk about their problems if the boys are there?'

'But it's when the boys are there that they'll learn to fight, isn't it? Aren't they supposed to be learning to put up a struggle, or have I misunderstood your feminist ideas? How are they supposed to do that if they haven't got anyone to learn to assert themselves against?' Hans was getting more and more engrossed in the subject, he was almost on the point of suggesting he should work with the girls himself, as he already had his ideas all worked out in concrete terms; what was more, he was rather taken by some of the girls, he found them very attractive, and he knew they liked his 'fatherly' manner. Although that was just what often infuriated him, for as a social worker, and the leader of the club into the bargain, anything which might have gone on between him and the girls was prohibited, and of course the little devils had figured that one out a long time ago. They took liberties with him, and in fact he often did them favours, but he had to remain sexually neutral, and he wondered whether that wasn't just what the girls liked so much about it all. . .

This time it was Tina Müller who jolted him out of his thoughts, 'Of course the boys are going to have to keep out, or what's the point in starting a girls' group? It's not just going to be confined to the appointed times, from five to seven in the evenings, either, a few things will have to change around here. It's precisely the fact that the boys will try to get into the girls' group which makes it particularly important to support the girls in keeping the boys out of their hair just once in the week. . . .' Tina was almost shouting, and there were tears in her eyes. Franz, one of the probationers, took her by the arm. 'If you're going to get so worked up one might almost think that it affects you personally. No one here's against the girls' group. Even Hans was for it, you heard him say so. And if the only problem is whether the boys can take part or not, then I'd suggest that I hold the motorbike group with the boys at the same time, most of them want to join in with that anyway, and they find that much more exciting than fussing about what the girls are doing, so we'll just be distracting their attention.'

Elke: 'But you certainly won't be able to solve the problem like that on a long-term basis, Franz; I also believe that the youth club should be at the disposal of all young people, we don't tell the Turkish people that they can't take part in particular events, of course, but somehow we've got to sort out just what this girls' group is supposed to be leading to, then we can talk about the organisational aspects too.' The question of the direction which their educational work ought to be taking was all too familiar to Tina — whatever the problem they were discussing, it was always used to stifle the topic whenever things got complicated. For everyone present knew that it was better not to ask questions about directions or goals in their team. The ideas of any given member, in so far as he or she had any at all, were bound to be different from those of the others. But it always sounded so clever to imply that one was also in pursuit of 'the fundamental objectives. . .'

And, sure enough, Heiner immediately inquired: 'I thought we were supposed to be dealing with this topic under "organisational"?' He was getting impatient, as he didn't really know if he had minuted the general feeling of the meeting. 'Elke's right, Tina should start on her work anyway, and then if there are difficulties, well, then we can give the thing a bigger spot on the agenda.'

That evening Tina had arranged to meet two women who were youth workers in a girls' home.

'Well then, let's hear what you're doing with the girls.'

'Well, it's like this . . .' Tina became embarrassed. 'I haven't actually started yet. I was at a meeting of the team today, and to start with I had to stand up to Hans, that's our custodian of order and expounder of so many pedagogic principles. I soon noticed how very subtle the resistance of the men in the team is to youth work placing an emphasis on girls. They don't say no straight out, they want everything to continue in the same old way, so instead they relieve themselves of the problem by reducing it to a question of rooms, or they say: "Tina, aren't you identifying yourself with this problem a bit too much?"

Because they realise that the problem really does concern me and that this in itself makes me vulnerable.'

'If you're starting up a girls' group now,' said Gerda, 'the best thing for you to do would be for you to sort out for yourself why you want to work with girls, and then just let reality take hold of you. If you don't think it's too much trouble you should get yourself some more information, too, by reading some more and talking to other women about it, ideally to women who are working with girls themselves, oh yes, and read the article which some women from Frankfurt wrote in the *Sozialmagazin*, September 1978.'

'I'd rather you told me what I should do with the girls on Friday, if anyone comes at all,' said Tina.

'Well, in weather like this I'd go out to a lake with them and get them to talk about mothers, for instance, or just about the situation of women in families. You should make them aware that you find women important and that your support extends even to their mothers. . . .'

'And to their grandmothers, if necessary,' Anne interrupted her.

'But why, a lot of them get really bad treatment from their mothers?' Tina asked.

'Right, and now along you come, as a wonderful girls' youth worker, and of course the girls think you're much better than their mothers, because in their eyes you're often just how they imagine a "liberated" woman to be, you can pick and choose your relationships with others, select your dependencies, you've got more social prestige than their mothers, and what's more, what you do to earn a living seems much more significant to them than the underpaid, undervalued, messy drudgery their mothers do. At home the girls rave about you and blame their mothers for being personal failures, just because they're not like you. The mothers'll probably react by getting angry, well, I'd react angrily, anyway, and rather competitively, too, most likely. Once it's got to that stage then you have hardly any chance of approaching the mothers any more, and in practice you'll hardly ever find fathers acting as responsible parents, at least not in the kind of environment you're dealing with.'

'Anyway,' Anne chipped in, 'it would be ridiculous if you accepted the rift between you and the mothers and didn't take the opportunity of involving them in your youth work with the girls, at least with regard to what the project consists of, while in other places — through the "Volkshochschule" [adult education college], the advice centres and so on — there are lots of women developing a feminist approach to working with mothers, and it's these same mothers they're working with.'

'OK, but the mothers often really aren't so very wonderful, am I supposed to tell the girls: "Grow up to be like your mothers?" ' Tina objected.

'No, you don't understand. The girls are meant to train for something and get a qualification, they're meant to learn to fight for an
improvement in the quality of their living conditions, but not in isolation from their mothers.'

'It's all right for you two,' groaned Tina, 'you only have to sit back
and react to events nowadays, but I've still got to find my feet — and
get the whole group off the ground, too.'

Photograph by
*Pam Bloor*

'The girls' group has been going for weeks now, Tina, and at every
team meeting you say you can't really tell us anything about it yet.
Could it be that you don't wish to discuss the matter with us any
more?' asked Hans pointedly.

'Of course I do — I'm trying to find out what's mutually important
for the girls and myself and to work out where and how we can go on
from there in concrete terms, trying to discuss the things we're doing
and to have fun at the same time, too,' replied Tina.

'I see. And what does all that mean, in practice?' asked Heiner
irritably. 'Perhaps we might be allowed to participate in your learning
process, because we'd like to support the girls too.'

Photograph by
*Pam Bloor*

Tina replied calmly: 'I think you'd do better to start some kind of discussion with the boys, they could really use it. If you want to support youth work with girls, then you ought to set the boys an example of an alternative male role, rather than worry about what the girls are doing. Instead of acting Mr Specially Nice Guy with that extra special sensitivity towards girls, I think you'd do better to start whittling down the boys' privileges. Why haven't you got the courage to put a few restrictions on their proprietary claims on the rooms, the girls, the billiard table and a sympathetic ear from all our colleagues here?'

'Now just a minute,' said Hans, 'next you'll be saying that we give preferential treatment to the boys, and it's our fault that what your girls most want to do is run after the boys. . . .'

Hans was sharply interrupted by Elke. 'What's that little gem supposed to mean, Hans? Tina's only just begun what she's doing, are you trying to employ some kind of time-scale to assess any noticeable change in the youngsters' behaviour, and if so, what's the time-limit? It takes three weeks in your music group till the kids who're taking part learn a single chord, and that sort of thing's a lot more concrete! Anyway. I was talking to two girls from the group. Whereas before they used to be under enormous pressure to tell me all about how marvellous their boyfriends were, now they don't seem to find it so central any more. They were telling me about a musical they're planning; it's about a girl who doesn't want to go to school any more, because she gets discovered by a record producer who wants to make her a pop singer, and about all the various things she goes through from then on . . .'

'Oh yes, and who's playing the producer? Could it be you, Tina?' Heiner was trying to be funny.

'The girls have no trouble playing a boy, on the contrary, they know every nuance of male behaviour. But maybe we'll take a boy for the part anyway, as it's an extremely repulsive one, and none of the girls wants to go near it — because whatever you think, what we're trying to achieve isn't merely a question of a crude exchange of roles,' said Tina cuttingly.

'Tina, I can't take any more of this aggression of yours. You're deliberately provoking us, and Elke's taking sides with you, what's more, though all Hans did was to ask a perfectly dispassionate question about what you and the girls are doing in this group. In fact you've been changing a good deal recently — I don't know whether I should congratulate you on your new self-assurance or whether I should conclude that you've been dishonest with us, because some-how you've been keeping something from us all the time — anyway I don't remember your ever being like this before. I'd be glad if we could start getting on with each other again as well as we used to a couple of months ago. If we're going to try to fight back against the oppression of girls, then it's no use fighting amongst ourselves. So, please, Tina, be your old self again!' Franz was gazing at her sincerely, he really meant it.

'Do you really believe you've got nothing to do with this oppression?' asked Tina quietly, 'do you really think that everything's differ-ent here in the team? If we really agree about what we're doing, then you've got to direct your opposition at men who are maintaining oppression, and not at women who are exploring new ground. May-be you should start by accepting that my problems are different to yours and that we're only getting in each other's way with our diver-gent expectations.'

'Oh, please, let's not turn this into a self-analysis session,' Hans interrupted. He hadn't heard everything that had been said and was afraid there was something going on behind his back. 'We've argued enough, now let's start being sensible again. We've still got to work out the duty schedule for a whole month.'

Tina Müller was on day-duty. It was six o'clock and the club had only been open for an hour. A few twelve-year-olds were playing cards in the entrance hall, and there were only a few kids in the coffee-bar. Outside on the wall in front of the club sat a few male regulars with beer bottles in their hands; they were waiting there to see who might come along. Tina was alone. Her colleagues weren't going to arrive until the film-show at eight. She went into the office and filled out forms about the allocation of rooms over the next few weeks.

She heard a muffled scream. She opened the door and stood in the corridor listening. The noise was coming from the girls' loo. She ran down there and saw Tom, an eighteen-year-old who was at the club nearly every day, and a girl she had never seen before; he had pulled her trousers down and was pushing her back across the washbasin and trying to rape her. Tina screamed, 'Tom, are you crazy?' He seemed startled, let go of the girl and became aggressive.

'Get out, Tina, go on, piss off! A new bit of talent always gets taken for a trial run in this place.' He moved towards her to push her away, and Tina punched him. Tom just swore at them — 'You cunts,' turned around, did up his flies with a tug, and went out.

'Well then, let's talk about the result of Tina's new level of awareness, shall we?' said Hans, when Elke had asked at the team meeting about points for the agenda.

'Now pull yourself together, Hans, if you're going to start like that we can save all the discussion and split into opposing camps right away,' replied Elke curtly.

'Oh, I see, you two have already agreed on where you stand, have you? The best thing for the two of you to do would be to start going to a karate club, so you'll be able to handle the boys here more easily in future.' It was patently obvious that the conflict was making Hans panic. The boys had complained to him and demanded that action be taken against Tina — an eighteen-year-old being 'clouted' by a woman youth-worker was something which had to be avenged, and they knew they could get Hans on their side. They too had heard of his disparaging remarks about Tina's girls' group and they had not been lost on them. But Hans was in a quandary, because the majority of the girls in the club had got together and written a wall poster in which they had drawn up a whole string of demands for activities of their own, beginning with a woman to teach them karate, a room of their own which they could use at any time, and so on. Hans didn't want to disappoint the girls, but on the whole he was annoyed with them when he saw how they, in their naivety, were suddenly allowing themselves to be towed along in Tina's wake. She seemed to have succeeded in getting them really stirred up. The girls were now spending half their time without the boys, but what did that have to do with emancipation? And in any case, the girls were tremendously important for the club's work with the boys, because if the girls weren't there for the boys, the boys might drift off to another youth club. After all, they couldn't all become gays, just because some of the girls had decided to behave like prudish old maids. He'd been doing this job for years now, after all, and had seen a lot of colleagues come and go. It was just no use taking such a stubborn view of things right from the start.

Franz raised his hand: 'Well, I think if we're going to have a serious discussion about this then we've got to consider it on two levels. One: whether, and for what reasons, we should allow ourselves to go so far as to hit a kid — or if not, why not; and two: the attempted rape . . .'

'Just a moment, it's only Tina who says he tried to rape her. He says they were just doing a bit of heavy petting . . .' interrupted Heiner.

'Then we've got to ask the girl,' replied Franz.

'She never came back again, of course, and Tina only asked her for her first name — sensible of her,' said Hans, with feigned indignation.

'Yes, that *is* a pity,' said Elke, 'she would have made such an interesting case for your statistics on visitors, Hans!'

'I don't think,' said Tina turning to Franz, 'that we can discuss the two things in isolation from one another; Tom was using violence and I reacted with violence. OK, Tom and I weren't in the same position, I'm a youth worker here, but he was in control of the situation by virtue of his brutality towards the girl, who wasn't able to deal with it herself any more — and who's certainly never learnt to fight back effectively.'

'But that doesn't mean you immediately have to hit him, because, after all, he'd already let go of her,' replied Hans. 'You could have just talked to him in a reasoned fashion, couldn't you, you've always got on fine with him otherwise, haven't you, or did you two have some old bone to pick with each other?' he asked.

'Rubbish!' said Tina. 'Don't you dare insinuate it was all my fault. I found the situation bad enough for me to clout him one. And apart from that I don't see why I should start "reasoned" discussions with rapists. How much am I supposed to take? A girl is sexually assaulted by way of welcome and I'm supposed to act the mother who clasps the boy to her bosom and says, "there, there. . . ." What do you actually expect of me? I'm not schizophrenic; how can one part of me get involved in the day-to-day struggles against sexism, while as soon as I get to work I'm supposed to let the boys' behaviour and your expectations of me drive a wedge between me and the girls.

'Do I stop being a woman once I'm here? — although it's just that, my femininity, that you're trying to take advantage of.'

'OK, OK, we didn't realise that we'd fallen foul of a feminist, all of a sudden,' Hans interrupted her.

'Well, well, at last you've revealed what you really think of youth work with girls,' said Elke thoughtfully.

'I feel bound to disagree with you on this point, Hans,' said Franz.

'Of course Tina's angry, that's understandable, and she's got every right to be a feminist, we can only learn from her in that respect. I don't think we men are really capable of judging a situation like the one Tina found herself in. And Tina has to have the right to experience what happens to her at work, and to feel affected by it, in exactly the same way as she does in her so-called free time. In any case we men never find ourselves in situations like that. . . .'

'Oh yes, we do, I can be beaten up in a pub too, or just recently, remember, Franz, when the "Alete Rockers" came round here and did their best to provoke a fight. . . . If I hadn't known just the right behaviour to adopt. . . .'

'Heiner, I don't think you've quite got the point; a rape is a form of violence which happens every day, but you men like to play it down by declaring it an exception or putting it down to high spirits — "boys will be boys" — as if you'd got drunk and broken a window,' said Elke.

'My friends, let's see what conclusions we can draw from our experience,' began Hans in fatherly tones. This was his pitiable attempt to clear the air a bit. Nobody took any notice of him, Franz leaned forward and spoke to Tina: 'What do you want to do? Shall we discuss the girls' demands or should we talk about the incident again?' he asked tentatively, aware of the delicacy of the situation. Before Tina could reply, Hans spoke again: 'Of course, I fully realise the importance of working with girls, and I think you're right to stand up for them the way you do; I would, however, find it excessive, and both educationally and politically unsound, to spend all our time from now on talking about whether everything that goes on in this youth club should be dictated by this particular problem, which is what's happening in our team at the moment. Therefore I would urge you, Tina, to struggle only in those areas where it's worth the effort, and to reduce the extent of your concentration on girls, or whatever you want to call it, to reasonable and manageable dimensions. You'd be doing us all a good turn.' He took a deep breath. This little speech was his contribution, as it were, to peace in the team, and he was very pleased with himself.

'I don't think that's possible,' said Tina. 'If you had come to realise that you have to fight back, then you wouldn't want to have your struggle restricted to certain times of the day. For us women and for the girls, concentrating on girls can only mean getting together and changing our everyday lives. My dear Hans, I can't promise you that I'll succeed in persuading the girls to develop a critical awareness only on Tuesdays and Fridays between five and eight, and otherwise guarantee peace and quiet between these four walls, the kind of peace and quiet which you seem to need so as to concentrate on working-class boys here.'

'Tina, you'll have to cut down on the extent of your work with the girls, at least until we've reached a point where we can discuss things calmly again,' said Hans sharply.

'If you start putting pressure on her nothing will happen calmly here, ever again,' Franz intervened.

Hans: 'I can't see how I'm going to straighten this one out. Who's supposed to have started all this, anyway, is it all supposed to be Tom's fault, or maybe even mine, am I the one who's to blame? Why won't Tina tell me what she really thinks? Am I not permitted to discuss anything with her because I'm a man? Why am I just a butt for your aggressions, why can't we have a constructive discussion of what's essentially at stake in this debate?'

He was cut short by Elke: 'Poor Hans, you make my heart bleed. Do you really think you're so indispensably central to this issue? You really are taking this as a personal insult, aren't you! Maybe you should try to deal with your own vanity before you do anything else. What do you think you've got to offer the girls? Have you ever made a serious practical attempt to raise their status, possibly even to the detriment of the boys, or to strengthen their position without thinking first about winning their admiration?'

'Aha, so now I'm being relegated to the chauvinists' corner. Great, that's what your sort always do when you run out of coherent arguments,' Hans shouted at Elke. 'And I'm not ashamed of being honest about my feelings. I may be a man but I'm still just as emotionally involved,' he added.

'You're scared, that's all,' Tina butted in, 'and you're putting up a fight because the last thing you want to have to do is change yourself. You wish the girls needed you, but they can do without you, and you know that though you won't admit it.'

'Tina, do they really need any one of us? Maybe this is the question we ought to be asking ourselves. Don't you think we all try to make ourselves indispensable to the kids? I hope the girls only need you to the extent that you're there to initiate learning processes — I trust you're not using that to make them dependent on you. . . . So there are a whole range of problems relating to the extent of our usefulness in society as social workers, and particularly to the significance of our practical work, and I don't think you can just attribute them all to Hans. That's going too far.'

'All right, Heiner,' said Tina, 'somehow I also feel that we've reached a point where we should stop. I've just had enough. I'm not trying to put the team under any pressure, but I feel I ought to mention that I'm not sure if I can see any point in my continuing to work in this team. I think the differences between us are just more than I can cope with.'

'But don't make any snap decisions, Tina. What are a few months when you're trying to overcome sex-specific differences?' replied Hans.

'Yes, but it's all such a struggle,' said Tina, 'I'll have to think about it.'

'Elke, I've decided to give up my job at the youth club. I can't handle it at the moment, I need some peace and quiet, and I've got to be able to concentrate my energies more on my own interests than on the day-to-day struggles to defend our position.'

'I do understand how you feel, but I can't really say I think you're doing the right thing. For instance, what's going to become of the girls at the club? And don't you think that at least Fritz and Heiner might learn from what happens here?'

'Yes, I'm sure they will, perhaps I'm just being too impatient at the moment. Maybe I am doing the wrong thing, too, maybe I'm just capitulating, but I want to find out what it's like to have to discuss working with girls only with other women.'

'Don't think that's going to demand any less energy, Tina.'

'Of course not, I know it won't, but it'll certainly be less frustrating, and in any case, I'm not trying to say that the path I've chosen is the right one. What you're doing is just as important, of course; but I've just reached the point where I have to decide for myself — and only for myself.' Elke sighed. Tina continued: 'Won't you carry on what I was doing with the girls for me? I think you've got more strength than I have in that respect, and anyway, you'd really be taking a load off my mind.'

'Well, well, Tina, so you do have a guilty conscience after all, don't you? But all right, I'll see if I can get anything going with the girls; I hope they'll still be interested, because they're already very attached to you, and your departure will make them all the more so. On the one hand it's hard to continue in this situation when everything's gone so wrong, but of course on the other hand you've already done such a lot of ground work. By the way, I was going to ask you, what are you going to do now? I suppose you're going on the dole?'

'No, I may be able to work in the women's refuge, they're looking for someone to help with the children.'

'I suppose we ought to try to get to know other women who are doing the same kind of work, so we'd be able to talk to each other about our experiences . . . but there aren't any of us who would have the time,' said Elke.

Tina laughed: 'The best thing to do would be to write a song and make a record about it!'


### Note

1   Originally published in 'Jahrbuch der Sozialarbeit 3' Copyright © 1979 by Rowohlt Taschenbuch Verlag GmbH, Reinbek bei Hamburg.